HARD TO PLACE

ONE FAMILY'S JOURNEY THROUGH ADOPTION

Hard to Place

One Family's Journey through Adoption

Marion Goldstein

To Terry,

Best Wishes

Marion Goldstein

NORTH STAR PRESS OF ST. CLOUD, INC.
St. Cloud, Minnesota

Previously Published

The poem, "Uncertainty Principle," was previously published in *Preaching the Poetry of the Gospels* by Elizabeth Michael Boyle for The Liturgical Press.

A section of Chapter 3, entitled "Two Roads Diverged" was previously published in *Ars Medica, A Journal of Medicine, The Arts, and Humanities* Vol. 4, No I, Fall 2007.

A section of Chapter 12, entitled "Shattered Glass" is scheduled for publication in the anthology *Transform* edited by Tim Wenzell.

Cover Design by Ron Travisano

ISBN-10: 0-87839-308-0
ISBN-13: 978-0-87839-308-4

First Edition

Printed in the United States of America.

Published by
North Star Press of St. Cloud, Inc.
P.O. Box 451
St. Cloud, Minnesota 56302
northstarpress.com
info@northstarpress.com

Dedication

*To John—the child who came like a meteor
one starry night and was gone*

To Robert, Kathleen, Dennis, Eddie, and Kurt

*And most of all, to Bob
who made this book
and everything else possible*

Acknowledgements

I would like to thank my first readers, Elaine Edelman and her writing class at the Writers Voice at the West Side YMCA in New York City. It was due to your enthusiasm and provocative questions that chapter after chapter of my story was teased from memory. To Sister Elizabeth Michael Boyle, for your countless readings of the manuscript in process, and for always believing in this project and in me. To Catherine Newell, for your research of the family and for sharing it with me in our innumerable conversations. To Christina Baker Kline, for your expertise in helping me pull the threads of many themes through the story, your careful editing and meticulous attention to detail. To Doris Radin who brought to her reading of the manuscript a poet's eye, and Pam Leggett, an adoptive mother, whom providence dropped into my life while I was looking for a publisher and who made my cause her cause, thank you. In addition to Bob, my children and their spouses, grateful thanks to my other early readers, Sylvia Cicetti, Emily Fenster, Claire Furlin, Lorraine and Steve Gordon, Frances Kaplan, Dena Olsen, Jane Quinn, Ron Travisano, Eileen and Lew Wayne, and Dorothy Winheim.

Uncertainty Principle

Faith is not
to know.
It is the iridescent scrim
of a pickerel
fin.
It weighs heavily
and it weighs nothing
slipping through your fingers
like froth on a mountain stream.

It is jealous of the crocus
anchored to the earth
and yearns for proof
reliable as tides
careening between continents.

It doubles back and plants itself
like a tree
gazing at galaxies.
It meditates on infinity
and takes pleasure in measuring.

It leaves no trace
which is to say cannot be measured
the way loss enters a body
infusing it with pain so exquisite
it is crushing under its weight.
And yet
it weighs nothing.

I have been to Lourdes.
I have counted crutches
hanging on the grotto walls
I have dipped my fingers in the spring
pouring from the living stones
I have read the book of miracles
and doubted.

We are all pilgrims
grasping each other by the hand
locked in each others' eyes
and in every language known
over and over
we long for the harmonies
a cosmic whisper
the smoldering ash
of the birth of time.

Home Left Them

O N A FREEZING FEBRUARY MORNING in 1971, in Yarmouth, Nova
Scotia, the young boys who would become my sons were rescued by
the Canadian Mounted Police from a childhood of overwhelming desper-
ation and neglect. Only two and three years old, my sons do not remember
that the door was unlocked and swinging on its hinges, and the only adult
at home lay unconscious in a downstairs bedroom. They do not remember
the broken jar of peanut butter that they scooped from in their crib, or the
sores on their buttocks or the feces in their hair. They do not remember the
shattered window in the attic room next to the crib, or the way the light
gave way to dark every twelve hours. They do not remember the little girl
with matted hair—their sister—crouched in the doorway, destined to find
them twenty-five years later. They did not know that their names were
Eddie and Kurt.

The social worker who took them to a place where they were bathed
and fed, as well as the doctor who documented the emptiness behind their
blank stares and the malnourished smallness of their rigid bodies, are both
beyond memory.

Kurt does not remember his trip to the hospital for the hernia that
the doctor found and his terror of the medical staff who tried to quiet him.

Eddie does not remember his panic at being alone, without the brother with whom he lived behind the bars of a dirty crib.

It wasn't until nearly twenty-five years later that I was able to piece together what happened to them during those early years, between May of 1967 and February of 1971. Reports from the only social service agency that existed in that small fishing village, a packet of letters from their foster mother, and patches of Kurt and Eddie's memories were all we had to go on. When their adoption file was finally unearthed from a Division of Youth and Family Services warehouse in New Jersey in 1997, the full extent of their deprivation as babies was revealed. Confronting and understanding truths long hidden has been an important step in the process of healing the deep, pervasive wounds of the past.

Several weeks after removing Kurt and Eddie from that attic room, the Canadian Social Service Department placed them with Ardis and Allen Morton, a young childless couple in Yarmouth. The courts had acted on the county's petition for protective custody, and a young social worker, Heather, made the children her cause. Piling them into her station wagon, she brought them to the little red house on a secluded tract of land on the outskirts of Yarmouth. Kurt and Eddie were the first of dozens of foster children whom Ardis and Allen would parent during their marriage. Good and simple people, they'd tried to conceive a child of their own, but Ardis was unable to get pregnant. As foster parents, they were prepared to take care of children, and perhaps eventually adopt them. Allen had an eighth-grade education, and worked with the maintenance department at the local hospital. When not at the hospital, he did forestry work in the timberland that surrounded the town. Ardis, who had completed ninth grade, remained at home and was looking forward to having children in the house.

The boys' first memory of their life as foster children was of Baron, the watery-eyed Labrador who came running down the icy patch of driveway in front of the little red house where Ardis and Allen lived. They each remember Baron as an instant friend, wagging his tail and nipping at their mittens as if to say, "Come and play." He dashed ahead, leading them to the doorway. Inside, the house was warm and neat. Neither of them could believe it when

Ardis showed them a cardboard box stacked with plastic trucks and a rocking horse standing next to it. Neither of them had ever had a toy of his own. Kurt even remembers the dried flowers, probably gathered from a nearby field the previous summer, arranged in a glazed pot on the kitchen table. Ardis took Eddie and Kurt and their little bags of belongings to the room where they would sleep. It contained a set of bunk beds where they would be tucked in each night under clean sheets and warm blankets. A window across from the bed was covered with cotton curtains. Beneath the curtains was a piece of clear plastic, pulled taut over the window and nailed in place to insulate the room from the cold. When warm weather came, Allen removed the plastic, and the boys were able to look out onto the huge trees and canopy of sky and stars that surrounded the house. Across a narrow hall was another bedroom where Ardis and Allen slept. The doors between the rooms were left open. At night, the soft murmur of conversation mingled with voices from the TV floated from the living room into the boys' room as they huddled with each other in the bottom bunk. These were the first images laid down like a plank in the scaffolding of memory around which the boys would construct a past. The architecture of a safe life was slowly being erected.

The trail into the woods that surrounded the house and a shack standing in a nearby cow pasture were two more images built into the fragile structure of their early memories. Here, the boys played with their little red plastic hammers amidst mufflers retrieved from worn-out trucks and tires waiting to be discarded at the dump. Rusted lawn mowers and an old washing machine were strewn in the high grasses, and the boys used their tools to fix them. Outdoors was their playhouse. Here, alone together, with cows mooing all around, they found a thin lath of happiness and nailed it down in memory.

Allen took the boys fishing. He taught them how to tie a string to a pole and bait the safety-pin hook with the fat bloodworms that emerged from the ground each evening. Every now and then, one of the boys would manage to haul in a catfish, and Allen would clean it and cook it for supper.

Sometimes Ardis took them beyond the pasture, deeper into the woods, to watch Allen at work. They followed the sound of the chainsaw and the trail of stamped down foliage that Allen and his friends had worn into the forest. Coming upon their foster father in the woods was both exhilarating and frightening. Trees were falling! Kurt and Eddie waited in the clearing, clutching Ardis's hand. After the long groan of the pine as it fell to the ground, the boys ran to Allen and quickly handed him his lunch-pail, before running back to the safety of Ardis. Sometimes they sat with Allen for a few minutes in a bed of pine needles as he ate his lunch, before he picked up his ax or buzz saw and headed for the next tree.

* * *

KURT AND EDDIE RARELY LEFT HOME. Occasionally they'd be allowed to ride to the dump in the back of the old pickup truck. They sat amidst the refuse, bumping down the gravel driveway onto dirt roads twisting into the hills, the wind blowing through their hair. Ardis watched them from the cab as they clung to the sides of the truck. "Hold on tight," she shouted as they giggled and shrieked with excitement. At the dump they each loaded up with a portion of the week's disposables and made a little procession from the truck to the huge swath of valley that swallowed and digested the town's garbage. Allen grasped the collars of their shirts or jackets so the force of the throw would not tumble them into the pit.

Trips to the hospital—the only other times the boys left the little red house on a regular basis—were less fun. They did not like the hospital, with its maze of corridors and people. They did not like the long hours with the psychiatrist, or the small testing room where each of them went separately. They did not like the tiny table or chair where the doctor sometimes squeezed himself so he could sit opposite one of them to play a game that was really not a game at all. Even the ride was less fun. Ardis and Allen told them to squat down in the back of the pickup so that no one in town would see them. They made a game of it: each time Allen slowed down, Ardis told the boys to pull the old wool blanket they kept in the bed of the truck over their heads. The explanation for this secretiveness was another piece of the puzzle that lay hidden in a sealed file for the next twenty-five years.

Sometimes peeking from under the blanket, the boys watched Ardis buy fish from one of the many markets that lined the harbor street. Nova

Scotia is a 350-mile-long peninsula protruding into the Atlantic Ocean like a giant lobster claw dangling off the Eastern Coast of Canada. Yarmouth is located at its southernmost tip. Here Kurt and Eddie could see the Atlantic coast and the seawall rugged with rocks. They were fascinated by the bracelet of lighthouses that wrapped around the coast, casting beams across the water for the many fishing boats that entered and exited the tiny port. One afternoon, standing on an empty beach, the waves lapping at their toes, the boys looked out at the great expanse of ocean that covered the whole horizon. Allen was pointing out the ferry docking in the harbor. He explained how it sailed for ten hours each night to transport tourists and their cars from Bar Harbor, Maine, in the United States, across the water into Canada. Of course, the boys did not understand this geography, only that the other side of the ocean was very far away.

It was the spring of 1971. Small as pebbles against the blue stretch of ocean, the boys breathed the sea air they would never forget. Small for their age, each boy looked about a year younger than he was. I imagine them standing together, shoulders touching through their washed cotton shirts, their hair, fine as corn silk, covering each head like a copper bowl.

* * *

DURING THAT SPRING, WHILE THE SONS I had not yet met were beginning to take their first tentative steps towards recovery from their traumatic early childhood, I was living in New Jersey. I can picture myself as I was then, deep in thought, folding laundry in the basement or standing at the kitchen counter spreading peanut butter and jelly on Wonder Bread. Robert, Kathleen, and Dennis, my three children, would come banging in the side door each day, hungry for lunch after a morning at school.

I was completely unaware that during those very days, providence was entwining my life with the lives of two little boys in another country who stood gazing at the sea.

ⳍ 2 ⳡ

Family Matters

IT WAS JUNE 10, 1970, THE DAY BEFORE my tenth wedding anniversary and one of those perfect spring mornings when the azalea bushes piled high with white buds looked like giant bowls of popcorn. Robert, Kathleen, and Dennis careened through the screen door to the kitchen in a flurry of hunger. They had about twenty-five minutes to gobble lunch and make the four-block walk back to school. It was the last day of school before summer vacation.

Dennis, age five, arrived first, a blond streak heading for the refrigerator, where he scooped a handful of carrots from the vegetable bin, bolted out the door and headed for the rabbit hutch in the backyard. Bandito was rocking his hutch on its cinder block stanchions, agitated in his wait for food. Dennis opened the latched door, and Bandito nibbled carrots out of his hand. Kathleen, age seven, was at the kitchen table pouring Hershey chocolate syrup into three glasses of milk. She was upset. A sixth-grade boy, a big kid, had walked behind her all the way home from school, stepping on the backs of her shoes, flipping them off her heel. She was near tears with shame and anger, and tripped over her words as she told me about "what a jerk he is." Robert, age eight, the last to arrive, was sitting on the floor sorting through his pile of baseball cards. He reluctantly threw them down when we heard Dennis shouting, "Bandito's loose," and I asked him to help his brother. Mumbling "Why

6

can't you just put the carrots in the rabbit hutch? You're a pain in the neck," Robert joined the chase, and finally they trapped the darting black-and-white ball of fur between the fence and the now-trampled tomato plants. Dennis didn't mind being a pain in the neck; it was a small price to pay for rescuing Bandito.

I stacked grilled cheese sandwiches on the kitchen table, my children eager and noisy and hungry around me. Happily, I thought, or rather felt, "This is a moment of being." I had been reading a biography of Virginia Woolf, and had been struck anew by her reverence for the ordinary moments of life. It was not the marked occasions, like a marriage or birth or death, where the living was done, she said, but rather those moments tucked into time where the things that really matter to you reside. I was determined to savor those moments.

I heaved myself into one of the chairs at the table, my belly so big I barely fit between the wall of the breakfast nook and the edge of the table. Lately, this was my favorite time of day. Chatter filled the kitchen as the morning drifted into the past. I looked forward to that patch of time I had each day after lunch when the children ran out the door and clustered with the other neighborhood kids walking back to school. I piled the dishes in the sink and, seven and a half months pregnant, took my huge self to the couch. Supporting my back with the firm, striped pillows that lined the sofa, I pulled my knees up and formed a pocket for the baby. This was our time. Picturing the little face, cupping the palm of my hand around the tiny foot galloping under my maternity blouse, I fell asleep for a blissful hour before the second half of the day started, when the children would crash into their rooms at 3:15, throw their clothes on their beds, and head outside with skates and baseball mitts and bikes.

My thoughts were interrupted by the warm water trickling down my thigh. It confused me at first. I grasped the side of the table and hoisted myself up to look for a puddle of tell-tale water or chocolate milk spilled onto the maple chair. There was none. Then the realization hit me: this water was *under* my clothes—it was coming from me. I quickly raised my feet and legs under the table and placed them on another chair, instinct telling me to reverse gravity. Panic seized me. Once I had witnessed a dam break after the steady April rains overflowed the lake. A trickle at first, it continued insistent. Within minutes it had worn a hole through the bags of sand the locals heaped in its path. It gained momentum until there was a steady stream and the final flooding through the torn wall. The water was relentless; nothing could stop that destruction while all around trees continued to bud, frogs kept up their croaking in the shoals, lily pads continued their slow dance on the surface of the lake. All of nature stood by, unaware and unconcerned.

Now not wanting to alarm the children, I managed to wait the five minutes or so until they planted kisses on my cheek and left for school. I called the doctor and my husband, Bob. I was annoyed with Bob. The previous night he had called to say he'd been invited to a baseball game. A business associate had great seats, and would I mind if he didn't come home for dinner? Although infrequent, this had been happening more and more lately. I did mind. Based on experience, I knew that Bob would drink beer, lose track of time, and come home very late. I would worry about his driving and get angry as I stayed up waiting for him to pull into the driveway. Predictably, we would argue, and he'd ask me why I didn't want him to have a good time.

He went to the game. But I resented Bob's failure to recognize that I needed an extra pair of hands for the bedtime ritual of baths and teeth and prayers that seemed to go on for hours before each of the children settled into sleep. I resented the fact that I was in for a long night of waiting.

The crisis I was now facing evaporated my anger the way a shadow disappears when the light shifts. The doctor told me he would meet me in the emergency room of the hospital. Bob drove home from work wildly. We took off for the hospital. Lying on the back seat of the car, my fingers sliding over the blue crystal beads of my rosary, prayers consumed my mind like a mantra. I stuffed towels under my maternity dress and between my legs as though they could hold back the seeping tide of water. I willed it to stop trickling from my womb. I prayed, "Don't let me lose this child." For this was the child who was saving me from myself.

I had learned in the past year, through therapy, that motherhood was the solution I had created for unnamed anxieties existing outside my awareness and stealing the joy from my life. Intimations of my unrest had their beginnings about eight months before I was pregnant. Dennis was approaching his fifth birthday, and was no longer a baby. I wanted to be pregnant again, but it had not happened. With my inability to conceive came feelings of loss, along with a belief that a fulfilling phase of my life was over. I woke to days when my time was my own, but I didn't know how to use it. By 9:00 a.m. each morning the beds were made, the dishwasher stacked, clothes were spinning in the washing machine, and the day stretched ahead of me devoid of purpose or promise. I felt useless.

As I struggled to find my way, my reason for being, an incredible sadness overcame me. My world grew smaller and smaller. As I fought the overwhelming sorrow, the God whom all my life I had accepted on blind faith vanished. I was truly lost. The existential questions that had eluded me while I was busy changing diapers and running after toddlers pounded like surf in my brain.

What is it all about?

Is there a God?

Is there an afterlife?

If there is no afterlife, does anything matter?

Is life an absurd joke?

These questions consumed me. I awoke in the night trembling with the fear that all I had believed in had been eradicated. Without God—what? A void opened up in me, a chasm so deep it was as though some alien had planted a flag in the desert of my being and claimed it for his own. As the weeks progressed into months I would awaken at 4:00 or 5:00 a.m., nauseous and unable to sleep. I would wander downstairs and sit on a corner of the couch and try to think my way out of my deep sorrow. Often Dennis would hear me and climb out of his bed. Wordlessly, he would find me and climb into my lap and snuggle. As I wrapped my arms around him, his warm body became an anchor to the sanity I felt I was losing.

I tried to help myself. I volunteered with the Red Cross and drove patients to medical appointments. I planted tomatoes in the yard. For a while, I invented a kind of surrogate motherhood through an association with the Essex

County Probation Department as I mentored a fourteen-year-old girl on probation for truancy. I had found a way through the labyrinth of county government to help sustain the role from which I believed fulfillment would arise. I would park in front of her apartment house. She'd emerge slowly through the front door, but not until she kept me waiting awhile. After breakfast and maybe some conversation, I took her to a local bowling alley. We rented shoes and chose a ball and bowled the morning away. Did this do her any good? I don't know. What I do know is that after a few weeks, Kathleen asked me one night, "Mommy, if someday I start missing school, will you take me bowling on Saturday?"

* * *

STILL MY FEELINGS OF USELESSNESS PERSISTED. A void filled the part of me that once believed my happiness was insured both in this life and the next. I seemed to exist outside myself, unable to climb back into the person I once was. The pain, though emotional, was as sharp and deep as physical pain. I continued to pray to the God who wasn't there to help me stay alive for my children's sake. "Keep me alive until Robert, Kathleen, and Dennis are all eighteen and don't need me any more."

Bob helped me find a psychiatrist, who diagnosed clinical depression, and referred me to a therapist. But what did I have to be depressed about? I was living my dream: a good husband, a safe home, and three children I loved beyond words. He told me therapy would help.

"You will start to feel better in about six months," he said.

I tried to believe him. Depression had slowed time to a crawl. Six months seemed interminable, but at least someone was offering me hope. He told me not to think about becoming pregnant, and I agreed. He made it clear: pregnancy was not the antidote to my depression.

But then it happened. A missed period and a different tiredness kicked the weariness that comes from depression up a notch. I was pregnant. My therapist was annoyed, but as the weeks passed, I felt the first twinges of what seemed like happiness. Yet I continued to keep my appointment with him each week. During those months of therapy I was coming to understand how I had plotted my life according to a myth entangled with motherhood. Perhaps the myth that finally came to dominate my life, that became a motivating core belief, the central narrative, was based on a series of coincidences and experiences strewn like wildflowers in my path.

I began to ask myself, where had my overwhelming need for motherhood come from? What was the force that drove me? Was I the modern incarnation of Rachel, one of the Old Testament wives of Jacob, who grieved her barrenness? Was I the mythical incarnation of Niobe, who gloried in her seven sons and seven daughters and counted herself richer than the gods? Did I believe an abundance of babies would insure my ultimate enrichment? I think not. More likely, the image fueling my desires was Mary, the Christian mother of the New Testament. Mary was the girl depicted in the picture of Da Vinci's *Madonna and Child* that hung above the blackboard in each of my parochial grade-school classrooms. Mary was the woman content to dwell in quiet anonymity and taste immortality when she accepted motherhood. Mary, in her blue robes, her tiny foot crushing the head of the serpent, her gaze compassionate, penetrated to the core of my unknowing. She was the mother of all children; her motherhood knew no limits. Mary embodied everything I wanted to be. As a child, she was as real to me as the mother who stood by the stove mixing meatloaf or browning pork chops each evening.

I had grown up in the small world of a Brooklyn neighborhood. Life was local. There was home, there was school, and there was church. Men got on the subway by 7:50 each morning and were whisked to the doors of factories and banks and insurance companies that grew like weeds along the city streets. Others were merchants on Liberty Avenue—that long stretch of shops that stood in the shadow of the elevated tracks where the train rumbled by every seven minutes. Each morning, punctual as clocks, they would turn the key in the glass door of the butcher shop or the drug store or the Economy Store where Fruit-of-the-Loom underwear was piled in dizzying rows of white. I cannot remember any men talking about their work. It seemed a private necessity. They earned money to put food on the table and buy the occasional Rheingold from Nathan's Bar and Grill on a Friday or Saturday night.

Women stayed home with the children. My mother was sandwiched between her four children and a bevy of maiden aunts and bachelor uncles, some of whom lived on the second floor of our two-family house with the green asphalt shingles. Others lived "around the corner" and made their way to my mother each day to dig like quiet clams into the narrow beach of her time. One after another, she nursed them, running up and down the stairs with homemade soup and medicine, taking them into downtown Brooklyn to see a doctor or to buy orthopedic shoes. Was she happy? It never occurred to me to ask. Sometimes I resented her availability to others because it made her less available to me. It was only in retrospect that I was able to see how I compensated for those "selfish feelings" by admiring her selflessness and sacrifice as I aspired to emulate her.

And so two role models defining the landscape of my early life drove the desires of my adult life: Mary, the Virgin Mother of the New Testament, and my own mother. Other possibilities were as small as that neighborhood tucked into a corner of Brooklyn. Manhattan, only a few subway stops away, the city where others were pursuing different dreams and embracing different myths, was as distant as if I lived on a farm in Idaho. My life was mostly austere, yet there was an economy of joy bubbling through the days that came from the knowledge that I had two parents who loved me and kept me safe.

Messages spoken and unspoken pervaded the mores of that neighborhood. First, do well in school, not because there was a bigger world out there whose doors would open through education, but because doing well was the right thing to do. Second, do your best in all things, and, more important, avoid bragging about any accomplishment, for that would nullify it. Third, find love, sooner rather than later (which meant around age twenty-one), marry, have children, and live happily ever after. There it was—the prescription for life.

The classroom and the church were entwined by the influence of the nuns, who, from the serenity of their long black robes, taught each of us how to conjugate verbs perfectly, multiply fractions, solve equations, and fear God. At night, I would fall asleep with Latin verbs echoing in my head; *amo, amas, amat, amamus, amatis, amant;* I love, you love, he loves, we love, they love, repeating like a metronome. The focus was on academics; arts and creativity were an afterthought. Success in drawing was measured by how many crayons you could return to the box unbroken. Musical ability was a God-given gift, and you had it or you didn't. Holy Days and holidays were celebrated with an assembly where the girls' choir performed its much-rehearsed songs. Miss Mae Etts, the music teacher, who smelled of lavender and Chiclets, took me aside and whispered, "Just move your lips; that'll be enough. We don't need to hear your voice."

Life was not about creating anew but in extracting meaning from the lives that had been lived. History had already happened. There was such a treasure trove in books and in museums that it was presumptuous to suppose oneself capable of a creative act, save one. But, ah, that was the ultimate one. And it would come later, much later, with the commitment to a Christian marriage, for it was marriage that gave you the right to create life and the responsibility to raise children in the image and likeness of God.

The nuns modeled a life of discipline and prayer. Walking quietly as cats in their black oxfords, their hands tucked into their habits, long wooden rosary beads mysteriously fastened at the waist, they were secure in God's love—and, oh, how I yearned for God to love me like he loved them! Sacrifice was the pearl to polish inside the shell of yourself. Thus emerged the conflict of my adolescence, what to sacrifice? Was God calling me? Was it my life he wanted? Was I rejecting the call? Did I have a "vocation?" Was I meant to be a bride of God? Or was I to model myself after his mother, Mary, the revered Christian mother of the New Testament? The choices carved like hieroglyphics on the doors that opened into my future were two: a classroom full of children, or a house full of children.

My desire for motherhood was probably enhanced by the birth of my youngest sister when I was thirteen years old. I graduated from dolls to babies in a few short years. My mother was in her early forties when she gave birth for the last time. Each night, exhausted from the day, she would clear the Formica table after supper and spend what seemed like hours with my nine-year-old brother, helping him with his reading. Probably dyslexic, in the days before dyslexia was identified, he suffered hours of torture as he tried but could not read the words in front of him. Tension ran high in the railroad rooms as the evening wound itself up, and then wore itself down in anger and frustration. By ten o'clock, Lorraine, the baby, would be in the full throes of colic, and I would pick her up and walk her back and forth down the narrow hallway between the kitchen and two bedrooms the six of us shared. I believe the mother in me awakened then, a small bud of longing. It could have been otherwise. Walking the floor with my colicky sister each night could have unleashed an aversion to babies. But it didn't. Rather it empowered me. I was no longer ancillary. I was necessary, I believed, to my little sister and, indeed, my mother, in those midnight hours. Being needed became intoxicating as I drank it in each evening. It was probably what sent me rushing to an obstetrician when I was barely twenty-two years old, to diagnose my supposed infertility. Having been married for almost a year without conceiving, I was in a hurry to meet my future.

Ten years later, I was once again rushing, seized with panic in the back of a speeding car. But this time I was desperate to hold back the future thrusting itself upon us.

This child kicking in my womb, and all he symbolized, was in the utmost danger. I contracted my pelvic muscles in an attempt to seal off the precious fluid, but I was no match for the contractions erupting spontaneously in my womb. From his perch in his cab, a truck driver in the next lane noticed the drama unfolding in the back seat of the car. He smiled and waved, and our eyes connected. He maneuvered his truck into another lane, allowing us to pass him. I took this as a good sign.

In the emergency room, a nurse handed me her stethoscope. "Here, listen to the heart beat. It's strong for eight months, very strong."

Oh, joy. The rhythm of that heart amidst the swooshing fluid was like nothing I've ever heard before. Surely this baby was going to live.

The doctor injected my arm with a solution. "Count backward from ten," he said.

By the time I got to seven, I was slurring, and at five I slipped into a deep well of timelessness. I awoke several hours later in a stainless-steel recovery room. I felt for my belly—it was shrunken as a dried-out pumpkin. An aide sat in a chair next to my feet, reading a movie magazine.

"How's my baby?" I asked.

"Go back to sleep. The doctor will be in later to talk to you."

"What did I have, a boy or girl?"

"You had a boy."

"Is he okay?'

"Go to sleep. The doctor will talk to you later."

"Please tell me. Is he okay? Were you there? Did you see him? Did he cry? He was six weeks early."

Silence.

"Please tell me."

"You have to wait for the doctor."

She did not deviate from her script. I could hear the pages of the magazine ripple as this programmed robot in green scrubs methodically turned them. I thought I would go mad.

Fear spread through me like mercury. Once, in the throes of a fever, I tripped, and the thermometer I was grasping between my fingers shattered on the floor. Shards of glass splintered on the tiles, but it was the mercury that worried me, lest one of the children gravitate to the shimmering poison. Using my fingers as delicate pincers I tried to pick it up, but it was impossible to gather the tiny silver balls. They separated at my touch and formed into tinier and tinier balls until there were only infinite points of fluid light. The mercury could not be grasped. My fear was like that poison, multiplying itself in my body, eluding all attempts to contain it.

I struck a bargain with the God I could not find. I counted the tiles in the ceiling. If there was an even number of tiles, my boy baby was alive, an odd number, he was not. I counted and recounted for what seemed like hours. I subtracted tiles that had been cut in half when I needed one less; I added slivers of tile in a corner when I needed one more. I made every total produce an even number. I kept begging the robot aide, "Tell me, please tell me, is my baby alive?"

Again, "You have to wait for the doctor."

Then suddenly I knew. I didn't know what I knew. But here was the part that I will never forget. From the spotlight over the gurney, a knowledge as clear and hard as a diamond entered my whole being. A presence filled the room. It flowed into me as pure knowledge. "There is a reason; you do not

15

know it, but it will unfold." I was filled with peace. It probably lasted no more than a minute before I was wild with fear again. Yet on some level, it lasted forever, and in my darkest moments I returned to it when there was nowhere else to go. This part of my experience matched no other, a transcendence that could never be undone and served as the bedrock of my belief.

Finally, the robot nurse wheeled me onto the elevator and then to the maternity ward. Nurses and aides were escorting babies in their little plastic bassinets to be fed by their mothers. My heart leaped as the door opened and I saw the bassinet. But it was not my baby, rather my new roommate's child.

Bob arrived. I recognized his footsteps in the corridor, the familiar, almost imperceptible timing between the one footfall and the other, as though he were bouncing a basketball, ready to pivot. He was trying to hold back tears. "The baby's very small," he said. "Only four and one-half pounds. But the doctor told me that's actually a good weight for seven and one-half months. There's a chance. It's his lungs. They're not developed, but the doctors are doing everything they can. The next twenty four hours will be critical."

There was nothing more to say. He left, and I fell into a drug-induced sleep. When I wakened, I climbed out of the bed and made my way towards the door. I was going to visit the nursery. A nurse intercepted me and returned me to the bed.

"How's my baby?"

"The doctor's with him now. He'll talk to you when he's finished."

Joy. My child made it through the night!

"What time is it?" I asked as she raised the bar on the hospital bed.

"It's 3:00 a.m."

It was the middle of the night, and the doctor was at the hospital with my baby. He hadn't made it through the night. I started to cry.

A few minutes later, the doctor arrived at my bedside.

"You're young. Have another baby," he said.

I didn't want another baby. I wanted this baby. Every cell in my body wanted this baby that lay stiff and still in a room not far from me, a room I had never even entered.

The next morning, the nurse asked if I wanted to see my dead infant,

16

but I was afraid. I didn't know what to do with the love he couldn't receive. I refused to name him, as though a name would create more of a reality than already existed. But the law would have none of that, and so Bob named him—John. I never looked at him or held him or attended his funeral. Later, much later, I learned to speak his name. John. He was the child who came and left like a meteor streaking across the starry night, leaving in his wake a life I could never have imagined.

* * *

June 11, 1970, John's brief life and death changed everything. The myth of motherhood that I had chosen, or perhaps that had chosen me, was short-circuited. Each day diminished itself with what was missing. I sometimes thought I heard the far-away cry of a baby. If not the mother of John, this child I enfolded into my dreams and with whom I envisioned my family's future, then who was I? There would be no more babies. I knew this from the moment I learned that my child was dead. Emotionally, I did not have the courage to carry another child inside me for nine months, to grow to love that child the way I grew to love John, knowing that the same fate could befall another pregnancy. What was I going to do with the rest of my life?

Summer was a blur. I was a mother on automatic pilot, navigating bruised knees and bologna sandwiches and the backyard sprinkler. It took enormous energy each day to quell the tears banked behind the dam of my eyes. The God of the hospital gurney had evaporated. I didn't want Robert, Kathleen, or Dennis to see me sad. I stuffed tissues inside my bra to absorb the milk that continued to gush from my stone breasts in spurts of longing whenever I thought of my dead child. Building a fortress around my grief, I pushed on. Women with infants asleep in the baskets of their grocery carts evoked a jealousy so intense that I turned away from them. I envied my friend Ginny even as she weeped beside the crib of her son who was born with Down syndrome.

I said, "I'll trade places with you."

Boxes of baby clothes I had saved were sealed, put out in front of the house, and picked up by the Salvation Army.

The door to the future snapped shut.

I doted on Robert, Kathleen, and Dennis. I became obsessed with their health, afraid that I would lose them, too. I didn't want to let them out of my sight. I tormented them with endless questions about their health. I developed sneaky ways of feeling their foreheads for fever by kissing them or casually brushing back their hair. But they were on to me. One night as I imposed my check-up on Robert while he lay in bed, he turned his head abruptly and said, "Leave me alone." As he moved away, my hand slipped and my fingernail ripped into his eye. My neurosis about his well-being ironically led to a regime of antibiotics, pain, an eye patch, and a scar that would flare once again into infection years later, when he was away at college.

I tried to pray, but it was as though I left God in the delivery room of the hospital. I read William James's *The Varieties of Religious Experience*. I wrote to Dr. Norman Vincent Peale, the great proponent of positive thinking, at his church in New York. He answered my letter, but the words could not penetrate my sadness.

Finally, the summer ended. The three children went off to school in a flurry of corduroy and vinyl book bags. I watched from the front stoop as they turned the corner and disappeared. Going back inside the house, I locked the door, truly alone for the first time since June. There would be no interruptions until the children returned for lunch, three hours later. I had no conscious plan, but found myself heading straight for the bedroom. I fell on top of the sheets and buried my face in a pillow. I heard myself sobbing. Unbidden, accumulated tears came and came. I couldn't stop them. I didn't try to stop them. For over two hours, I cried with abandon. I feared I was breaking down, whatever that meant.

At some point, I reached for an envelope on the nightstand and rummaged through the drawer for a pencil in the still, shade-darkened room. Some impulse to write had emerged from the grief. A poem poured forth from the deepest part of my being, a simple poem about a mother and the son she could not have. I had never written a poem before, nor had I ever thought about doing so, but as if possessed, I found myself scribbling madly on the back of an envelope. As I did, the fog began to lift, revealing to me a moment of faith in the existence of another world and the futility of trying to comprehend it in the present one.

18

This is what I wrote—

I wonder oh my little one
If you know how much you're loved
Of all my thoughts about you
And what it would be like
To have you here to love and share
This puzzle which is life
The joy, the ache, the love, and pain
That would never cease to grow
That sometimes seems to choke me
When I allow it to do so
There are feelings deep within me
Reserved for only you
That will always be a part of me
No matter what I do.
It's painful to remember
But that serves a purpose too
It puts me in touch with a wonder
The reality of you.
Will I know your little face?
Will it greet me with a grin?
In some far and distant place
When we're all at one with Him.
I wonder?

By the time I wrote the last word, I stopped crying. I still didn't have my child, but in a strange way, I did. Although he could not exist in my world, he existed on the page; he existed in the poem. Here was a record. He was born, he was loved, he was real and he would never be forgotten. The poem told me I had hope. It was a hope of knowing him in another dimension. I no longer had to keep him fastened like a little button to the forefront of my mind where I couldn't lose him. I could let go and keep him at the same time. All at once, absence and presence were co-mingled.

In a subtle way, through the rhythms and language permitted by a poem, I had finally prayed. It was in writing that poem, my prayer poem, that I took another tentative step forward in my struggle with faith. A long time would pass before I realized that others had discovered the secret I thought was mine alone, that the act of writing mediated pain; the act of writing healed; the act of writing could be a prayer.

John's brief existence would lead me to poetry, and then to the emerging field of poetry therapy, and eventually to a graduate degree in psychology and a career in psychotherapy. But more importantly, before that, John's brief existence would lead me to a dirt road in Yarmouth, and two little boys, who, like me, during that summer of grief, also could not cry. John's brief existence would lead me to my whole self.

* * *

THAT SEPTEMBER MORNING, AS MY GRIEF finally turned to tears, and my tears to prayer, there were other tears frozen behind other eyes. A packet of letters, yet to be written, would one day tell us about a rickety school bus clanking up a dirt road in a fishing village in Yarmouth, Nova Scotia. They would describe a small boy shivering with fright, reluctantly and obediently stepping out of the shadows of the dark green fir trees. His little legs barely managed the steps as he tentatively climbed into the cavernous bus. He carried an orange plastic lunch pail, the same lunch pail he would one day fill with plastic tools and cart to the United States. His brother, a year younger, still wearing his cotton pajamas under a woolen sweater, stood by the road-side. Sucking anxiously on his left thumb, he watched as the yellow bus, coughing gusts of billowing smoke swallowed his brother and backed down the dirt road. The boys did not cry. For eight hours each day, they wondered about and yearned for each other. Although they never quite believed it would, the bus returned each afternoon to the grove of fir trees, and they ran to each other, full of relief and joy.

ಸ 3 ೞ

The Road to Adoption

Ⓘ**T IS THE COLOR BLUE THAT RECOMPOSED** the canvas of January 9, 1971, like a still life in my mind. Kathleen wore a navy blue jump suit with red piping. It was her Christmas outfit, and today was her eighth birthday, so she was allowed to wear it to school. It had been seven months since the baby's death. Cupcakes were packed in a foil-lined blue box from Hahnes Department Store. Pale-blue stars made of sugar decorated the vanilla icing. But mostly, it was the bolt out of the blue, the strike of lightning that changed her life forever, that fastened the blue day in my memory.

"Hurry up. Let me in. I have to go," Kathleen yelled through the bathroom door to her brother Dennis, who was busy floating a salamander in the sink.

"I can't wait. Hurry, hurry," and with the next breath, "I'm so thirsty" as she ran to the tap, half filled a glass and started to gulp down the water. When she came home at three o'clock, it was the same thing. She dashed for the bathroom, darted for water. During the night I heard her at 10:00 p.m., and 2:00 a.m, and 6:00 a.m. I heard the toilet flush and water running in the sink. In the morning, three paper cups in the wicker wastebasket attested to her ongoing thirst. This went on for three days and three nights.

I made an appointment with the pediatrician. The nurse sent Kathleen into the bathroom to urinate in a paper cup before ushering us into the examin-

21

ing room. Kathleen was embarrassed, mumbling how disgusting it was. It was such a primitive act to her; she refused to touch the cup. The nurse dipped a strip of yellow paper into the urine, and I watched as it turned from the color of buttercups to a bluish-green and then to a deep forest-green. Was this good or bad? I didn't know. The nurse left the examining room, and the pediatrician came in. He took one look at the colored strip and sighed heavily.

There is in almost every life the moment before the moment. It happens surreptitiously, while the kettle is boiling on the stove or the radio is playing the same old song. There is no drum roll to announce its arrival, and the sky doesn't turn an ominous black. But everything changes. Time is divided into before and after.

The urine tested positive for sugar. "No, there's no mistake," the doctor said. "No, it's not just a fluke from having a candy bar after school. No, it won't go away if she stops eating sugar." No, no, no. She has juvenile diabetes.

We had to act quickly. She could go into a diabetic coma. The pediatrician called a specialist. Stunned, that night Bob and I made our way to the endocrinologist's office. He spoke directly to Kathleen, his sentences bypassing Bob and me as though we were the long way around the mountain. He told her he was going to give her an injection of insulin, and then we would all talk some more. Kathleen tried to be brave as she leaned against her dad, who was telling her silly stories with a shaking voice. I closed my eyes in a reflex born of denial. The doctor gave her a choice: "Do you want the injection in the arm, the leg, or the stomach?"

She looked at me with frightened eyes. "The arm," I said through gritted teeth. He injected her. She didn't cry.

Next, the doctor reached into a basket of oranges he kept in the treatment room.

"Here, mother," he says, "I'm going to teach you how to administer a shot. You can practice with an orange, and tomorrow I want you back here by 7:00 a.m. You can give your daughter the injection." I did as I was told. I followed his instructions with the orange, all the while silently screaming, "I can't do this."

It was barbaric. But the only way to exit that office that night, the only way to avoid having Kathleen hospitalized, was to stay calm, to prove I could

22

handle this, obey. I operated like a robot. This was not like other medicines she or her brothers had taken for a sore throat or cough. These injections would stalk her every day for the rest of her life. One moment she was a carefree eight-year-old, and the next she was chained to a regime of injections and a rigid timetable of meals and snacks on which her very life depended.

The specialist began to educate the three of us that night. Every morsel of food consumed by Kathleen had to be counted in terms of carbohydrate content. Each carbohydrate had to be compensated for by the amount of insulin injected. Sitting behind the big cluttered desk, he scribbled a list of foods on lined yellow paper and handed it to Kathleen. Her eyes, welling with tears, sought mine, then Bob's. She didn't understand.

There are "slow-acting" carbohydrates like bread that require insulin in three hours, "medium-acting" carbohydrates like milk that call for insulin in about one hour, and "fast-acting" carbohydrates like candy or juice that require immediate insulin. There are fast-acting, slow, and intermediate-acting insulins. A combination of insulin could be mixed in the syringe by drawing part of an injection from one bottle and the other part of the injection from another.

"You will learn to do that, Kathleen," the doctor said. "We'll start with one shot a day." What he didn't mention was that by the time she left for college, she would be injecting herself four times a day; first thing in the morning, before lunch, before dinner, and before bed. From that day forward, she needed to test her urine four times a day by dipping a strip of treated paper into it. She learned to evaluate the color and adjust her dose of insulin.

Her day was precarious. When her blood sugar dropped rapidly because a meal was five minutes late, or play was more rigorous, or she was upset, or had a fight with her brother, or was getting a cold, or from just plain anything, she could have a reaction. The antidote for a reaction was to ingest sugar. Left untreated, a reaction could quickly morph into unconsciousness.

"My legs feel funny," was the way it generally began. Freckles sprinkled across her nose would disappear as if caught in an undertow of white paste. She would reach for a Life Saver to suck on or a can of apple juice to drink. Within minutes the color would return to her cheeks and her legs would feel strong again . . . or they would not . . . and the reaction would continue in a relentless tide of symptoms. Beads of perspiration would begin to soak her hairline, she would get progressively weaker, her thinking would become compromised, she would get angry or cry and not know why, her stomach would hurt, and she might vomit the juice she had drunk to offset the insulin that had sent her blood sugar plummeting.

For a child, diabetes is a balancing act on a high wire strung across each day and each night. Trial and error are the two instructors, and they are not compassionate. And always in the background, the litany of complications that lay in wait in the future: blindness, and kidney, and heart disease. I did not want to hear about them, and I did not want her to hear about them, but the doctor insisted. "Ultimately, she is responsible for her own health, Mother," he said. "You can't be with her all the time. She has to learn." I wanted to smack him.

The specter of those complications haunted me. Bob tried to help. As a mathematician, he had always been able to find solutions in numbers, and he gave me all the reasons the actuarial statistics on diabetes did not apply to Kathleen. He carefully explained how the statistics included cases that were undiagnosed, and cases of inadequate treatment, and cases of people who refused to take insulin or watch their diet. Somehow, after allowing for all the variables that did not apply to Kathleen, my fear was assuaged—until it reared its ugly head again.

I was angry with God. I made futile attempts to understand the randomness of my child being inflicted. I went through months of magical thinking—a vague dialogue with the powers that be, to take diabetes away from my daughter and give it to me. I bargained with God, the God who continued to remain hidden from me since that numinous moment in the delivery room, to keep Kathleen safe. My bargain: I would get down on my knees and pray, even as I searched for God, as an act of worship, every night for the rest of my life. In return, I beseeched, "Keep my child safe; don't let the complications of diabetes harm her." Often in the two minutes it took me to keep that promise, kneeling by the side of the bed, exhausted from worry, I fell asleep and awakened with a start a few seconds later. Or I heard Bob say "Are you asleep down there?" Often as not, I was asleep. But it was my bargain, my ritual, something I needed to do. I couldn't prove it was helping my daughter, but nor could it be proven otherwise.

In spite of the strictures diabetes imposed, the doctor told Kathleen, "You can lead a normal life. You can do anything anyone else does; you just have to account for insulin." These were the words she wove into her personality like gold threads in whole cloth.

During the first spring after she was diagnosed, Bob and I struggled with Kathleen's need for independence. Her life was measured into time periods that aligned with insulin metabolizing in her body. She began to wear a watch. Often she went off on her bike to ride the trails in a wooded area near home. She knew that as dinnertime approached, her insulin started to drop. This was when she was most vulnerable to a reaction. Often I was out on the front steps, looking for her biking up the hill towards home. One day, she was about ten minutes late. Robert was playing basketball at the hoop mounted on the garage.

"What's the matter, Mom?" he shouted, my son who would have you believe he never noticed anything.

"Kathleen's late. Have you seen her?"

"No, she'll show up soon," he said.

I started to get on my bike. "She doesn't have juice with her." He knew what that meant. "I'm going to look for her," I said, as I tossed a can of apple juice into the basket of the bike. But before I finished my sentence, Robert stuffed his basketball behind a shrub and jumped onto his bike.

"I'm coming with you," he said. We both tore down the street. I can still see him standing on the pedals as we flew alongside the cars bringing neighbors home from work, his blond hair flying, his eyes squinting in the dusk as he sought out his sister. And mostly, I remember the tears on his cheeks.

Three months after she was diagnosed, there was an overnight trip to girl-scout camp. I did not want her to go, but Kathleen and Bob double-teamed me. Her concession was to allow me to be a volunteer counselor for the weekend.

After having packed her insulin in an insulated bag, she woke herself up in the morning, ten minutes before roll-call, and tiptoed over the sleeping bags lined up on the wooden floor of the camp barracks. The yawning and stretching and giggling of the other girls would start soon. She huddled in a corner under a moose head, secretly measuring insulin into the syringe, hoping no one would wake and see her. Then she crawled back to her sleeping bag, ready to participate in the waking-up ritual of girls.

They say a family is like a mobile, each individual separate yet connected. Picture the quilted animals that hang over a baby's crib. Each one wears itself easily, held in equilibrium, balanced. Watch the baby kick one of those figures and disrupt the balance. The animals sway and wobble, and all is chaos. So it was with our family. The effects of diabetes rocked our every day. Life went on, but it was different, more fragile.

Yet, unbeknownst to us, in the midst of that sorrow lay the seeds of transformation for all of us.

* * *

DURING THAT SAME MONTH of January 1971, those blue days, when Kathleen was diagnosed with juvenile diabetes, a social worker named Heather, hundreds of miles away in Nova Scotia, Canada, labored late into the night, composing a black-and-white canvas of words. It was those words that were the first ripples in a stream of events that would bring more change into our lives.

When I met Heather, Thanksgiving week, 1972, she told me about the report she wrote on that freezing winter night. Icicles hung like stalactites from her kitchen window, and as the logs in her fireplace burned to embers, she typed page after page of a history of abuse and neglect. She knew that a few miles away, in the outskirts of Yarmouth, there stood a dilapidated building banked in snow drifts. She could picture children huddled together, seeking warmth from each other under the one shredded blanket they shared. Heather was determined to get her words before a judge. Only her words could rescue those little ones. She typed on and on.

* * *

MILES AWAY IN NEW JERSEY, a journalist typed a headline.
WESTFIELD AGENCY HUNTS
HOMES FOR HARD-TO-PLACE

The headline caught my attention as I leafed through the newspaper one winter morning. I was drawn to this human-interest story. It remained in my mind for days, simmering like a pot on the back of a stove. It told of a social worker named Lillian Kawet who once worked for the State Bureau of Children's Services. She was quoted as having become acutely aware of the major tragedies happening in the lives of homeless children who had little or no hope of being adopted. These were children with disabilities and illnesses like cerebral palsy and congenital heart disease, children with mental and emotional and behavioral problems. These were the babies who had been ineligible for adoption until they were three or four years old. In a society where infants were the most sought after age group for placement, these children were often over-looked and forgotten. They were the children who got shuffled from foster home to foster home, becoming sources of income in an already overwrought and struggling family. These were older black children who were the most difficult to place in the current culture.

This travesty of the forgotten children, whom she called "the living dead," caused Ms. Kawet to quit her job with the state and found an agency for hard-to-place children. It was a no-frills operation funded by private donations and grants from foundations. She and her four part-time case workers operated out of a one-family house on Main Street in Westfield, New Jersey. According to the article, Spaulding for Children, as the agency was named, had in the previous six months placed sixty-six children from as far away as Nevada and Canada into adoptive homes.

* * *

BOB READ THE ARTICLE that same evening, but it was not until several days later that it came up in conversation. Each of us had been captured by its message, and the possibilities had taken root in each of us, separately.

It was late on a Saturday morning. We had already been to the endocrinologist's office with Kathleen for her three-month check up, and the doctor found her to be healthy and in good control of her diabetes. Now we were settled at the kitchen table with a pot of coffee and the newspapers between us. We could see Kathleen through the kitchen window flying as high as her legs would pump on the backyard swing. Our hearts were easy. After bagels and the papers, with the day stretching ahead of us like a blank sheet of paper, there was time for slow talk. I said to Bob, "I read this interesting article earlier this week about an adoption agency devoted to hard-to-place children."

"So did I," he said. "I can't believe there are so many children that no one wants."

"I know," I said. "It makes me think, if something happened to us, no one would want Kathleen because of her diabetes."

The room got very quiet. Bob's eyes met mine over his coffee cup.

"Are you thinking what I'm thinking?"

"What are you thinking?"

"About that article."

Neither of us wanted to be the first one to say the words aloud. This was big.

"Do you think there might be a diabetic infant out there that no one wants?" we asked each other tentatively, as those longings on the underside of consciousness were spoken. And like the force that caused the compass needle to move, each of us in turn felt the shift that Saturday morning.

As the children played in the backyard, the slow listening over the incubator of the kitchen table allowed our free-floating thoughts to germinate and be converted into words. It was as though the idea of adoption had been hidden in the coffee grinds or in the pine trees framing the swing set, and each of us suddenly discovered it. Longing was transformed into possibility.

We called Spaulding for Children and told them of our grand plan. We requested a child with chronic illness, specifically a child with juvenile diabetes. To our shock and dismay, they denied our request. No, they did not have any children with diabetes. No, they had never placed a child with diabetes before. No, they doubted such a need would develop any time soon. No, they did not consider diabetes a chronic illness; they dealt with more debilitating physical problems. Then we were asked, "Would you consider a hard-to-place child that we do have available?"

Bob and I had fantasized this perfect match with a diabetic child's needs and our recently acquired ability to meet those needs. Letting go of that idea was hard, but the concept of adoption had taken root. We took a day or two to talk about it with each other, and then called back and said, "Yes, we would consider adopting another hard-to-place child."

Within weeks, a case worker visited us at home. She asked questions about our motives, our health, our histories, and our marriage. She walked through the house and observed the living conditions.

We asked questions. "Do we need to have a separate room for a child?"

"No."

"How much will this cost us?"

"Nothing. If you want to make a donation, it'll be accepted, but we charge no fee."

"How long does this take?"

"A couple of months."

We waited, half believing that it would never come to be. We told no one. We were afraid that family members and friends would try to discourage us or react with doubt and warnings. Questions like "You already have three children, why would you want to adopt another?" were bound to be asked. We were asking them of ourselves! Yet it was difficult to articulate an answer. There was a gut feeling, some undercurrent sweeping us forward. "There's a reason for this," echoed unconsciously in every thing that happened to us since losing the baby. And so Bob and I kept our plan to ourselves, sensing that sharing it with others would siphon the energy and joy from it.

About six months later, a call came from a social worker at the agency. An infant girl, ten days old, was available for adoption. Born with a harelip and cleft palate, she needed to be tube-fed because she was unable to suck. She would need a series of operations as she developed. We could have her within a few days.

We said yes. The next day, I called our pediatrician to discuss the medical care of this new baby. He asked us to come to the office without Robert, Kathleen, or Dennis, and he educated us on what we could expect. He explained the difficulty the baby would have swallowing and how visually it would be very disturbing to the other children. He discouraged us, and reminded us that diabetes already imposed its own food restrictions and scheduling structure to meals in our family. He told us that by adopting this baby, we would be taking on a problem that would complicate the care of our three children. Of course, he was right. We could see it immediately, once he drew the picture for us. We went home and called the agency. We told them we had changed our minds.

A few months later, we received another call. Three American Indian children, who had been in a series of foster homes out west, were available for adoption. They had serious behavior problems, but there was hope that, with a stable environment, they would improve. This placement scared us from the beginning. Three children, doubling the size of the family, were overwhelming. The ages were all wrong. Each of our three children would lose their place in the family hierarchy. We said no the same day, but as we did we wondered if we were deluding ourselves. Were we going to find some excuse to refuse each child offered to us?

∽ 4 ∾

Further along the Road

I WAS ON A LADDER IN THE KITCHEN, painting cabinets, when the agency called for the last time. It was spring of 1972. Physical work had become one of my antidotes for loss, a Band-Aid on the emptiness that still visited occasionally since John's death, and the sadness inherent in injecting Kathleen with insulin. Choosing paint and wallpaper made me feel creative. I clung to the words of the psychologist Rollo May, "Creativity builds on the innate facet of every person's inheritance, the will to live, for to create is in some sense to be born again." In another sense, I was also re-creating myself.

Since losing John in 1970, it had been difficult to tease apart clinical depression from normal grief. I was still going once a week to see the psychologist I had started seeing when depression hit me, in those months before I was pregnant with John. While he never gave advice or explicitly told me what to do, his misgivings and cautions about adoption and once again relying on motherhood for fulfillment, generally expressed by probing questions and raised eyebrows, were abundant.

Early in my treatment, this man had gently elicited my feelings about going back to college. He had recognized as loss, my forfeiture of an education, after attending one year of night school when I was nineteen, to pursue marriage and motherhood. He encouraged me to return to school. I enrolled

31

in a local college as a non-matriculating student, and my mind was being opened to the world beyond my home, the world beyond motherhood.

I loved the mental stimulation of the courses. When I came in at 10:00 p.m., energized by a lecture in philosophy or history, the children were asleep, and the house was quiet. Bob turned off the TV and listened to me as I re-interpreted the lecture to him. We discussed what had, or had not, engaged me. I began to have opinions, and began to care about things of which I had previously been unaware. The very act of verbalizing the concepts that filled my notebooks was a learning tool for me.

The Woman's Movement was happening all around me. Although I was not consciously involved, the internal need that was driving me, a recognition that life was about more than my parochial world view allowed, was probably being influenced by that agenda. I was gaining insight into the fact that it was the confines of the insulated life, the limited horizons of my Brooklyn childhood that tethered me to my preoccupation with the myth of motherhood.

As part of my college course work, I studied poetry. The poem I wrote when grief found its way into words in 1970, three months after John's short life, had stirred an academic interest in poetry for me. I yearned to be able to re-experience the shift toward peace that took place in me that morning. By reading other poets, I found a vehicle that opened me to my own questions. Gerald Manly Hopkins was inspired to write, "The world is charged with the grandeur of God." Dylan Thomas asked, "What is the force that fuels the flowers?" In my own way, I was asking the same question. I began to reconnect with the world and myself through the poetry of others, as poetry provided the impetus to give voice to my own unarticulated questions.

The classroom and the therapy room both nourished my depleted spirit. I found I wasn't alone. Others were asking the same questions, in books, in conversations, in lectures, in poetry. At college, I met a brilliant teacher, a Dominican nun, Sister Elizabeth Michael, who, years earlier, had grappled with questions of faith. She would become a spiritual mentor and a lifelong friend. From her, I learned that every attempt to name God must be an approximation, since God transcends all human categories of experience. I began to come to terms with the idea that faith was a leap into the unknowable. The infinite could not be contained within our finite minds. She taught me to appreciate metaphor, for it is metaphor above all else that approximates the shades of deepest feelings for which there are no words. For me, metaphor became the way of saying the unsayable and an avenue to the spiritual. My own poetry, stored in vaguest thoughts and questions, and slippery as ice, began to emerge into words.

Many years later, I was drawn to a quote by the poet Kathleen Norris that spoke to what was probably the core issue of my spiritual life: "What we glimpse of the divine is always exactly enough and never enough." This put into words what poetry provided for me; those moments of insight, the flash of belief like sparks in stubble, that extinguished doubt: even though embers of unbelief would ignite again, for the moment all was peace.

I was on a journey and no longer desperate for immediate answers. I was finding my way to a new kind of emotional health.

* * *

THE DAY OF THAT LAST PHONE CALL from the adoption agency was a good day. As I painted, the pure white satin finish glowed as it covered the scratches and dents that scarred the old pine kitchen cabinets. The olive-green trim and new copper hinges matched the colonial-print wallpaper standing in rolls against the tile of the breakfast nook. Climbing down the ladder, tripping on the big oak kitchen table I had pushed into the center of the room, I dove for the phone.

The adoption agency had another placement for us, two little boys from a small fishing village in Canada. They were natural brothers, ages three and four. They had an older sister, but she had already been adopted by a minister and his wife who, when they saw her, had formed an immediate attachment. I held my breath as I listened. The agency was trying to keep the two boys together. Since most adopting families requested an infant, and one child, it was felt the two boys were "hard to place," thus their availability through Spaulding.

The background information on the boys was sparse. I was told that these young brothers had been removed from the home of their biological parents in February of 1971, due to neglect. Three specific incidents of neglect were enumerated: an attic room with no heat, a broken jar of peanut butter in a crib, no bed linens or diapers or shirts. Neglect. This small word attached to three examples seeped like a toxic gas through the earpiece of the phone.

In September of 1971, the Province of Nova Scotia filed with the court to have the boys become wards of the province, the process needed to make them eligible for adoption. During this seven-month period, the boys had been placed together in foster care. Their names were Eddie and Kurt. If we were interested, we could come in for an appointment. There was a photograph of them, sent from Canada, in the file.

This felt right and my paint splattered hands trembled as I dialed the phone to call Bob. He dashed home from work, and we called Spaulding back within an hour and made arrangements to drive to the agency the following day.

It was over two full years since we had lost the baby, and sixteen months since Kathleen had been diagnosed with diabetes. Yet, all the while, those months of loss had been propelling Bob and me toward this bright Indian summer day, toward a tiny office, an overwhelmed social worker, and the thin manila folder on her desk.

The caseworker smiled as she extended one hand in greeting and picked up the folder with her free hand. She motioned us toward two chairs in front of her desk and opened the file. Attached with a paper clip to the inside front cover were three photographs of two small boys taken by the foster mother over the winter.

Bob and I leaned forward, our heads nearly bumping as we strained to absorb every detail of the two faces peering out of the pictures. The first photo was two inches by two inches, with a quarter-inch white border on each side so the actual image was even smaller. It had been focused from a distance. Eddie and Kurt were standing in the far right-hand corner of what looked like a snow-splotched yard. A corner of a house overshadowed by enormous green fir trees was in the background. Each child held a hockey stick limply in his hands. The pose looked defeated and bewildered. Each was wearing a snow jacket, with a woolen scarf wrapped around his neck. Knitted hats covered their heads, and even with a magnifying glass it was impossible to make out their features. The boys looked straight into the camera, their shoulders touching, still as little snowmen with their hockey sticks and scarves.

The photo seemed like a metaphor for their lives. Alone, in the far corner of an icy landscape, faces indistinguishable against the whiteness of the snow, wind whipping their scarves, they stood together. Bob and I were mesmerized. The realization that we might be looking at our future, at two children that might actually be ours someday, descended upon us in a wave of gratitude.

The second and third photos were close-ups. Written on the back of each print was the name and birth date of each child. We laid them side by side on the desk and drank in their faces. Each was fair-skinned, with medium blond hair that would probably turn darker, the way Robert's and Dennis's had turned from platinum to yellow to dark-blond. Their hair was cut short, revealing perfect little round heads. Each had a wide brow with a high forehead and large brown eyes. Kurt was staring full face into the camera. He was half lying on a brown and beige flowered upholstered sofa, one hand on his knee, the other holding the arm of the couch, as if to anchor himself. His gaze was open and serious. Eddie was posed on the same sofa, bent slightly forward. Both hands were clasped in his lap, as though someone had told him to be a good boy. He was looking slightly away from the camera, and his face seemed less relaxed than his brother's. They could have passed for twins, and they were beautiful.

The "yes" we had uttered the previous day was confirmed and reconfirmed as we sat and looked at those pictures. We could barely comprehend the opportunity being offered to us. The residual sorrows of our separate selves broke free that morning. Joy was our passenger in the old Buick station wagon as we drove home. The wet spring that had caused softball games to be cancelled and mud to accumulate in the soccer fields had produced an abundance of flowers blossoming in backyards, and canopies of green overflowing the highway. The world seemed to be shouting a new beginning.

After Robert, Kathleen, and Dennis were tucked in bed, Bob and I took the snapshots out of the small white envelope and spread them on the table in the quiet kitchen. As if in a dream we talked about how right Kurt and Eddie seemed for our family. At ages four and five, they would be entering the family as the youngest children, the way nature did it. Robert, at age ten, would remain the oldest; Kathleen, who was nine, would remain second and retain her position as the only girl; and Dennis, not quite seven, would move to the middle, following a natural progression, as if another biological child had been born. Bob and I talked long into the night, all the while squinting at the photographs while falling in love.

The question that loomed largest was how to prepare the other children for this incredible change in the family. This was a decision on which the rest of our lives would turn. We tried to put ourselves in our children's position. We asked ourselves, would one or all of them ask now or years from now, "Were we not enough for you? Did you need to go out and adopt children because something was lacking in us?" Or would they view this experience as one that enhanced their lives and contributed to their development as good and caring people?

I had learned over the years that love does not divide, it multiplies. When I was pregnant with my second child, I could not imagine how I would love that child as much as the first. It was as though I thought I would have to divide love from some pre-filled container and siphon it from one child to give to the other. But then, the wonder of it all—I found that, like a field of wild violets, love multiplies, seeding itself over and over.

We had to do it right.

✳ ✳ ✳

WE DEVELOPED A PLAN THAT INVOLVED two of our closest friends, Gail and Charlie Barry. Over the years Gail had visited numerous obstetricians and fertility doctors in a fruitless attempt to conceive a child. With the birth of each of my children, she would arrive with little knitted outfits and swoon over the new infant. Never bitter about the void that being childless made in her own life, she was able to give herself generously and openly to my children. By 1971, she and Charlie had decided to adopt, and it was around this fact that the plan took shape. However, our plan was based on a lie!

The question from the children had come up in the past, "How come Mr. and Mrs. Barry don't have their own baby?"

"They want a baby, but God has not sent them one yet."

"Why not?"

"I don't know."

Now we needed a reason to introduce our children to the idea of adoption, and we used our friend's situation. Though Bob and I questioned whether we were doing the right thing, we convinced ourselves that the "story" we were preparing to tell the children was really just another version of a fairy tale, but in this case, a fairy tale with an ending they could help create. One night, shortly after making the decision to adopt, as the children were getting ready to say their nighttime prayers, I said, "Guess what?

As I got their attention I went on. "There are two little brothers in Canada who have no mother or father, and Mr. and Mrs. Barry might adopt them."

The children were excited, and the questions started.

"Really?"

"How did they hear about the boys?"

"What happened to the boys?"

"Why don't they have a mother and father?"

"How old are they?"

"What do they look like?"

"Are they scared?"

"Who's taking care of them now?"

We told them the version of the truth we had told ourselves, filling in the gaps in the story as the mind inserts missing letters into a misspelled word. Our own attempts to understand, plus the paucity of information available from the adoption agency, led us to construct a narrative for our children based on what we did know, one that made sense to us.

We told Robert, Kathleen, and Dennis that Kurt and Eddie's parents forgot to buy food or cook for the boys; they forgot to wash their clothes or keep the house warm in the winter. Sometimes they forgot to come home until very late at night, and the boys would cry because they were alone in the house. We told our children that any parents who forget so much were probably sick and that was why Kurt and Eddie were going to be adopted by someone who could take better care of them. This was the simple version we would tell and tell again.

Robert, Kathleen, and Dennis listened with rapt attention. We told them that the two boys had just turned four and five years old. Speaking simply, we explained that Kurt and Eddie were poor and didn't have many toys, and that all that had happened had made them confused and scared. We explained that the two brothers were living in a foster home. Our children had never heard of the terms "foster home" or "foster parents." They asked us why the foster parents did not keep Kurt and Eddie. We told them what we had been told, "Because the foster parents were going to have their own baby."

They listened. Each of them knew that Mr. and Mrs. Barry wanted a baby, and that the two little boys would be lucky to have the Barrys for parents. They began to include a prayer for the adoption with their prayers each night.

"Dear God, please watch over Mommy and Daddy, my sister and brothers, my grandmas and grandpas all my aunts and uncles and cousins and make me a good boy/girl. Amen."

And then the codicil—

"And help Mr. and Mrs. Barry to adopt Eddie and Kurt, the brothers from Canada."

Most often, they said prayers together, in the boys' room, and Kathleen came from her room to join her brothers. And so it went, each night another question or the same questions calling for a more elaborate answer, as they knelt next to one of the beds, their sleepy heads on the quilt, their toes curling into the shag rug.

Eddie and Kurt became their favorite bedtime story, but it was not a fairy tale; it was real and they understood it was real. They wanted to know more and more. When they suggested that we send some of their toys to Canada, I knew my faith in my children had been well-founded. Of course, sharing toys was one thing, sharing parents quite another, but we were on the right track, one that would end with our asking for their approval to adopt Eddie and Kurt.

It was the Fourth of July in 1972 when we told them the whole truth. They had spent the day at the backyard pool of friends. There had been hot dogs, and ice cream, and jumping and diving. At 10:00 p.m., they were exhausted as they got undressed for bed. It was one of those nights when the prayer ritual was replaced with the ritual of Noxzema applications to sunburned shoulders.

As Kathleen began to make her way back to her own room, and Robert and Dennis fell into bed, a question was whispered. "Are Mr. and Mrs. Barry going to adopt the boys?" Perhaps it was their fun-filled day that made them reflect on those two boys without parents or toys. Providence seemed to dictate this moment, and I found myself saying, "No, Mr. and Mrs. Barry would really like an infant, so they're going to wait for a little baby."

The boys sat up in their beds. Stricken. Kathleen turned around in her little summer nightgown and came back into the boys' room.

"Well, what'll happen to Eddie and Kurt?" someone asked.

"I don't know."

"Are the foster parents going to keep them now?"

"No, they're going to have their own baby."

Silence.

"It's not fair. Where will they go?"

Their brains were working overtime, trying to achieve an "and everyone lived happily ever after" ending before giving themselves over to sleep.

More silence.

I took a deep breath. "What would you think if we adopted them?" I said dizzyingly, knowing what hinged on their reply.

The three trusting faces of my children took it in, the biggest question of their combined lives. It hung in the air like a red balloon for about thirty seconds and then they grabbed it.

"That would be okay," Robert said. Dennis agreed. "Yes, let's do it," from Kathleen.

Now they could turn over and sleep.

"Shall we tell Daddy?" I said.

"Yes, let's call him in here."

We called Bob and he came. "Guess what? We're going to take Kurt and Eddie to live with us because Mr. and Mrs. Barry want a little baby," Dennis said to his father.

"That's a great idea," Bob responded, as we looked at each other in amazement over the three sleepy heads. We were overwhelmed with joy at the generous hearts of our children, innocent in their beds amid the wet towels and chlorine-scented bathing suits littering the floor.

* * *

IT HAD BEEN SO EASY, but of course it wasn't over. There were bound to be more discussions, and questions and reassurances. The next day we brought it up again.

"So, what do you really think about our family adopting the boys?"

As I look back, all these years later, I see that the reservations expressed by each of them at ages ten, nine, and six took the same form their concerns crystallized into as adults.

Robert went first. "Can we afford it?"

We had never imagined discussing our finances with a ten-year-old, but unusual circumstances called for unusual responses. It was a good question. We were not rich, and Robert knew it. When his shiny red Schwinn bicycle was stolen two weeks after his birthday, we told him he would have to save money from his allowance for a new one.

We had asked ourselves the same question. Part of the answer had come from a bit of family lore passed down from my father. I can see him in the living room of our home in Brooklyn, the big pink cabbage-patch roses blooming on the gray wallpaper making a garden of that windowless row-house room. He was handing my uncle a Rheingold. He was celebrating. My mother had delivered her fourth child that day, and he was telling my uncle how every time they had another baby he seemed to coincidently get a promotion at his job. "God always provides," I heard him say to my uncle from the dining room where I, at thirteen, was solving algebra equations. I thought, "Is it alchemy or is it God?" Subliminally, I chose God, and my adolescent belief in providence had taken root.

We reassured Robert. We could live in the same house, and we would buy a second set of bunk beds. The boys could all share the same room for

40

now, and pretty soon we would refinish the attic, giving us another bedroom. We had lots of clothes and toys to share, and we always had enough to eat. He listened, and asked, and listened.

Kathleen was next. Her questions: "Would the family still have the same kind of fun together? Could we still go to the zoo and the circus and take a vacation with the Barrys? Could we still ride paddle boats in the park with Grandma and Grandpa?"

"Yes" we reassured her. "We have a station wagon, and it holds a lot of kids. Remember how many kids from the girls' softball team we drove to the ice cream parlor after a game?" We told her she would still be the "only petunia in the onion patch."

Then it was Dennis's turn, my smiling tow-headed son who then and now adapts like a chameleon to any situation. It was Dennis who had run home from school in June with his first-grade report card flapping in his pocket. "Mom, you just want me to be a normal average kid right?"

"Right," I said.

"Good, I got all C's, I'm average," and he was off on his bike.

At almost seven he was too young to think of anything but two new playmates. "It will be great," he offered without hesitation.

Approval was ours!

❧ 5 ❧

Learning Their History

I WROTE THE FIRST LETTER TO EDDIE and Kurt in mid July. Heather told the foster parents, Ardis and Allen, to expect to hear from me. It was a simple letter written for a four- and five-year-old, keeping in mind their inability to comprehend words like adoption, and the finality of leaving Ardis and Allen. I told them about Robert, Kathleen, and Dennis, and about the toys they were saving for their new brothers. I asked basic questions I thought would engage them and which they could respond to through Ardis. "What is your favorite food? Do you like ice cream? What is your favorite TV show?" I told them how excited we all were that they would be coming to live with us.

A few weeks later I found in my mailbox the first onionskin airmail envelope, with its red-and-blue stripes and Canadian stamps. It contained four pages of dense script written on both sides of the delicate paper. Breathless, I read the letter over and over, unable to get enough of these first sentences linking me to Kurt and Eddie. Ardis had written for the boys. Yes, they too were happy that they were going to have a new family and were excited, anticipating two brothers and a sister to play with. Peanut butter and jelly were their favorite foods, and they had the most fun watching *Captain Kangaroo* on television. The red plastic tools they played with in the cowshed at the back of their property were their favorite toys.

42

Ardis wrote that Kurt and Eddie were musical and sang all the time. She told us they loved her father, whom they call Grand-pops, and she wrote proudly about how Eddie killed a deer when Grand-pops took him hunting. I pictured a five-year-old with a rifle and couldn't help but wonder how Eddie felt as he was applauded for his bounty.

I wrote back and sent photographs of Bob and myself, another of Robert, Kathleen, and Dennis. I enclosed pictures of the room with red-and-blue plaid wall-paper and a red-flocked baseball player border where they would sleep in a new set of bunk beds. I sent pictures of a gleaming red fire engine and a shiny tricycle that Robert, Kathleen, and Dennis had retrieved from storage in the basement and scrubbed and polished for them.

I told them about our rabbit hutch and the pet rabbit, "Bandito," and about the dog, "Poo," a curly black poodle who refused to wear bows in her ears and was afraid of the color orange. We mailed them teddy bears, and Ardis responded with how they loved their bears from New Jersey. Acknowledging every sentence in my letters, Ardis told us how good Kurt and Eddie were, how they brushed their own teeth and dressed themselves.

As August drifted into September, the letters became more frequent, often crossing in the mail. Each day, one of the children asked if I'd heard from Canada. When a letter arrived from "the brothers," as they were now calling them, I read it aloud to everyone at dinnertime. Kathleen began to write her own letters to Kurt and Eddie. She arduously poured all nine years of herself onto the page in big block letters, telling them big sister things, like, "I can teach you to play the piano, and I will push you on the swings in the park." Ardis quickly answered Kathleen with her very own letter that she tucked into the envelope with the one to me.

We all shopped together for toys to send to Canada. Two wooden puzzles, one a blue polar bear and the other a red train that Ardis would later repack with their little bundle of belongings when they left her. She sent us photographs of Kurt and Eddie, close-ups we read like a bible, absorbing every aspect of their intense faces as we tried to read the story behind the eyes looking out at us. We hung their pictures on the refrigerator, the shrine for precious things like finger paintings and circus tickets. Each day was infused

43

with meaning for us as we drew closer to meeting our boys. I felt connected to a plan that I never even imagined before I lost John.

As the days turned into weeks, and we had no word of when we would be going to Canada to pick them up, fear seized me. Perhaps Ardis and Allen decided to adopt the boys themselves! They had been caring for Kurt and Eddie for almost fifteen months, a long time. I could not help but contrast the joy I was feeling as I anticipated the boys coming to us with what it must be like for Ardis and Allen as they prepared to let them go. I began to worry that Kurt and Eddie would be snatched from us at the last moment, the way John, the baby had been taken two years before.

By late September, Bob and I were more than ready to deliver to Spaulding the packet of documents that we had accumulated. This included our five birth certificates, our marriage certificate, income tax filings, Kurt and Eddie's wardship papers, a set of certified fingerprints for Bob and me and a copy of the Petition to Classify an Orphan as an Immediate Relative that was filed with the United States Government. As we made our way to the office located in a small second-story bedroom of the house that served as the agency for Spaulding, I noticed a sign tacked onto the bulletin board. A child had decorated it with yellow-and-green daisies, making it eye-catching and inviting.

PARENTS' SUPPORT GROUP
Meets every Tuesday at 7:00 p.m. Open discussion of behavioral problems.

About twenty families had already signed up. I secretly congratulated myself on our good fortune in finding Eddie and Kurt as I thought of the myriad problems that came through this agency's doors. We had gone to a "hard to place" agency anticipating a child others might not want, and were now miraculously in the process of adopting two perfect little boys. The sequence of events that had gotten us this far—the loss of John, Kathleen's diagnosis of juvenile diabetes, our inability to say "yes" to the other children offered to us through Spaulding, and the sustaining belief that there must be a reason for our grief, all converged. I wondered aloud, "How are we so lucky to find not only one, but two perfect little boys? Why is it that no one else scooped them up?" It was more a statement than a question.

The social worker paused momentarily. She seemed ready to say something, and then thought better of it.

"What?" I asked. "Is there something we don't know?"

She hesitated.

"Tell me," I said, feeling a chill crawl up my spine. *Ardis and Allen are keeping them,* I thought in panic.

She looked up from behind her glasses and sighed, an internal struggle written in her furrowed brow.

"Well, there are some indications of problems, but we feel they'll self-correct."

"Problems? What kind of problems?"

"Well, you have to understand, children who suffer such enormous neglect and deprivations are often delayed in their development."

"Such enormous neglect and deprivations? Do you have more details of their past?"

More hesitation. Then . . . "There is some concern about IQ tests that were administered." Inwardly, I froze. Outwardly, like a robot, I continued to function and asked, "Are the boys normal?"

"It's hard to say. I think so, but I was not sent the complete reports."

Panic rose in my chest.

"Can you find out?" Bob asked as his eyes met mine over the corner of the desk.

"I'll call the agency in Canada and see if I can get more information for you. Give me a couple of days."

Stunned with fear and disbelief, we made our way to the car. I revisited a time when I had experienced similar feelings. Bob and I had been on vacation, feeling lighthearted and happy. The bus taking us to the hotel in the mountains of Virginia took a wrong turn in heavy fog. The winding dirt road was treacherous, and the driver decided to make a "U" turn without giving us an opportunity to get off the bus. Suddenly the back of the bus was hanging over the side of an embankment, the wheels spinning in mid-air, the ground literally swept from under us. Fog, thick as soup, was pasted to the windows, and we could only imagine the plummet to the bottom awaiting us. Pictures of Robert, Kathleen, and

Dennis, bereft and orphaned flashed in my imagination. Eventually, the bus driver got traction as the belly of the bus ripped along the edge of the road but not before I had bargained with God for some kind of protection.

Now I was emotionally back on the bus and already I was bargaining with God. *Let them be normal and I will never lose my temper again. Let them be normal and I will pray every day. Let them be normal and I will, I will, I will . . .*

We waited.

The caseworker called a week later and told us she had more information and asked us to come in to talk to her. Driving to that meeting on a steamy September day, the car wheels drumming on the road matched the drumming in my head. *Let it be okay, let it be okay.*

The room where we met the caseworker was small and cluttered with photos taped to the wall, pictures that, in my preoccupation with Kurt and Eddie, I'd never before noticed. There were children in wheelchairs sharing hot dogs at a picnic, a Down Syndrome child holding the hands of a man and woman who obviously adored him. A girl with braces on both legs stood proudly between a man and woman, each of whom supported one of her elbows. Suddenly, I realized how my on-going enchantment with Kurt and Eddie had blindsided me to the disabilities that were the reality of "hard-to-place" children. I saw the trusting faces of Robert, Kathleen, and Dennis in my mind's eye and was terrified by what we were doing.

Sounds of a fan whirring on the floor melded into the street noises floating through the open window, breaking the silence that hung in the room. The caseworker offered us water and small talk, but we wanted neither. Her tone was serious as she began, "At the time Kurt and Eddie were picked up by social services, they had not received any inoculations or vaccinations. Kurt needed a hernia operation. There was no history of illness, but that doesn't mean they weren't sick prior to being made wards of the Province, just that there are no medical records."

She hesitated, letting us absorb her words. Then her tone lightened. "The record reads, 'Physically healthy' for both of them. They've been examined and found to be in good health, very good health."

Bob and I listened, barely breathing. In her low, steady voice, she continued, "Unfortunately, the intelligence tests are another matter."

My heart dropped. It was not the thing I feared, a change of heart by Ardis and Allen that was thwarting us, but nonetheless, I sensed our happiness was about to explode. And yet a part of me knew that whatever was coming, it was too late to turn back.

The caseworker began by using a specific word "echolalia," that carried a medical definition and needed to be explained to us. Adverbs like "improved" were like buoys that kept us afloat and prevented our drowning in the language. "Improved echolalia"—is this the good news or the bad?

Stressing the fact that severe neglect was the condition that led to the separation of the children from their biological parents, she continued, "It was evident to the social welfare investigators from the very beginning that something was not right with the children. They documented bizarre behavior, but the report doesn't give examples of that behavior, so I have no way of knowing exactly what they're referring to."

By now my heart was racing as questions flooded my mind. Did they bang their heads against the floor? Did they destroy things in outbursts of frustration? Did they fail to respond to affection?

As if from some far away place, I heard Bob ask, "What is echolalia?"

"It's a parroting of language, a repetition of phrases and sentences rather than a response to language."

"What does it come from?"

"It's sometimes seen in schizophrenia. It's a form of regression whereby a person merely reacts in reflexive or short-circuited ways that do not involve his will center. Another way of putting it is that he learns to react to stimuli with inactivity and to simply repeat or echo what he hears, rather than process it in his mind, and respond."

"I'm not sure I understand," Bob said. "Could you give us an example?"

She thought a minute, "If Kurt or Eddie hear a typical sentence, for example, 'Did you see the dog?' instead of responding with another sentence that indicates engagement and moves the conversation forward, they just repeat or echo the same sentence, using the same intonation as the speaker, mimicking rather than participating in conversation."

I tried to comprehend what she was telling us. I had seen infants mimic sounds as language began to develop in the first year of life. However, an infant was engaged with language, and within days learned to initiate the sound on his own. What did this echolalia, incorporated into the language of a four- and five-year-old, signify?

Conflicting emotions bombarded me. I was baffled. It sounded bad. Was it a mental condition? Was it an emotional condition? We had requested a "hard to place" child. Was this going to be too hard? At the same time, I felt hypocritical. Perhaps under my altruistic heart lay a heart of tin. And I was angry. Why hadn't we been told this information weeks ago? Were these facts deliberately hidden from us, or just overlooked in a genuine belief that the behaviors would dissipate in time? Looming like a mushroom cloud in my mind was the ultimate question, what would happen to our family if we went through with this?

"You mentioned psychological testing," Bob said. "Do you have copies of those tests?"

"No, the agency in Canada is unable to release the actual tests." She went on to assure us that the psychologist who examined Eddie and Kurt indicated in his report that the aberrations in behavior were consistent with gross neglect and would dissipate over time. In addition there had definitely been improvement documented since the boys had been placed in foster care.

I held on to that thought like a falling man grasping air. It certainly seemed true. We had a stack of letters from Ardis telling us about the boys. She never mentioned any serious behavioral or mental problems. Now I asked myself, could we believe those letters? It seemed impossible that the boys we began to love, the boys of the onion-skin letters, who played in a shed with plastic tools and ran to Allen in the nearby forest, were the same children being described in this conversation about bizarre behavior and echolalia.

As the case worker shuffled through her papers looking for the scant information she had on the IQ tests, I remembered phrases from those letters. The boys were excited about being adopted and coming to New Jersey. How naive I was to believe that. Of course the boys were not looking forward to adoption, to having their lives uprooted once again. They were barely four and five years old and could not begin to comprehend what adoption meant. We worried that even Robert, Kathleen, and Dennis, years older, could not grasp the full implications of adoption. If one used the right tone of voice even to a dog, one could tell it that it's being banished to the North Pole and it will lick your fingers and roll over in happiness. At best, Kurt and Eddie were accommodating their response to Ardis's positive presentation of information. At worst, we were being deceived. A teddy bear, a wooden puzzle, and a few letters do not a family make.

The social worker found the report she was looking for.

"About the IQ tests," she said. "There were a series of three tests administered to each of the boys. The first took place in March of 1971, a month after their being removed from the building where they were barely surviving with their biological parents."

As she spoke, Bob began to take notes on the back of an envelope. The results forwarded to Spaulding were summaries, cryptic and brief. In March of 1971, Eddie's IQ was 50; Kurt was untestable.

Bob reached across the space separating our two chairs and put his hand on my shoulder as if to hold together the shards of my shattering dream. We had done a bit of research in the previous few days, and we knew that with an IQ of 50, Eddie was retarded. They could not even administer the test to Kurt, which seemed to put him in a category less than human.

Without looking up from her notes and before we could utter a response, the social worker continued. "Kurt was tested again one month later in April of 1971. At that time, he was described as alert, cooperative, understandable and slightly retarded." My mind regrouped. There was no number assigned to the IQ test result. Was this a reason to be hopeful? At least he was no longer untestable. We sat rigid in our chairs, as she continued.

In June of 1971, they were both tested again. The summary of the report indicated that Eddie's speech had improved, and he was easygoing and affectionate. His IQ was 78. At that same time, Kurt was described as curious, and it was noted that he related to the tester. His IQ was 70, and he was functioning in the two-year, one-month range."

49

Bob did a quick calculation in response to my "How old was he at that time?" The answer: Three years and one month.

Finally, in January of 1972, approximately six months later, Eddie was tested again. He was observed to be "Eager, attentive, and cooperative, with an IQ of 80." He was functioning in the three-year range, and he was actually four years and eight months old.

Affectionate, eager, cooperative, alert—these words were beacons in a dark and vast sea. Other than the very broad and cursory understanding of Intelligence Quotients we had researched the previous week, our knowledge was limited. We wondered about all the words not listed in that report. There were hundreds of words with positive connotations like "Unlimited," "Reasonable," "Willing," "Motivated," and words with negative connotations like "Angry," "Obtuse," "Boisterous," and Demanding"—conspicuous by their absence. The fact that both Kurt's and Eddie's scores improved was encouraging to us as we sat there, hoping against hope.

We left that meeting with numbers and adjectives wreaking havoc in our minds. Now began the work of trying to interpret them. We called a friend in Boston who was a child psychologist. He educated us. He confirmed that the final IQ scores given to us indicated the boys were slightly retarded and/or borderline retarded. "Are the numbers going to change? Will they improve?" we asked. He couldn't tell us; he did not know. "As a rule, these scores remain consistent over time," he said. It came down to the nature/nurture conundrum.

The psychiatric literature confirmed what our own common sense told us. Nurturing was vital to a baby. If no one was present to tend to its needs, to comfort and soothe it, then the baby must learn to do that for himself, a daunting task. If he did not learn to do it for himself, he might literally die. Of course, the behavior a baby could engage in by himself was limited. He might learn to comfort himself by rocking endlessly while staring into space. He might avoid eye contact or play with his own feces. What seemed like bizarre behaviors to an observer were really survivor skills. Studies done with orphaned children linked a "failure to survive" with severe neglect. Secondary to physical death was emotional death, whereby the child's will and feelings became numbed. It was as though the child grew a hard outer shell to protect himself from painful feeling and then carried the pain, frozen at some primitive level, with him throughout his life.

Common sense told us that if no one was interacting with a child, if no one told him that a table was a table and a chair was a chair, and if no one showed him how to use a spoon or a dish, then there was no way he could recognize or name these simple objects. Of course his IQ must be affected. The more global the deprivation in the environment, the more damaging to the child. It seemed clear that mental stimulation was not a part of the environment of children found alone and naked in a cold attic.

Embedded, like a splinter in my mind, was the "nature" factor. What genetic mischief might have been at play here? We knew that the biological parents must be psychologically, and possibly physically, unwell. We knew their father was passed out when the boys were taken. We wondered about alcohol or drug addiction. No mention of physical illness and no specifically stated mental diagnosis had been revealed to us.

Echolalia was seen in schizophrenia, we were told. Schizophrenia was rumbling in my mind like distant thunder. Was there some sort of psychosis present that put one or both of the biological parents out of touch with reality?" The likelihood of a genetic predisposition to a disease like schizophrenia coupled with the environmental factor of gross neglect was a fearful combination.

The questions we were left with in the days that followed tormented us. Was environmental damage reversible? Would the boys continue to improve mentally? If IQ's remained stable over time, would they be able to lead normal lives? Did we have the strength and resources to address the needs of handicapped children? And finally—if our worst fears were realized, how would adopting these two little waifs affect our other three children?

In the days that followed, although our hearts were beating a steady "yes," there continued in our minds and conversation the constant static of doubt and fear. Never before had we made a decision based on so many unknowns. When one of us became overwhelmed by the enormity of our plans, the other reminded that we still had choices, "We can pull out of it now. We don't have to go through with it."

I prayed, although I found it difficult to believe in a personal God who would involve himself in my idiosyncratic decision. It was difficult to focus, and often my attempts at prayer culminated in "worst possible scenario" thinking.

At some point, the words of a poem that I'd known since childhood came back to me with startling clarity. I found I was able to calm some of my fears by repeating it to myself. The poem was "The Road Less Traveled" by Robert Frost. It was especially the first and last lines that gave me comfort and assurance.

> Two roads diverged in a yellow wood
> and sorry I could not travel both . . .
> I took the one less traveled by
> and that has made all the difference.

I heard these words like a trumpet call to trust the instinct that had placed us on this road in the first place. My heart filled with compassion as I considered what a difference we could make in Kurt and Eddie's life and swelled with gratitude when I thought of the way two little boys would complete our family.

Here was risk. And here was opportunity. Like the fairy tale of the Lady and the Tiger, there were two doors from which to choose; each would change our future in different ways. Yet some intuition, a knowing without knowing, took root. Like faith, an abstraction that by its very nature refused to offer proof, we believed in the boys. No one could make the decision for us, yet the reality was that the decision had already been made. We made it during those weeks of the onion-skin letters.

Now I shored up our decision by once again dipping into myth. Romulus and Remus called to me in those weeks of doubt. Was I the she-wolf who would rescue these two cubs from a wilderness of neglect? Would they mature into men of substance, as solid as Rome? Although there was no question in my mind that this myth did not operate on any conscious level, who could say what combination of memory, archetype, desire, and faith bubbled from underground springs and flooded the heart in a "yes" it hardly knew it was uttering?

೫ 6 ೫

Meeting Our Boys

THE FRIDAY BEFORE THANKSGIVING in 1972, the house was quiet. The children were all in school, and I had a few hours to work on a paper I was writing for a course in philosophy. In my research, I had discovered Emerson, and I was gathering his thoughts the way a bird gathers bits of grass and earth and twigs to construct a nest for its young. In his writings, Emerson encourages the reader to "Trust the instinct to the end, though you cannot tell why or see why." Now I was happily preparing my heart for Kurt and Eddie. Emerson's words not only validated my sense of knowing that the decision to adopt was the right one, but also dissolved my fear and replaced it with anticipation. I read, "Every secret wish and every desire of the mind is a prayer," and again felt a confluence of thought and feelings.

The call came from Spaulding. The Canadian court had severed the parental relationship. The boys could be released to us. It was as though we had been rehearsing a script for the past several months and were suddenly called to the stage for opening night. We dropped everything and sprang into action. We told Robert, Kathleen, and Dennis that their brothers were finally coming, and helped each of them pack a traveling bag. We arranged for airline tickets, five to Canada and seven for the return flight and reserved connecting hotel rooms in Halifax for the two nights we needed to stay. We notified the school about taking the children

53

out for a few days. We told our next-door neighbors, who publicly shared our joy, and privately we later learned, wondered about our sanity.

We drove to Long Island to tell my parents. After they hugged the kids and offered us bagels that Sunday morning, I said in my most light-hearted voice "We have something to tell you. We're all going to Canada this week to pick up two little boys that we're going to adopt."

The blood drained from my mother's face. She was sitting on the edge of a kitchen chair, and for a few moments she was speechless as she took in the news. The room got quiet. A bowl of fat red apples on the table seemed to absorb the momentary doubt I felt.

Bob filled the silence. "We have pictures to show you. Wait until you see these boys. They're wonderful."

My mother's eyes started to register fright. "Why would you do such a thing?" she finally said, looking from me to Bob. "You're asking for trouble. You can't afford more children. Are you thinking of your own children? What will it do to these children if it doesn't work out?" she said, extending her arms to gather them close to her, as if to shield them from our wild notions.

My father was less emphatic, although when it came to family matters, he generally deferred to my mother. I could tell from the look in his eyes that, in spite of being astounded, a part of him was bubbling with delight, but the part of him that honored my mother's feelings was keeping his under control. For my father, whose hobby was restoring old furniture, much of life was dedicated to finding value in remnants disguised by time and misuse. He found treasure where others failed to notice, and he always had an eye out for what could be salvaged.

I thought of the old, scarred oak table he had hauled from Nathan's Bar and Grill the day Nathan closed his doors for the last time. Each night after dinner he disappeared into the cellar to work on it. Sometimes I helped. First he stripped the varnish, and we watched it bubble up like silt in a pond after rain. The layers of varnish and grease turned into a thick pasty liquid that we peeled off with our scrapers. We repeated the process over and over until, as if from behind a gauze curtain, the grain of the golden oak revealed itself.

We sanded it by hand. First with sandpaper number nine, the roughest paper needed to remove the deepest burns, and then with sandpaper number one, for a delicate finish. The air was thick with dust. It made its way up the stairs in a mist that passed through small cracks around the basement door into my mother's kitchen. She protested. Still we kept sanding. "Always sand with the grain, never against it. Be patient," my father said as he rubbed his hand over the surface. And so we worked side by side under the naked light bulb hanging from the basement socket. We were midwives, ministering to a holy moment. "Just look at that," he said as he admired our work. "Who would believe that something so beautiful was hidden under all that goop?"

I knew that this man who could invest such care and joy into salvaging a table would soon be won over to my boys. Of course, my parents were trying to protect us. Later we would learn from our friends that my family was not the only ones who thought we were crazy, but they were the only ones who said it out loud. Thankfully, we were beyond the point where we could be influenced. We were following a star and had willingly entered its shining orbit.

✻ ✻ ✻

THE DAY FINALLY ARRIVED. Our plane landed with a thud. It was freezing cold, three days before Thanksgiving, as Bob and I, Robert, Kathleen, and Dennis followed a handful of passengers disembarking from the American Airlines plane that flew us to Halifax. Heather was to have driven Kurt and Eddie the three hundred miles from Yarmouth across Nova Scotia into Halifax the previous day. She was supposed to be waiting at the gate with them for our plane to land. Mounds of snow were heaped along the chain link fence separating the runway from the terminal buildings. Each footfall clanged as we descended the steep steel staircase that connected the plane to the tarmac. The swirling wind turned each of us into a battering ram as we tried to slice through it, making the three-hundred-yard walk across the airfield seem endless. Corralling the children against gusts that threatened to lift them off the ground, I was exquisitely aware of how young and vulnerable they were as they followed us into a decision destined to change their lives.

Suddenly, the wind changed direction. At our backs, it propelled us through the heavy glass doors of the terminal. Barely inside, I scanned the terminal but did not see a woman with two small children. At the same time, I heard our name being paged over the airport speaker system. "Will the Goldstein party please report to a customs agent?"

Bob and I were startled and apprehensive, but for different reasons. "Was that us being paged?" I said in disbelief. Bob nodded. I thought— *What's wrong? Why are we being paged? Why are they not here waiting for us?* We were so close. Here in a foreign airport, submerged in snow, in a country where we knew not one soul, was the whole thing going to fall apart?

But Bob's apprehension was about the bureaucracy. The thing he felt most powerless about was the paperwork and procedures written in stone by government agencies. Now he was afraid that an "i" hadn't been dotted or a "t" crossed, and we were in for a battle with some government agency that could take weeks.

We found the customs officer. He had a few routine questions about our newly issued passports, and a message for us. He pointed down the terminal. "There's an empty gate a few hundred yards in front of you. Your party's waiting for you there."

Flooded with relief, we hurried. It was happening. Heather and the boys were in the building. They were waiting for us. I could feel tears of happiness gathering behind my eyes. The terminal seemed endless as we scanned the gates that grew less and less crowded as we walked. And then we saw them. From under the glare of the fluorescent lights, we saw a young woman standing at an empty gate. She was holding the hand of a small boy in a light-blue hooded parka. But there was only one child clutching her hand. With racing heart I followed her gaze and saw, several feet away, another child in a red jacket. He had found a machine that dispensed little toy airplanes and was kicking it violently, ignoring the woman's pleas to return to her. Both children looked so small, like two-year-olds, not a four- and five-year-old. We started to run. Heather saw our family approaching and instinctively moved towards us.

In the whirlwind of smiles and tears and greetings that followed, Eddie never let go of her hand. At Heather's suggestion and without any eye contact or emotion, he whispered, "Hello, New Mommy. Hello, New Daddy."

His little formal handshake foreshadowed what must have been heavy coaching to be a good boy so we would like him, keep him. That would be in evidence over the next several months before it all cracked like an eggshell. Following the lead of this toddler, I offered him my hand and felt for the first time the thrill of his fingers slipping into my palm.

We all made our way to Kurt, who was kicking more intensely now. Bob bribed his attention by giving him coins to feed into the toy airplane machine. He looked at the toys but refused to make eye contact with us as he too, at Heather's bidding, finally said, "Hello, New Mommy. Hello, New Daddy." Some intuition informed the moment, and Bob and I instinctively rejected the impulse to scoop the boys up in our arms and hug them. It was obvious they were not ready for hugs or kisses.

Robert, Kathleen, and Dennis, in the meantime, were clustered together, a little to the side. Had we forgotten about them? Robert's face turned scarlet as he watched Bob try to calm the kicking Kurt. This was a scene, as in "Don't make a scene." Kathleen was tentatively making her way towards Eddie, who was still clutching Heather's hand and averting his eyes to the hem of her coat. The freckles across the bridge of Kathleen's nose had disappeared, and her face was pasty white. The excitement, plus the need for lunch, was causing her blood sugar to plummet. I pulled a can of apple juice from my pocketbook.

"Here, drink this," I said, watching the color return to her face as she gulped the juice and bent down to talk to Eddie, one of her pen-pals of the last six months. Meanwhile, Dennis had inched his way next to me, jiggling and hopping from one foot to the other.

"I have to go to the bathroom," he whispered. Such a simple statement, yet it sent me into the first of those mind-bending dialogues in my head that for years would swirl around every small decision I made as I attempted to show no favoritism between my biological and adopted children. Do I leave the boys within the first fifteen minutes of meeting them to take my biological child to the bathroom? Do I send Dennis alone? Do I send Robert with him? Is that fair to Robert?

Finally, "Can you wait a few minutes?" I asked Dennis. He could.

Heather suggested lunch, which would give us the needed space and opportunity to begin to interact with the boys. Kurt and Eddie did not know what a restaurant was except that it was a place to get "pop," the Canadian word for soda.

"Pop, pop," Kurt chanted as he continued to wildly kick his way across the terminal. Robert hung back, the ten-year-old big brother, embarrassed at the scene we were making.

"Pop, pop," Kurt continued to chant as we sat down at two Formica tables that had been shoved together to accommodate the eight of us. Even before we were all seated, Kurt flung the shiny silverware across the room with his toy planes. The waitress cringed and sent disapproving glances towards Bob and me. A few minutes later, Eddie, unaccustomed to the choreography that went on between a waitress and the people she served, chose the wrong moment to stretch his leg into the space alongside the table. The waitress tripped and "pop" went splashing all over her tray and the floor. Eddie looked terrified. After, "It's okay. It's okay. It's only soda," and the clean up, and a few bites of food, Eddie indicated to Heather that he needed to use the bathroom.

"I'll go with him," I said, jumping up quickly to catch him as he sped from the table. I reached for his hand, but he pulled it away. He wanted no help. I followed him and watched him go into a stall and close the door. As I stood guard outside, I heard the awful retching as he vomited and vomited.

"Are you sick?" No answer. "Let me help you," I pleaded. No answer. Finally, the door opened. Eddie pretended that nothing unusual had happened. He showed no emotion, and I began to comprehend that the veneer of self-sufficiency was, in truth, fear fossilized in his heart.

How different this was from Robert, Kathleen, or Dennis, who shouted "Mommy, I'm going to throw up," knowing I would run to them with a bucket and hold them tight across the back and shoulders until their bodies stopped shaking with the retching and I could mop the slop from the pale face. This five-year-old was taking care of himself, letting me know not only how self-sufficient he was, but more significant, that he preferred not to be touched.

The rest of that day was spent on official business. There was the trip to the medical doctor for an exit check-up, required by the U.S. Government before allowing immigrants into the country. Kurt and Eddie wanted Heather to accompany them into the examining room. They did not want me. They did not want Bob. We waited in the outer office, praying for no last-minute snafu, while the doctor examined them and signed the necessary papers. We stood in line at the Department of Immigration where their passports were finalized. There were endless papers to sign. The day finally ended, everything accomplished.

Heather was leaving. She handed over their belongings, carted from Yarmouth in the back of her station wagon in two brown paper bags. There were a few pairs of underwear, two pairs of pants, and two shirts. Each child had one pair of ski pajamas and a toothbrush. There was a *Thomas the Tank Engine* book and two wooden puzzles. There were two stuffed animals. There was an orange plastic lunch pail that Eddie had taken with him on the bus to kindergarten. There were his workbooks, where, in what looked like primitive hieroglyphics, he had tried to print some letters. There were ragged cutout pictures of a house and a dog he had tried to color and paste in his book. That was it. The transfer was made. We stood, the seven of us, waving good-bye as Heather disappeared in her station wagon for the long ride back to Yarmouth.

Eddie and Kurt could not control the sobs racking their little bodies as the enormity of the situation hit them. Heather was truly gone, and they were left with five strangers. Neither Bob nor I could console them; it was the other children who helped. First Robert, digging in his pockets for his precious baseball cards, offered cautiously. "Here, want to hold my cards?"

Kathleen and Dennis bent towards the boys. Kathleen stroked Kurt's back. "Don't cry. It'll be okay," Dennis said. "Mom and Dad are nice."

Eventually the sobbing gave way to whimpering, and the whimpering to a final sigh. These were their last sobs for a long, long while, as their fate and their feelings froze in that parking lot. Neither Kurt nor Eddie would cry again for the next eight months.

* * *

WE HAD BOOKED TWO ADJOINING ROOMS at the Holiday Inn, each with two double beds, for our first night together. Getting ready for bed, the older children did what children do; threw their clothes on the floor. Amazed, we watched as Kurt and Eddie methodically folded their shirts, pants, underwear, and "stockings" and stacked them neatly in a pile. The shoes were placed alongside the pile. They brushed their teeth for a full five minutes. Each filled up the wash-basin, inserted the plug, and vigorously rubbed soap on his hands. How different this was from the older children who were haphazardly going through the motions with their toothbrushes and wash-cloths. In just this one day, it became obvious to Bob and me that the need to be good, to be neat, to be no trouble, had been drummed into these boys. I could not help but wonder what combination of fantasy and reality about adoption was motivating their behavior.

Our plan that night was to have Robert and Dennis share one double bed, Kurt and Eddie the other, and Kathleen was to sleep in the other double bed in our room. When the boys tentatively started to jump up and down on their beds, Kathleen, already in her flannel nightgown, heard the ruckus and asked if she could join them. Although this was not a normal bedtime ritual or a thing we would ordinarily encourage, in view of the circumstances, the pent up emotion in each of them, it seemed like a good idea. In retrospect, this was their first act of "play" together, the five of them whooping it up at the Holiday Inn in a bonding ritual familiar to most families.

The insulated drapes with a cobalt-blue geometric pattern were thick, but the neon light flashing in the parking lot outside the window cast an eerie glow throughout the night. Bob and I lay awake, alert with jumbled thoughts and listening for sounds of a nightmare or feet padding across the stained rug. Heather had warned us that Kurt and Eddie might regress to bedwetting with the changes they were encountering, but what we didn't expect that night was the evidence of upheaval in the older children. At about two o'clock in the morning, Robert woke up sick to his stomach and vomited. There were wet sheets and wet pajamas in the bathtub that morning, but it was our two older boys whose bodies betrayed them during the night, manifesting the turmoil everyone was feeling.

* * *

IT WAS STILL DARK as we made our way out of the rooms for breakfast.

"Don't run in the hallway. People are still asleep," Bob said to Kurt and Eddie, as they raced like little banshees down the long corridor. And then,

"Stop pushing the elevator button," as they took turns pressing it like a doorbell.

"Leave them alone. At least they're happy," I said, a forecast of the negotiating we would do over the years, negotiating that would sometimes erupt into accusations: "You're too hard." "You're too easy."

We were both right as often as wrong, as we continued to navigate without a compass. We questioned ourselves, and we questioned each other, looking for any disparity between our handling of situations with our biological and adopted children. We tried to be consistent, to foster the same rules and know when it was more important to let the rules slide.

One of the first things we noticed about the boys was that they used pronouns indiscriminately. At times each referred to a male as "she" and a female as "he." The singular and plural pronouns were also mixed-up, resulting in the use of "they" for "me" and "we" for "them." "You" floated around their speech like an impromptu visitor and might be substituted for any other pronoun. Bob and I did not know how to evaluate these language oddities. We hoped they were simply quirks but feared they indicated a deeper problem with understanding and intelligence, one predicted by the IQ tests. Correcting the grammar was momentarily successful at best or a manifestation of echolalia, at worst. Both Kurt and Eddie repeated the sentence with the correct pronoun, but neither could retain the grammatical rule and, unaware, went right back to using the pronoun incorrectly.

Finally, paperwork in order, it was mid afternoon and we headed for the airport. As we made our way toward the ramp to enter the plane, the boys were excited. "New Daddy, look. New Mommy, look. There plane. Where go?" they sang in the November air. Heads turned and people smiled as they skirted around us, until it seemed everyone knew something wonderful was happening. Our fellow travelers asked questions, offered to switch seats, wished us luck, and gave us advice. We were a movable puzzle trying to fit together in the crowded plane.

At last, we were strapped into our seats with coloring books and crayons at the ready, and the plane took off. The "borderline retarded" results of the IQ tests were a persistent itch I wanted to scratch in the back of my mind. Sitting with Kurt, I secretly tested him with colors as he scribbled the pages of a coloring book. He identified red and blue and yellow and green, but purple was a problem. He consistently called it "marble," so we played our first word game—hiding and asking for the purple crayon. I was saving "marble" for another day. That purple crayon took on enormous proportions for me. It became a symbol. I knew that children generally recognize colors around age two. If I could teach Kurt to identify the color purple by the time we got to Boston, he was not retarded. On the other hand, purple did sound like marble. He probably just heard it wrong. He was not retarded; any fool could see that, I cautiously thought, as he made an attempt to color the arm of the airplane seat.

We arrived at the Boston airport for the shuttle back to New York at about 5:00 p.m. on Thanksgiving Eve. We tried to make our way through customs amidst a professional hockey team that had come in on another flight with their equipment slung over their shoulders in enormous canvas bags. There must have been thirty of them rolling down the corridor in a huge wave. We seemed to grow smaller as they jostled each other, and their booming voices filled the cavernous customs arena.

Then I heard other voices, higher pitched but nonetheless loud, shouting, "New Mommy, where New Daddy? New Mommy, where New Daddy?" as Bob and I get separated in the throng. And while Robert blushed as his hockey heroes took notice of our family, I saw player after player nudge one another and nod towards Kurt and Eddie. And then, amazingly, the team parted like the Red Sea. The Boston Bruins stood aside and made a space for two brand-new little brothers on their way home.

At Customs, the last bureaucratic process where something could go wrong, questions abounded.

"Why are you entering the country?"

"Which of these children are citizens?"

"Let me see all the passports again," said the customs agent, and he looked from the passport photos to the five tired little faces peering up at him. Finally he closed the passports and a smile lit up his face.

"Okay, Mrs. Deveau, you and the children can go through now!"

Just when everything was officially under control, it wasn't. "No, no," I said, "You have it wrong. I'm not Mrs. Deveau. I'm adopting two boys with that last name. I'm their new mother."

"Yes, yes," he said, as he waved us through; and it really didn't matter who he thought anyone was. We were in the country! Next we had to get to New York. It seemed as if every college student in Boston was heading home for Thanksgiving and they were all trying to get on the Boston shuttle. The airport was bedlam. Students tossed Frisbees over each other's heads. Some slept on the floor, using their knapsacks for pillows. The air was charged. Every mother's child was on his way "home for the holiday."

There are moments in life that are so intense that they remain engraved in memory like etchings on a cave wall. Such a scene for me was the picture of Robert and Kathleen transforming themselves into a big brother and big sister on that shuttle line. Kurt and Eddie were exhausted, and after standing for over an hour could not stand any longer. Bob and I were maneuvering the luggage, trying to keep all five children close to us in the midst of the chaos. Robert, all of ten years old, carried Eddie, their tousled blond hair mingling as Eddie slept on his shoulder. Kathleen held Kurt, talking to him privately about the piano she would teach him to play when they got home to New Jersey.

Once on the plane, Kurt and Eddie slept, even though the noise of students on holiday rivaled a party in a college dorm. At last the plane banked, and the New York skyline, ablaze in a million lights, rose out of the darkness to greet us.

"We're here," we said as we gently woke them and carried them through the temporary corrugated tin corridor of an airport under construction.

"Is this York? Is this Jersey?" they asked.

How different the names of the states sounded, separated from their modifiers. So fresh, so unknown. So new.

❧ 7 ❧

The First Year

A S WE PULLED INTO THE DRIVEWAY THAT Thanksgiving eve night, our attention was drawn to the big white cardboard "Welcome Home!" sign tacked to the front door. Our next-door neighbors and their four children had created it with watercolors and paper streamers. There it was, shouting a happy welcome to Kurt and Eddie.

"What that?" each of them whispered sleepily. We explained as we unfastened the sign from the door and brought it inside to hang up. That was the first "what that." It became the question asked over and over again during those first weeks. Contractions were not in their repertoire.

The first piece of furniture each of them saw when we opened the front door was the piano. "What that?" they shouted as they ran for it and banged on the keys. Before any of us could answer, they were running around the room, touching everything in sight, asking, "What that?"

At first we tried to answer, "That's a dishwasher."

"What dishwasher?"

"It's a machine that washes the dishes."

"What machine?"

"Something that's automatic."

"What automatic?"

"It goes by itself."

Kurt and Eddie gave us a quizzical look, and then were on to something else. "What that?"

We finally gave up trying to answer the streaming questions. Our mission became focused. Just get everyone to bed. Let the trip be over.

Kurt and Eddie were to share a bedroom with Robert and Dennis, referred to as "the boys' room." The best part of the room was a large cedar closet shaped like an Old Dutch barn, with its own small window overlooking the patch of grass and chain-link fence on the side of the house. The closet was packed with toys that had been removed from the room in order to make space for the additional set of bunk beds now filling its opposite corners. Robert and Dennis, in their new role as older brothers, had already started sleeping in the top bunks.

Bob and I eventually got them all to bed. Alone together for the first time in five days, we put our feet up and heaved a joint sigh of relief. "We did it," Bob said from his prone position in the lounge chair that he had been craving for the past twenty-four hours. In Halifax he had whispered to me, "I can't wait to get everyone home. I'm longing for the moment when they're all safely tucked into bed and we can put our feet up and relax."

The moment had arrived. We sat in wonder, counting the blessings of the two boys entrusted to us. Tired as we were, we stayed up talking, reliving the past five days. We wanted to make the experiences last and bask in what felt like the greatest accomplishment of our lives.

Bob told me how Eddie had started to tremble in the taxi on the drive home from the airport and how he had taken him onto his lap, held him tight, and said, "You will never have to be afraid. I will always take care of you." He described how Eddie calmed and let himself settle into the crook of Bob's arm. Our hearts were nearly bursting as we recounted the scene at the airport in Boston—the image of the vulnerable heads of our five children, the older ones carrying their new brothers, inching forward to the shuttle. Still counting our blessings we made our way up the stairs, paused at their bedrooms, watched each of them breathing deeply in sleep, caught our breath at the beauty of it, and finally fell into bed.

* * *

THE NEXT MORNING THE WEATHER joined forces with our lives. It was Thanksgiving Day, 1972, and we awoke to the season's first snow covering the neighborhood in drifting waves of white. Everything looked new. It was a good diversion, and the kids wanted out early to make a snowman and angels in the snow. The phone rang fifteen minutes later. It was our sign-making neighbors who were watching the frolicking in our backyard from their own house, about twenty feet from ours. They heard Kurt and Eddie singing "Frosty the Snowman" and they told us it was the voices, the perfect pitch that drew them to the window.

We cracked open our kitchen window and listened. Robert, Kathleen, and Dennis had stopped their own play and were standing in their rubber boots, listening. Bob and I looked at each other in amazement. "What that?" Bob said laughingly as the pure notes coming from their throats hung in the morning sun and we got our first glimpse of Kurt and Eddie's musical inheritance, a talent the rest of our tone-deaf family could only aspire to.

Around noon, two sets of grandparents and my sisters arrived. "Where are they?" everyone asked in unison as they pulled into the driveway and got out of the car. I pointed to the yard where the dark green branches on the fir trees, heavy with last night's snow, dipped their shoulders to the ground as if bending to greet the newcomers. Kneeling at the rabbit hutch were Dennis, Kurt, and Eddie, each with a fistful of lettuce and carrots. Six woolen mittens were sprawled like starfish on the crust of the snow. Dennis was teaching them how to feed Bandito, who was at that moment doing the "Bandito Dance" as she went from hand to hand, feasting on the abundance from the three care-takers. Everyone's hats and scarves were off by now, strewn around the yard. Kathleen was wrapping her scarf around the neck of a snowman newly birthed by the four of them and already melting in the sun. Their heads were damp with perspiration from play and the sun's dazzle on the white snow. Robert, peeled down to a sweatshirt, hockey stick at the ready, was standing by the gate of the chain-link fence, with a group of "big kids." I heard him say proudly, "There they are, my new brothers."

"Wow," from a chorus of ten-year-old boys.

The first day home.

Grandma and Grandpa and my sisters tentatively made their way into the yard, and Robert, Kathleen, and Dennis ran up to them with hugs. Kurt and Eddie hung back, watching. Then Kathleen moved aside and said, "Our new brothers are here." And Grandpa said, "Well isn't that great. Will you introduce us to them?"

And with these simple words began the love affair between the once-reluctant grandparents and their newly acquired grandchildren. Before the end of the day something ignited between Kurt and my father. Kurt attached himself to Grandpa's lap. At dinnertime, he plopped himself in a chair next to him at the Thanksgiving table, initiating a ritual that would be repeated throughout the years.

Wet and tired, the five children finally came in for lunch, and Kurt and Eddie resumed their chorus of, "What that?" It continued like a drum beat.

"That's a cord to open the curtains." I pulled it to demonstrate, and the white sheers part.

"What cord?"

"It's a long string that attaches to the curtain rod."

"What rod."

"The rod holds the curtains above the window."

"Me do?"

"No, only mommies and daddies pull the cord."

A confused look.

"If children pull too hard on the cord, it could break, and the curtains will fall down."

The naming of things was endless. Sometimes, exhausted from the sheer bombardment of questions, we were tempted to say, "Just because," or, "I don't know." The incessant, "What that?" combined with the misplaced pronouns often left Bob and me confused. As time went on, we learned to maintain a delicate balance between correcting the language mistakes and letting them go, knowing that constantly correcting could be more disruptive to their overall sense of themselves than speaking incorrectly. Gradually we all developed our own "translating system" to fill in our momentary gaps in comprehension.

And we had helpers. One evening around dusk, I overheard Dennis and Kurt talking to each other on the front stoop. Dennis was explaining how a switch inside the house controlled the outside light. Kurt seemed to think this was quite magical. It was equally magical for Bob and me to observe how Kurt and Eddie were absorbing the urban world of New Jersey.

It was hard for them to understand the reasoning behind some of our explanations. Often it was necessary for the boys to experience something in order to absorb it. It wasn't until Eddie hung on the drapery cord and the nails holding the rod in the wall loosened in a rain of plaster dust that he learned why "only Mommy pulls the cord for the curtains." When confronted with the results of such behavior, each of their instincts was to deny any involvement.

"Did you pull the curtains off the wall?"

"They just fell," from the guilty little face.

Our most difficult task was to teach them to take responsibility. Bob and I gradually learned that if they broke something or disobeyed a rule in their foster home, they were hit with a strap by their foster father, often hours after the incident. In addition we had no way of knowing what happened in those destitute and chaos-filled years spent with their biological family.

It was natural that the boys wanted to protect themselves from punishment. Their ability to discern when a lie might work and when it was obvious to us was absent. We talked to them about how telling a lie was worse than breaking something or disobeying a rule. Each of them sat still, quiet as a stone, while we explained— "There are no straps, no hitting, and no beatings ever. You can tell us when something bad happens." But it had to seem to them that lying was effective because there were also no beatings when they did lie.

Fear was a parasite thriving under their skin. Each became paralyzed with anxiety when confronted with an incident he knew was "bad." Sometimes they ran and hid in their room rather than face Bob or me. Mostly they froze in place, endlessly mute in spite of our attempts to get at the truth. As the months progressed, there were more and more incidents. I found myself exasperated and distraught by their denials as they stood in front of me like soldiers being reprimanded by a commanding officer, eyes downcast or focused on some distant object, jaws set, never flinching, never crying. It was not normal.

I could not reach the place where the fear resided, the core of the engine driving this behavior. While they were progressing on a developmental level, I was unable to tap into the emotional level where the past had written itself deep in their psyches. I did not know how to break through. I did not know how to get them to trust me.

* * *

I continued to exchange letters with Ardis and Allen that first year.

"What do you want to tell Ardis?" I asked the boys.

"About my new fire engine" or "about the piano" one of them told me. When a letter arrived from Ardis, I read it to them. This was a conscious decision on my part. I wanted them to maintain the connection to these foster parents, believing that, for each of us, the knowledge that there are others in the world who care about us is as necessary as air.

The boys never asked to go back to Yarmouth or showed signs of yearning in that first year, or if they did, I missed the cues. Having each other was probably the single most important factor in their adjustment. Where I'd find one, I'd find the other. It was KurtandEddie or EddieandKurt, sitting in the same beanbag chair watching *Sesame Street*, next to each other in the sandbox or on the piano bench. Some of the neighbors never got them straight. KurtandEddie—EddieandKurt become one interchangeable word.

Every so often, an image of their sister, amorphous as smoke and cowering in the attic room with them, crossed my mind. I wondered about her life without her brothers, and felt a sudden panic for retaining the secret of her existence. As quickly as the thought came, another surfaced of her as the only child of loving and doting parents. This was the image that prevailed. Bob and I reasoned that we had no right to interrupt the family in Canada by reaching out to her. They obviously knew of Kurt and Eddie's existence but we didn't know if they told their little girl about her brothers. Not wanting to add one more loss to those already being endured by Kurt and Eddie, we kept the secret.

✳ ✳ ✳

THINKING IT WAS THE AGE-APPROPRIATE thing to do, and after consulting with the principal at the local grammar school, we enrolled Eddie in kindergarten in January. Kurt, on the other hand, was home alone with me five mornings a week. The separation from "New Mommy" only weeks after arriving in New Jersey was, in retrospect, not a positive experience for Eddie.

Since Eddie was a year older than Kurt, he had an extra year's worth of exposure to deprivation in that attic room in Canada; another whole year for the neglect to do its dirty work. The paucity of attention, the lack of mental stimulation, the scarcity of food, the unsanitary conditions, and inconsistent messages or no messages at all from parents, all had disastrous effects on his developing sense of self and his place in the world. For Eddie, the ability to establish an appropriate sense of boundaries was affected.

He took to following me around like a puppy. I often did not know that he was standing at my heels until I turned around with a pot full of boiling spaghetti or a stack of dishes in my hands and found myself tripping over him. His sense of the appropriate physical distance to maintain with others was off even for a five-year-old. For him, it was like pouring a glass of water and having no internal mechanism telling him the glass was about to overflow.

Sometimes the older kids got embarrassed. "Eddie's hugging the crossing guard on the corner or hugging the mailman," one or another would tell me. The ability to discriminate between who it was appropriate to hug and

The first year—Dennis, Kurt, Kathleen, Eddie, and Robert.

when a smile would do, was missing in him. The line between private and public was fuzzy. While all growing children test limits as they construct their own boundaries, Eddie's struggle was the hardest and took the most attention and reinforcing from Bob and me.

"Do you ever see any other kids hug the mailman?" I asked Eddie during a bedtime chat, the time I usually saved for private discussion with one or the other of the children.

He thought about it, and then asked, "What about hugging my teacher?"

This was a good question. I saw his struggle as he tried to differentiate the categories of public and private. Of course he had seen others hug a teacher, and yet the teacher was not a member of the family. And so we agreed, sometimes it was appropriate. It depended on the situation. Just as with practice a child learned to color within the lines, Eddie was learning how to identify and respect social and personal boundaries.

Often, Bob and I found ourselves carrying Kurt and Eddie. New situations alarmed them, and their bodies tensed as fright registered in their eyes. An examination by our pediatrician revealed the omissions in the original medical report given to us before the adoption. Screaming and thrashing under the mural of Little Bo Peep painted on the wall next to the examining table, first Eddie, and then Kurt, roiled in fear as the doctor examined them. Afterwards, the pediatrician educated me, explaining how neglect not only affects IQ, but actually stunts physical growth as well. Kurt and Eddie's bodies were equivalent to children eighteen months younger than their actual ages. This probably accounted for our inclination to respond to them as if they were still toddlers. It seemed natural to scoop them up in our arms even when chronological age might dictate otherwise.

The first time we brought them to church with us, Kurt was settled in Bob's arms in order to see around the throng of people in the rows in front of us. During the ritual of the Mass, the priest raised the host and the cup of wine and prayed, "This is my body, this is my blood." Upon hearing these words, Kurt stiffened in Bob's arms and blurted out, "This place is dangerous." While the other children either blushed or giggled, Bob and I were made exquisitely aware of how any new situation could be interpreted as fearful by our new little boys.

Eddie was terrified of the shower. Each time it was turned on, he shuddered violently. His little barrel chest trembled, and his eyes darted back and forth around the room like a frightened rabbit. He could not tell us why. For months we just let him use the bathtub. Every so often we made sure he observed one of the other kids in the shower. The boys danced and clowned under the jets, and Eddie watched from across the room.

"See, there's nothing to be afraid of," Bob or I said to Eddie as he cowered on the other side of the room, his arms crossed against his chest in a protective gesture.

"Come on in with me," Robert said. "I'll take care of you."

But for months, Eddie remained unconvinced. In time his fear abated, although its root cause, the incident that caused the fear, remained unknown.

Kurt loved his thumb. Perhaps he found it while still in the womb, the way present-day sonograms reveal a fetus, snug in the amniotic fluid, sucking contentedly. Perhaps he found it as an infant when he was hungry and there was no parent and no milk, or when Eddie got on a school bus and left him standing in the grove of pine trees. When he went to bed each night, the thumb automatically found its way into his mouth. The dentist told me his front teeth were in jeopardy of protruding. Each night I went into his room and removed the thumb and tucked his hand beneath the blanket, but that thumb made its way back into his mouth during sleep. Finally, the dentist suggested we paint the

Kurt sucking his thumb.

offending thumb with iodine because the bitter taste would keep him from putting it in his mouth. Kurt didn't want anyone else in the family to know about his struggle, and so for weeks, each night before bed, I painted his thumb bright, bitter, iodine orange, and he placed in under his pillow before trying to find sleep. My heart broke for him as I witnessed how hard it was to relinquish the world he had created for himself with that magic thumb. Finally, he gave it up.

Kurt's and Eddie's memory of the first three and four years of their lives seemed nonexistent. Access to a sketchy past began with their placement with

Ardis and Allen. It was often heart-wrenching to see them struggle to be equal participants around the dinner table when Robert, Kathleen, or Dennis spontaneously talked about something that happened before Kurt and Eddie were with us. "Remember the funny hat Grandpa had on when we went to Sterling Forest?" "Yeah, and remember how Grandma kept telling him to take it off?"

Kurt and Eddie looked puzzled and got very quiet. Butterflies fluttered in my stomach, as I was torn between interrupting memories the other children were enjoying so the boys did not feel excluded or waiting and then trying to engage the boys with some of their own memories. "Tell us some things you remember that we don't know about." I interjected. And so it was at the dinner table, through their fragmented stories that pieces of the past slowly emerged.

The food requirements imposed by Kathleen's insulin compelled me to make sure dinner was ready at the same time every evening. While this rigid structure often seemed burdensome, it turned out to be a blessing. It let the children know that each of them was expected at the table at 6:00 p.m. and that each was important and would be missed if not present. We counted on one another to be there every night. I think, in a subtle way, this laid the foundation for them to count on each other to be there in their lives.

One night there was a lull at the dinner table, and Kurt announced, "I was shot when I lived in Canada." That was a conversation stopper. A chorus of, "You were not!" from the others.

"I was so. I'll show you. I was shot by a pellet, and I have a pellet wound." He pulled up his shirt and pointed to a tiny scar on his abdomen.

I had seen it before, but we'd never talked about it. I attributed it to a fall or some other benign incident. Although it seemed unlikely, he thought he had been shot, and I guess that was as bad as being shot. So we treated it seriously. Of course, we never found out where that scar came from. By the time he was a teenager he was able to tolerate teasing about it.

"Let's see your pellet wound, Kurt," Robert would tease, and Kurt would smile his slow smile that started in his eyes, and worked its way, like a secret waiting to be discovered into the corners of his mouth.

* * *

"I SAW SOMEONE DIE," EDDIE blurted out one night. "Me too," from Kurt, as the statement jogged his memory. They described to us how they'd witnessed

Ardis's father have a heart attack, interrupting each other as they tried to get the story out. Their three siblings were kept spellbound.

"Everyone was running around crazy," said Eddie.

"Except Grand-pops. He didn't move."

"They made us go outside and wouldn't let us back in. Frazier was there."

"He took us to the wood shed. It was scary."

"Then everyone was crying and we never saw Grand-pops again because he died."

We were all quiet for a moment and then Kathleen said, "Who's Frazier?"

"He was a big kid, about Robert's age. We went hunting with him."

"Hunting?"

"Yeah, when I killed the deer," offered Eddie.

"You killed a deer?" from Dennis, in awe and horror.

In a rush, Eddie remembered, and it all came tumbling out. His feelings emerged, like a groundswell from under his chest, where they were lodged in all their gory details. He wasn't proud. He told us about a nameless red face and the huge hand that clapped him on the back and said, "You killed it. Now clean it," an act more fearful to him than shooting. He described how he joined the others hovering over the dead animal and, with his little hand grasping the knife, helped slip it under the skin and peel the coat back like a rug to reveal the pink flesh. As the others pulled the entrails, still bloody with life, out of the carcass, he helped dig the hole in which to bury them. After butchering the still-warm animal, its eyes frozen in a glassy stare, they had divided it among a few families to eat during the winter months.

That was how our family, stunned to silence, learned the details about the five-year-old Eddie butchering a deer.

* * *

A crucial incident occurred one hot July day, a day all three of us remember. It was the quiet that alerted me. Robert, Kathleen, and Dennis were outside riding bicycles and playing hockey. Kurt and Ed were in the living room watching TV. I could hear Mr. Rogers putting on his sweater, saying good-bye to the neighborhood. One or both of them usually appeared in the

75

kitchen minutes after the show ended for a little ritual check-in or to have their way with me for a pre-dinner snack. I looked up from the meatloaf I was patting into a pan, realizing some fifteen minutes had gone by without a word from either of them.

I called from the kitchen, "What are you guys doing?"

Silence.

Again "Ed, Kurt?"

More silence. I walked into the living room. The scene was dizzying. The pale yellow walls and the beige rug were streaked with purple and yellow magic marker. Circles and zigzags and lopsided squares in incandescent primary colors were everywhere.

"What are you doing?" I shouted as I lunged for the markers still in their hands.

"I didn't do it," each of them offered, even as the rainbow of luminous stains glowed on their fingers.

"Of course you did it!" I shouted in anger and disbelief.

No response. No emotion. No words.

"Admit it. Tell the truth," I continued in a shaking voice, as eight months of patience and reasonableness erupted like a volcano. I lost all composure. Whether I believed it was my failure or theirs remains blurred in my memory, but what I do remember is that I lost control. I shouted as though a wall could never be repainted, as though a rug could never be replaced, as though a lie could never be undone.

"You know it's not okay to write on the walls. Why did you do it?" I shouted angrily.

No reaction—no movement except a short glance between them that confirmed their mutual commitment to denial and to each other.

Just acknowledge it's wrong. Just let me know you know. What is this cold, numb response? They would not look at me. It was as though I was a piece of furniture or some other inanimate object that had started to rant. Now I was frightening them. They'd never seen me so upset. Suddenly, they bolted up the stairs and into the bedroom. I followed like a crazy woman, determined to avenge the great wrong done to my living room walls. They were sitting next to each other on the blue shag carpet, their eyes downcast, and their bodies still. I got down on the floor with them and put my hands on their shoulders.

"Look at me," I said as I shook each of them like a rag doll for a good fifteen seconds. "Why don't you cry? It's okay to cry when you get hollered at, when you do something wrong."

Neither one raised his eyes off the carpet. I was a runaway train headed for a wreck. I could not slow myself down, and their resolute silence was the wall into which I was crashing. They should react. Underneath that thought was my personal fear, the unspoken fear hibernating all winter deep in the cavern of my mind: Perhaps they were not normal. Perhaps the early damage could never be compensated for.

Suddenly, as if the act of admitting that to myself was the key unlocking a mystery, they began to tremble. Kurt first, his lower lip going up like a suction cup and pulling the upper lip down. Tears welled up in his eyes. Eddie seemed to absorb the sadness through some brotherly osmosis. His barrel chest started to heave, his mouth quivered, and they both looked up at me in the same moment as tears erupted in a great flood that streamed down their cheeks. They were crying. It was over! I gathered them into my arms. I stroked their hair, kissed their foreheads, and told them, "It's okay. It's all over now. Tears are good when you're afraid."

We rocked together while the meatloaf dried out in the oven, and the other children kept their distance. All three of us were sobbing, huddled close on the blue-shag carpet, as each small body nested between one of my knees and thigh. I held them long and tight. I crooned, and the sounds that came from my throat were as unfamiliar as a fifteenth-century instrument that I had never heard.

We sat there, clinging to each other on the floor. "Let the tears come," I kept repeating through the rocking and crooning and sobbing. It was as though a fissure deep in a glacier was finally erupting on the surface of the ice and sending great frozen chunks into the ocean to float off and dissipate.

This was a day etched in memory for all three of us. I recall it with shame, but also with thanksgiving. They recall it with fright, but also with gratitude. This was the day when Kurt and Eddie found the feelings that were buried somewhere on the rocky coast of Canada. This was the day trust was born.

* * *

WE WERE LIVING IN A SORT OF LIMBO that first year, knowing the boys were not truly ours and could not be unassailably ours for at least six months, the period of time required by law before petitioning the court to finalize an adoption. Up until the days preceding the court date, all the children believed the adoption was a *fait acompli*. We did not want to burden them with our fears that something might go wrong. Because I had been corresponding with Ardis, I had some alarming news. Filtered through her letters were vague references to their biological mother, who was still making herself known to the Children's Service Agency in Yarmouth. The biological mother frightened me by her very existence. Yet this fear paled in comparison to the way she would subsume my life in the future. On July 20 the U.S. court finally responded to our petition and scheduled August 17 as our court date. A few days prior to the appointed date, we received another letter, changing the date to August 21. Panicked, we needed reassurance from our attorney that this was nothing ominous, just a shifting of the judge's calendar.

When we arrived at the court house we were ushered into the judge's chambers.

There was a half circle of eight chairs forming a horseshoe around his huge walnut desk, one for our lawyer and one for each of the five children and one each for Bob and me. The judge, wearing a dark-blue business suit, was standing behind his desk as we entered the room. He tried to make us comfortable with small talk about the children—how they all looked alike with their blond hair and fair skin.

"Which of you boys are the adopted children?" he asked. Kurt and Eddie shyly raised their hands.

The judge asked them a few benign questions. "Does everyone think you look alike? Do you go to school? Do you get along with your sister and brothers?" And then, shuffling through the file, he turned toward me. Peering over the reading glasses balanced on the tip of his nose, he said, "I see here that you go to school at night."

"Well, yes," I answered, taken aback by the question. No one before this judge had shown the slightest interest in my plodding along toward a degree. Why was it coming up now?

"How many nights are you away from the house?"

"Only one," I answered.

"And who's home with these five children while you are at school?"

"I am," said Bob.

Turning toward Bob, the judge said, "It must be difficult for you."

I did not hear Bob's reply, the part where he said, "No, it's not hard. I actually like being Mr. Mom one night a week."

I was fervently preparing a soliloquy that would have equaled Shakespeare in which I pleaded my case with something like, "I'll quit school. I don't care about college. It doesn't mean half as much to me as Kurt and Eddie." But I never had to deliver my plea. I realized the judge had his pen in his hand and was smiling as he signed the papers. School was just small talk, and Kurt and Eddie were from that moment on forever ours.

* * *

I WAS FULL OF SPONTANEOUS GRATITUDE all through this year. There was a perpetual thank you in my heart for the grace of my blended family. My periodic uncertainties about God, especially those questions that related to an after-life, diminished. I often found myself having a wordless internal dialogue with John. My happiness seemed directly connected to his birth and death. Had it not been for him, Bob and I would never have opened our lives to Kurt and Eddie. This infant whom I never had the courage to hold in my arms was present to me like luster from another realm.

Eddie and Kurt holding hands.

As I went through my ordinary days with Kurt and Eddie, I was aware of a Divine Presence in my life. From the first days of the onion skin envelopes, through the "What that's," through the mystified Eddie hugging the crossing guard, through Kurt's battle with his thumb, through the mysterious incandescent purple markings on my wall—every day overflowed with a kind of grace during those small events when I felt with the boys or with one of the other children who were opening their generous hearts to their new siblings. Paradoxically, when strangers become aware of the background of our blended family, I heard praise about how special Bob and I were. This embarrassed me. The reality, that at the time I could not begin to explain or understand, was that I was receiving so much more than I was giving.

* * *

IT WAS MANY YEARS LATER, while reading Karen Armstrong that my experience during that year was named for me. Armstrong writes about practical compassion as the common thread linking the worlds' major religious traditions. She describes it as the ability to let go of ego and truly feel with another. She demonstrates how this self-emptying brings one close to an encounter with a transcendent experience or a divine presence. Whether the experience is called God, Tao, Brahman, Nirvana or the Sacred, the path of practical compassion is the same and unites all faiths. Her words echo the Jewish scholar, Abraham Heschel who said, "When we put ourselves at the opposite pole of ego—we are in the place where God is." What opportunities my children were offering me to live in the place where God is!

8

Life Finds Its Own Routine

As Kurt and Eddie's questions about their adoption surfaced, we answered them. We tried to be straightforward and non-judgmental. We explained that their parents had been sick and did not know how to take care of children. "They forgot to feed you and forgot to change your diapers and wash your clothes. Somebody has to take care of children because they can't take care of themselves. That's why the policeman took you and had to find a mommy and daddy who were not sick and knew how to take care of children." The boys listened cautiously.

We had no choice but to accept the paucity of information available to us in 1972. Adoption was a sea of uncharted waters. Bob and I were trusting of a system we rightfully believed had the best interest of the child at heart. After asking for more comprehensive information about their past and for official documents, we accepted the minimal amount of information. We turned our gaze forward rather than backward.

Perhaps, in a naive sort of way, we wanted to obliterate the part of their past that harmed them, the parts out of our control. Neither Bob nor I had experience with children other than our own, and lacked the psychological sophistication to anticipate any future demands for answers to questions sealed in a file of documents in Canada. Reasoning that there was nothing we could do to change the past, we never dug deeper.

I had come to believe that Lucienne and Eric, those faceless names appearing on the official papers, were mentally ill. It was the only way I could account for the way they had failed to take care of their children. But we deliberately did not attach "mental" to their sickness when we spoke to Eddie and Kurt. Intuition told us that children could leap from mental illness to labels like "crazy" and "nuts." We wanted to protect them from any association with those pejorative labels. "Sick" seemed all-encompassing, a wide net that neglect could seep through, like water, without entangling the debris of details accumulated in the first years of our boys' lives. I believed this explanation would allow them to go through life with empathy for sick parents rather than an anger that could be debilitating. But I learned otherwise.

✻ ✻ ✻

LIKE WATER FINDING ITS LEVEL, life found its routine. The household ran on a September to August calendar, with back-to-school haircuts, newly sharpened pencils, and spiral notebooks—all symbols of the challenges and milestones to be achieved in the upcoming school year. There was the inevitable homework each night. Kurt and Eddie needed more help than their siblings. Bob worked with one of them at the dining room table while I worked with the other at the kitchen table. Often Kathleen sat with one of her brothers and helped him through math or reading. Intermingled with the school-work were the endless celebrations that the seasons brought. One after another, holidays and birthdays orbited like suns around the year.

On rainy days there were roller-derby tournaments around the beanbag chairs scattered on the plaid indoor-outdoor carpeting in the basement. Each of them strapped on a helmet and ball-bearing skates and circled the steel beams holding up the house.

Behind the playroom was the furnace room. Snuggly warm, it doubled one winter as the home for a family of gerbils living in a lucite maze of a cage. The pink, eraser-sized newborns escaped endlessly. "Find them!" Bob or I commanded from the kitchen. The kids complained and accused each other of causing the escape. Yet together they found a unique way of rounding the rodents up. Instinct prompted the hairless mice to run through a tube. Setting the flexible hose of the shop vacuum on the floor enticed the miniature rodents through the tube and plummeted them into the canister of the vacuum. The three younger boys tenderly scooped them up and transported them back to the maze until the next escape.

During those years, my father took to picking Dennis, Kurt, and Eddie up early on Saturday mornings as he made his way from Long Island to his little cabin in northern New Jersey. Here, in the country, Kurt and Eddie felt a kinship with nature, reminiscent of the woods and lakes of Canada. They worked with my father, clearing the lot of stones, shoveling manure into barrels for carting to his tomato garden, priming the pump, painting the outhouse, helping him get the place ready for summer. At the end of a day, each of them felt proud as they received a dollar in payment. But their real earnings were the memories stored and the lessons learned from those long days with Grandpa.

The doubts Bob and I had about Kurt and Eddie's intelligence and potential to lead normal lives dissolved like snow in the sun. The stimulation of a home environment, filled with three energetic older siblings who played with them and talked with them, compensated for the early deprivation that inhibited their growth and development. The boys' use of pronouns gradually took the correct form. They learned to read and they learned math. Relaxing into their lives, they even took to throwing their clothes on the floor and walking over them, like their brothers and sister. How different from those first nights in Canada, when the ritual piling of each article of clothing, with shoes and "stockings" on top, was so meticulous. When I insisted in frustration one Saturday morning that they all pick up their rooms, Kurt and Eddie chanted, "You taught us to be messy." And so I did.

There were fights; sibling rivalry could erupt between any of the five of them indiscriminately. It was often a challenge to keep the peace. One day Kurt and Eddie were fighting over a record, both claiming ownership and I stumbled on a consequence of questionable behavior that worked then and continued to work in the future. "I can't understand both of you talking at once. Write it out," I said as a last resort.

That's when the writing did its magic! Oh, how they hated it. It took too much time—it was stupid, they told me. Using big block letters so that a few sentences appeared like many, Eddie handed me his explanation—"It's my record and he took it and that's not fair because he's a jerk and that's why I threw the book at him and I didn't even hit him with it I missed and he's just trying to get me in trouble and last week he took my basketball . . ." and on and on. Kurt wrote a similar paragraph. By the time they were finished they were no longer mad at each other, but mad at me for being so inept at settling their differences. During the record incident, Kurt mumbled, "Why can't you just hit us like other mothers," and we all three laughed as the irony of the situation was revealed even to their ten-year-old selves.

Music was everywhere! Eddie played the piano by ear; Kurt, from the moment he picked up Robert's guitar, could tease any song he wanted out of it. The rest of us were amazed. We arranged for them to have music lessons, and with those lessons and their innate ability, the doors to a world acknowledging each of them as gifted and talented was opened.

One evening, I overheard a conversation drifting up from the basement. Kurt was strumming his guitar and singing when Kathleen asked, "Kurt, when I get married someday, will you sing at my wedding?"

"Sure," he answered instinctively, making a promise to his sister that would not be easy for him to keep.

* * *

WE WERE BURSTING OUT OF OUR six-room house. We refinished the attic into a larger bedroom with a dormer ceiling. The walls were pine paneled; the floor and stairs were covered in a red-and-black shag rug. As the construction was going on, Bob and I didn't know which of the boys to put in the room. We asked ourselves, *Are Kurt and Eddie too young to move to the third floor? Will Robert and Dennis feel displaced if they are evicted from the bedroom they shared long before their brothers were even a thought on the horizon?* From the few facts we knew about Kurt and Eddie's infancy, "attic room" held huge negative connotations. Would we repeat a trauma by having them sleep in the attic? And so it went. Always the soul-searching conversation between Bob and me to insure ourselves against favoritism for our biological children or favoritism for the waifs we had embraced.

We loved our life with the five children. Each day was a whirlwind of activity. We were tired beyond measure, but it was a good tired. Life was predictable and secure. Bob and I had our own little game for survival among the five of them—See Saw. One of us slept for an extra hour or two on Saturday morning and the other on Sunday morning. The luxury of those hours away from the fray recharged our depleted energy. Bob and I were in it together, a team supporting and outwitting that other team, "the kids."

For years, each Saturday morning Kathleen found her brothers and got their orders for the sandwiches they would take to school that week. After an outing with her father to the local butcher shop and the bakery, Bob sliced twenty-five rolls in half and placed them on the kitchen table. In assembly-line fashion, he and Kathleen doled out the ham, bologna, cheese, roast-beef, or some combination of the above. The sandwiches went into the freezer and were ready for the mad rush of the upcoming week's school-day mornings.

And then there was the phrase Bob coined for them, "watching is helping." He used it when he was trying to undertake a complicated job, like fixing a sink or painting a room. It was his way of including one of them in a fix-it job, as he talked to them about whatever it was he was doing and, at the same time, guarding against someone's foot winding up in the paint can or the last piece of hardware disappearing into thin air.

* * *

FIVE YEARS AFTER Kurt and Eddie entered the country, they were finally eligible to become naturalized citizens. We were not prepared for the crowd vying for seats in the courtroom that morning. In the weeks prior to the scheduled date, our dinner conversations were sprinkled with civics lessons—how special it was to be an American and what an honor it was for Kurt and Eddie to be citizens of two countries.

People who had immigrated from all corners of the globe were waiting in the courtroom to be sworn in. Unlike Kurt and Eddie, who because of their adoption were becoming naturalized citizens, these people had studied hard, passed tests, and were fulfilling a dream. Some were accompanied by lawyers with leather briefcases and three-piece suits. Some were alone and some had family members holding them by the elbow, steering them to a seat in the overflowing courtroom. Others had extended families swarming around them, trying to be of assistance—brushing dandruff off a jacket, straightening a tie. A man with the rough red hands of a bricklayer was buttoning a suit jacket that had been cleaned so many times it glowed. A white straw hat with a branch of red cherries across its brim framed the ebony brow of a woman whose face was a map of wrinkles and joy.

The courtroom felt like a holy place. A reverence reserved for a church or temple seemed to fill the spaces between the gathering assembly. Some people whispered. Most were quiet. Others betrayed their nervousness as they shifted in their seats, while keeping their eyes on the door to the right of the huge bench with its brass engraved sign, "JUDGE'S CHAMBER." Finally, a hush, as the judge, stately in his long black robe, entered the courtroom and took his seat at the bench, under the red, white, and blue of the American flag. On cue from his clerk, we all stood. He greeted us enthusiastically and asked us to be seated. As the judge spoke to us about the privilege and responsibility of being a Untied States citizen, I watched the upturned faces of my five children. All were spellbound as they listened to the words booming across that courtroom, words fostering another link binding us to one another. Finally, the candidates were asked to stand once again. The judge asked the few questions requiring a group answer. We watched as ten-year-old Kurt and eleven-year-old Eddie voiced their rehearsed responses.

"Do you want to become a citizen of the United States?"

"Yes."

"Do you promise to defend this country?"

"Yes."

And then the Pledge of Allegiance. It was as though I'd never heard it before. This band of new citizens, broken English tumbling from their tongues, eyes riveted onto the flag, hands over hearts, my two sons standing tall among them, were reborn American citizens partaking in "liberty and justice for all."

* * *

ALTHOUGH LIFE WAS TURNING on the wheels of happiness, as the older children entered adolescence and Kurt and Eddie approached it, undercurrents of concern were surfacing within me. I realized the losses in Kurt and Eddie's early years contained the seeds for rebellion in their adolescence and for

A family portrait—Eddie, Kurt, Robert, Kathleen, Marion, Bob, and Dennis.

depression in the future. Questions about their past were becoming more frequent and I was unsure of how to answer them. I knew first-hand how clinical depression could infiltrate itself like a poisonous gas, paralyzing the mind while racking the body with a physical pain that was difficult to describe. I wanted to do everything I could to insure the emotional and mental health of my boys—to protect them.

In addition, my heart cracked a little every day as I watched Kathleen's need for insulin change until she was injecting herself three times a day, morning, noon and night. I was constantly aware of the potential for her blood sugar to plummet and cause a reaction, or skyrocket if she ate the wrong combination of foods. My impulse to control what only she could control caused friction between us. I asked myself how diabetes and all the structure that it imposed on Kathleen's life were affecting her. I wondered if my growing pre-occupation with her health was causing a hidden anger in the other children.

I also felt a sense of vulnerability for Robert and Dennis. Juvenile diabetes is a genetic disease, and I worried that one or both of them would develop symptoms, and that I would not detect them. If either of them seemed excessively thirsty or seemed to be urinating more frequently, I asked them to urinate in a paper cup, and I tested the urine. They balked, they got angry, and they hated my interference.

Although there were no indications of resentment from Robert, Kathleen, and Dennis about the adoption, I wondered if negative feelings might someday surface. My antennae were always up for signs of jealousy or discontent. I asked myself if they could ever feel cheated at having to share their parents or if they might feel they were not enough for us.

I also began to wonder about alcoholism and the genetic potential for it to surface in all of the children. I had no way of knowing if alcohol or drugs were involved in Kurt and Eddie's biological background. I suspected that they had been, from having been told their father had been "passed out" the day they were removed from that attic room. I did know there were problems with alcohol in Bob's background that might put Robert, Kathleen, and Dennis at risk. Bob's father had had a serious drinking problem that had its inception before Bob was born. A binge drinker who could not sustain a job, he had lost days at a time drinking in his room, leaving only to buy more rye at the local liquor store. Ashamed and embarrassed by his father, Bob rarely spoke about the hurt he and his family endured because of the drinking.

Yet in the year or so before I miscarried our baby John, there were an increasing number of nights when Bob's intention to come home from a business meeting or a ball game by 10:00 or 11:00 p.m. were forgotten or ignored. The hours blurred together as time was distorted by beer, and he'd arrive home long after midnight, having drunk too much. We argued about the anguish and sleeplessness he caused me, and about my fear that our life would be a repeat of his parents'. He would express remorse and promise to stop drinking. He would try, and life would return to normal, but then a few weeks later the whole pattern would repeat.

I knew Bob detested what alcohol could do to a family, and I naively believed this was my insurance policy, my guarantee that he would never let himself succumb to the addictive elements of alcohol. I believed he could control his drinking and took it as a personal assault early in our marriage when he drank too much and came home late from a hockey game or baseball game. I would notice the subtle changes in his speech, the bleary look in his eyes and detect the sour smell of beer even as he obscured it with mint or gum. I would get angry and accuse him of being "just like your father." These words hurt him even as they foretold my most fearful prediction. I used them like a weapon. "I am nothing like my father," he would insist, "I only drink beer, and he drank hard liquor. Why don't you want me to have a good time?"

My anger was in the category of "preventive." I never believed Bob was anything like his father. Bob was a happy drinker, the party guy, everyone's best friend. His father was a binge drinker who drank alone, at home, for days at a time. Bob never drank alone. There were no hidden bottles in the basement or garage. He never missed a day of work. He had established his own business, and it was doing well. He would arrive home as punctual as a clock to coach baseball and basketball. He got up at 4:00 a.m. to take the kids to ice-hockey practice. He was active in the church, working on building campaigns and going to classes to help prepare the children for First Communion.

But life was confusing. In the year after I lost the baby I had become aware that Bob was sometimes drinking at lunch. Each week there were sports events he attended that ended up with our fighting about how much he did or did not drink, and sports events I talked him out of attending in my attempts to control his drinking. I started keeping a record of the drinking incidents. I threatened to end the marriage. One weekend, in anger and spite, I left with the three children and went away with my sister-in-law. This frightened Bob. When faced with the calendar of accumulated dates that were evidence of his coming home drunk a few times a month, he saw the dangerous path he was on. He admitted he had a problem, called AA and faithfully went to meetings for about six months. Thankfully, the incidents of drinking ended; there was no more slurred speech, no more bleary eyes or beer breath. Our life stabilized. And then came the early wondrous years of Kurt and Eddie and our blended family when our future seemed safe and secure.

All of this family history with alcohol, plus the current family dynamics, translated into urgency on my part to be constantly vigilant. On some level I believed my vigilance could thwart danger, protect me and my family, and even somehow control the future. This took enormous energy and often left me drained and exhausted. Once again, I was unable to find peace through prayer. I resumed therapy as I realized there was more I needed to know about myself and my previous vulnerability to depression, which had lain like tinder in a dry field, leaping into flames when I was in my late twenties and least expected it.

As I struggled with my growing anxieties, therapy and college were sources of research for my questions and concerns, a part of my vigilance. They were also a place where my spiritual journey continued as I confronted the existential questions that caused me to doubt God and challenge my faith. I discussed them in therapy. I chose subjects at college and topics to research that related to my questions in an intellectual pursuit of God.

My relationship with Sister Elizabeth deepened, and it was she who opened my eyes to a new reality; my struggle with God was indeed a relationship with God. She sent me to Rilke. Here I found the words that would get me through my darkest moments of doubt. In his *Letter to a Young Poet*, Rilke urges,

> . . . have patience with everything unresolved in your heart. Try to love the questions themselves . . . Don't search for answers . . . live everything . . . live the questions now. Perhaps then someday . . . you will gradually, without even noticing it live your way into the answers.

These words lifted a burden from me. My need to understand what I could not understand was gradually replaced by an invitation to flourish in uncertainty, to live with what the poet John Keats called Negative Capability—the ability to embrace mystery and doubt without an irritable reaching after fact or reason. I was learning to trust that efforts to comprehend God could never be exhausted.

Poetry continued to be my avenue to prayer. I was drawn to poets, like Theodore Roethke and Mary Oliver, whose spiritual life was nurtured through the particulars of the natural world, who believed it was through the natural world that we came to know the transcendent—that which gave life meaning. The poetry I was reading sprang a latch on memories long dormant that seeped into consciousness like the first stirrings of an orchestra. I learned through my work in cognition that feelings were stored around images and it was the image that had the power and the potential to lead us back to the original experience.

I got up early in the morning, before the house was abuzz with the noise of my children, and tried to enter and write about those experiences with nature that once created a sense of the sacred in me. The ice-encrusted trees that turned the countryside to crystal, the pickerel flashing under the canoe in the muddy waters of the lake, pussy willows standing in a swamp and the canopy of silver as buds burst open in the April sun, the armfuls of lilacs I gathered from roadside bushes, and a huge rock covered with moss, an emerald cushion where I lay on my back under a canopy of trees. These images came back to me as if from some distant place, the small things that pointed to something larger. The poems generated by these memories felt like prayers. Although the personal omnipotent God of my childhood had receded into the shadows, the pull towards nature that had often quickened my pulse in ways I did not understand was now offering me images to reconnect to each of those spiritual experiences. They echoed Emerson: "What is beyond nature is revealed through nature . . . the inner life is revealed through the life of the senses." Sometimes I was writing to myself, sometimes to God—even when I felt no God was there. With each of these poems I experienced that momentary joy—as though I had come close to something important—and that was enough.

෨ 9 ෬

Intimations of Unrest

B Y THE TIME KURT AND EDDIE WERE READY for sixth and seventh grade, we
had outgrown our house. The move to a larger house in a town just a few
miles away involved a change in school districts. Bob and I felt this was a good
time to make the move. Eddie was scheduled to transition to middle school;
Dennis was ready to enter high school as a ninth grader; Robert and Kathleen
were firmly ensconced in a parochial high school where they could remain regardless of what town we lived in. We convinced ourselves the disruption would be
minimal, but we were wrong. Both Kurt and Eddie found themselves among a
large population of students instead of the insulated small classes of the previous neighborhood school and found the transition hard. They both had trouble
with math and science. After a year of parent-teacher consultations, we felt the
curriculum offered in the town school that put more emphasis on the arts would
serve them better. So another move to another school took place. It was disastrous for Kurt. He rebelled. He didn't do homework because he "forgot his
books." He cut classes and "hung out" in the nurse's office with creative illnesses. He told us what we wanted to hear, and then went his own way. We exhausted the public school system and failed to harness his impulse to rebel.

By this time, Dennis had gotten himself admitted to a private school.
Dennis was my easygoing son, the peacemaker and the middle son. He was the

one who didn't care how many hits he got in the game or how many times he fell on the ice, happy just to be on a team. Working behind the scenes, whether constructing sets for the school play or pulling ropes on the red velvet curtain so others could take a bow, he was content. Or at least I thought he was content. One day when he was nearing the end of his freshman year, I received a call from the admissions officer at a private school within walking distance of our house. After introducing herself to me, somewhat apologetically, she told me: "Your son Dennis stopped by the school today and asked for an interview. In all my twenty years in this school, I have never met a student who came on his own to seek admission. I had to pursue it with you."

It seemed Dennis wasn't happy following in his popular brother's and sister's footsteps at high school. He was bored and the upperclassmen teased him. When I asked him what they teased him about, he told me the awful truth. He walked too fast! He had never told us, or perhaps he had and we hadn't taken him seriously. He found his own solution, my middle child, and he transformed his place in the hierarchy of siblings into an opportunity for independence and academic excellence. He not only got himself admitted to the private school but studied himself into the Ivy League. "Walking too fast" led him to the cross-country track team at his new school, where a lifelong love of running had its inception.

Dennis loved his new school. It cost more than we could afford, but somehow we were managing. Feeling that Kurt was at a turning point, and believing the lower student-teacher-ratio would be good for him, we placed him in the seventh grade of this private elementary school. Academically, he was less than a shoo-in, but shored up by Dennis's reputation and performance, the school accepted Kurt. The music director immediately recognized Kurt's talent and took him under his wing. For the next six years, he would engage Kurt in a spontaneous music game. If a truck backed up on the road outside the school, or a bird was chirping outside the window, he stopped the class and asked Kurt, "What note is that?" and Kurt listened to the *beep beep beep* or *chirp chirp chirp* and identified it—F sharp, B flat, whatever—dazzling the class with his ear for music. The attention and praise he received for his voice with perfect pitch and his all-round music ability released Kurt from feelings of "not being good enough." His self-esteem soared, his motivation improved, and his downward spiral seemed to cease. For a while things were stable.

By the time he was thirteen, he had his own band, and with it a following of little-girl groupies in fuzzy sweaters and tiny skirts. One Friday night, he told us his band was going to perform at the middle school. We purchased tickets, and the whole family arrived at the auditorium early enough to get a bird's-eye view.

His navel was the first thing I saw. Skinny ribs were exposed under his white skin. The long-sleeved shirt I'd ironed two hours earlier was unbuttoned and flying at his waist as he did a sound check on speakers bigger that he was. His guitar flashed in the spotlight that encircled all sixty-six pounds of him in its glow. Little girls were swooning in the aisles. He was barely thirteen years old, and he was a "star."

Bob and I found it funny. Robert, the older brother, saw it differently. He shook his head in disbelief at my attitude. "Mom, he's headed for trouble, and you can't see it," he said more than once. He was right. I couldn't see it.

* * *

AN INCIDENT OCCURRED WHILE KURT was in eighth grade that both alarmed and excited me. There was a policy at the school that allowed prospective students the opportunity to visit and spend a day before enrolling. One afternoon, Kurt came home and, looking pensive, said, "Mom, you won't believe this, but there was a third-grade kid visiting school today. I saw him at lunch in the cafeteria. Mom, it was weird. He looked just like me. I felt like I was looking in the mirror. I couldn't stop staring at him."

As Kurt spoke between gulps of orange juice and cookies, I was flooded with thoughts. I knew that their mother was at the hospital in labor with her fourth child the day the boys and their older sister were taken into protective custody. We were told that the infant was to be placed for adoption. The order of protection was separate and subsequent to the boys' order, since this unborn child was not part of the same actions by the Social Service department. Could this possibly be another biological child of Kurt and Eddie's parents?

I thought about calling the principal and trying to get information on this third grader. Yet I realized that even if she gave it to me, which I doubted, I would be in a position of causing turmoil in another family. There was no way of knowing if the inquiry would be welcomed or rejected. However, as I thought about this third graders' age, I convinced myself he could not be a sibling. He was too young. But then my mind leaped forward—Was it possible that their biological mother gave birth after that, to yet another younger child? In the end, I did nothing, yet I continued to wonder. I periodically asked Kurt about the boy, but he never saw him again.

This incident made me acutely aware of two things. First, that somewhere in Kurt's unconscious, the seeds of a question about other siblings was present, and second, that I was keeping a secret about their sister Catherine, while advocating a "no secrets" policy in the family. I wondered how they would feel if the day ever came when that secret was revealed.

* * *

AS KURT AND EDDIE GREW older they asked more questions about their past. We added the few details we knew: how they were found naked and malnourished, the danger of a broken peanut butter jar in a crib, the cold coming through the cardboard-covered window of the attic room, the soiled mattresses and empty refrigerator.

As they reached puberty, their questions became more complicated. Eventually we found ourselves explaining the early IQ tests that found them retarded. We told them how the months spent with Ardis and Allen had begun to reverse the damage of their first four and five years. I told Kurt about my quizzing him on the difference between purple and marble on the plane ride home from Canada and made the whole episode a joke on me. We assured them that they were as normal and bright as everyone else and, when it came to music, were far beyond not only their siblings, but Bob and me as well. We revisited a question they had each asked in earlier years. It came at low moments, as though another confirmation of their worst fantasy that they were unlovable and unwanted—"Why didn't Ardis and Allen try to adopt us?" It was a question we asked ourselves. We believed Ardis and Allen loved them, and we told them that. It was written in a thousand ways between the lines of every letter Ardis wrote. We did not know why they didn't attempt to adopt them. We knew from her letters that she was pregnant when they left Yarmouth, and told the boys we believed the pregnancy had something to do with it. The real answer to that question lay in wait for us, an answer so simple yet so complicated it never crossed the radar of our minds.

We were open with the boys from the earliest years and told them we would help, when and if they decided to search for their biological parents. Suspecting—from what little information we did have about their past—that the process would be lengthy and traumatic, we wanted them to have the support of the whole family. We asked two things of them in this regard. One was that they wait until they were eighteen and had gone through the tumult of adolescence before initiating a search. We were afraid that the lure of a simple life in Yarmouth, where school was abandoned by many after eighth grade and fishing was the main industry, could be too enticing if the identity crisis that was sure to infuse adolescence got too hard. In addition, we asked that they seek out their parents together. We discussed how hurtful it could be for either one of them to confront the past if he was not ready at the same time as his brother.

It was this second condition that delayed the process. Kurt and Eddie each vacillated between a readiness and a reluctance to undertake a search. A deep bond of love existed between them and, throughout the years, each had been able to acknowledge the vulnerability of the other in opening up a history that was sure to ooze pain. There were times when one or the other went through a difficult period and the subject came up. They talked to each other and the whole question got put off. It was Eddie who, during his sophomore year of high school, was overtaken by feelings he could not understand, feelings that thrust him in the direction of Yarmouth and his hidden past.

* * *

AS I APPROACHED GRADUATION from college in 1978, Sister Elizabeth, who continued to be a major influence both academically and spiritually, made it possible for me to earn my last two credits in a course called Introduction to Poetry Therapy, being offered at the New School in New York City. She recognized long before I did that poetry and psychology were propelling me along a parallel path. It was while attending this course that I found the passion for a career I never knew existed. My avocation with poetry became my vocation as I embraced poetry therapy and was welcomed into a community of people who would become my future colleagues and friends. This new-

Marion's graduation from college. Bottom row: Kurt and Eddie; Top row: Dennis, Robert, Marion, Bob, and Kathleen.

found direction led me to enroll in a Masters Degree program at the New School. I began commuting one night a week into the city to work on a graduate degree in psychology.

By the winter of 1978, I was offered a job as a part-time poetry therapist at Carrier Foundation, a psychiatric hospital in New Jersey. It was here that my clinical training really began. As a member of the creative arts department, I was sent to different units in the hospital, where I worked with carefully selected poems to help patients recognize and express their feelings. My exposure to mental and emotional illness covered a wide spectrum as I rotated through the array of therapeutic programs. Among the populations I worked with were anxiety disorders, anorexia, adolescents, alcohol, geriatric, women's trauma, and the general psychiatric population.

This work gave me insight into the dynamics of my own family, its health and its problems. Over the years I found myself at the dinner table, recreating, in disguised form to the five children, incidents that had contributed to the hospitalization of others, particularly the adolescent patients. These stories were meant to illustrate how a wrong choice like drinking, drugs, fast driving, staying out all night, or lying, could culminate in disaster. The kids listened intently, maybe asked a few questions. I ended my "report" with a not so subtle, "This could happen to any of you." They all rolled their eyes, exasperated at my conclusion. "But it didn't happen to us," they sang in a chorus. Even so, I felt on some level I was getting through to them with these reminders about how easy it was for a child, any child, to fall.

This exposure and training in ameliorating the pain in the faltering lives of others affected me deeply. I became exquisitely aware of how random life was and could not help but ask "why" as I witnessed the emotional pain that others were enduring. I found myself thinking, *There but for the grace of God go I,* knowing full well that given the same circumstances I could very well be the patient and not the therapist in this milieu.

✳ ✳ ✳

AS EDDIE MOVED THROUGH ADOLESCENCE, it became obvious that some losses could never be compensated for. There was a void he carried within him, an empty hole where his biological family belonged. It crystallized in feelings of not really belonging that bubbled to the surface and attached themselves to his mind like a skin of algae covering a pond. When studying the hereditary patterns of the fruit fly in science, the homework assignment was: Observe your parents. Who do you resemble? Is your hair the same color as your mother's or your father's? Whose eyes do you have? Eddie had a stomachache the morning that assignment was due, and I let him stay home.

He simply told me, "I don't know what to say."

In high school biology, the subject of genetic predisposition caused beads of perspiration to erupt on his forehead. In the past, we had all acknowledged those musical genes inherited from his parents that made him special. But now, for the first time, he was considering what genetic time bombs might be planted in his genes.

"I don't know where I come from," he said mournfully one afternoon as I drove him home from ice hockey, when his Canadian heritage had failed him as he tried and tried to score a goal. "You don't know what it's like not to know whose stomach you grew in," he said. "It's like I was just dropped from outer space."

He was right. I could never know that feeling. I could conjure images and imagine it, but I could never experience it, never really know it. A few months later, Eddie's home-room teacher, Mr. Frey, called the house one morning. "Did you know," he asked, "that Eddie's bringing wrapped rolls of coins to school and giving them away to classmates?"

I was stunned. After a few minutes of confusion, I realized that Eddie must have helped himself to the loose change and foreign coins that Bob collected and regularly left in an empty glass pretzel jar in his home office. But why? What was compelling him to steal?

Angry thoughts of, *How could he? And what punishment will make enough of an impression to insure that he will never do it again?* gave way to a deep concern in the hours I waited for the school bus to drop him off. I heard the back door slam as he came inside, his shirt half out of his khaki pants, the usual blue splotches from his ball-point pen staining its pocket. He threw his bulging backpack on the floor of the back hall, drank half a quart of orange juice, and headed for his room. I stopped him at the foot of the stairs and told him that his teacher had called me. Eddie looked away. He knew what was coming.

"Why did you take money from Daddy's office?"

"I just borrowed it. I'm going to give it back."

"But you gave it away to other people. You can't give it back."

"No, I didn't," he said, a rabbit caught in a snare.

"Look at me."

He tried, but he could not meet my eyes. Meanwhile, the other children were coming home and sensing trouble. They started to hang around and ask questions. Edging Eddie onto the porch for privacy, I closed the door and asked again, "Why did you steal money and give it away?"

He kept denying and I kept asking. "Mr. Frey called me. He saw you. He took the coins from the kids in the lunchroom and has them in his desk to give back to Daddy."

Nothing.

Finally, I said, "We're going to stay here until you tell me what's going on." We waited a good five minutes. He was stoic. Only his eyes betrayed him. Suddenly, without warning, his foot started to tremble, and then his leg. It was vibrating three times as fast as the second hand on a clock. We were sitting alongside each other on the big red geranium-print cushions of the wicker couch. I felt his tremors through the pillows before I saw them. Reaching across the couch, I put my arms around his shoulders and held him tightly to stop the awful shaking. His head collapsed into my shoulder. Now he was sobbing, tears running down his cheeks and over the stubble beginning to grow on his boy chin.

"What's happening?" I asked.

"They threw me away like a piece of garbage in a garbage can," he said. "They didn't want me, and put me out like the garbage. That's what I am, garbage."

"Who threw you away?" I said, even as I felt sure I knew the answer. I was buying time, an extra moment to figure out how to counter his raw pain.

"You know," he said, sobbing, "my mother and my father."

"No, they were sick, so sick. They didn't know how to take care of children. They didn't throw you away. You are not garbage, and we all love you."

But it was going to take more than my words to dissipate the anger and rejection gripping him. The tip of an iceberg had revealed itself, and with it, a glimpse of its size.

As adolescence progressed, Eddie continued taking things, mostly from Robert's room, a Sting album, a baseball mitt, a shoelace from one of his sneakers. I heard Robert bellow, "I can't find my comb . . . Eddieeeee," as he made a bee-line to Eddie's room, where the comb was lying in full view amidst the clutter on his desk. "I borrowed it. What's the big deal?" I heard Eddie say. Robert muttered and told him what a jerk he was. I got involved and talked to Eddie, but a week later they were once more embroiled in accusations about a missing baseball card or some other personal item.

Perhaps these skirmishes were Eddie's way of getting attention from his big brother who was a hero to the four who followed him. It was negative attention, but attention nonetheless. More likely, Eddie was attempting to fill the void he carried within, compensating for loss with objects that temporarily filled his emptiness. As Eddie coveted Robert's possessions, Robert took to booby trapping his room, arranging things in an ordered disorder—a book balanced on a nest of balls that would spill like a waterfall if the door was opened. Some mornings he tied a string from the doorknob to the brass light fixture attached to the wall outside his room. There were other incidents at home when one of us realized something was missing or recognized that a drawer has been rifled or a closet disturbed. Accusations escalated into arguments. Each time, Eddie resolutely denied his involvement—but his face gave him away. He could not make eye contact, could not look at his accuser.

These skirmishes resulted in my trying to reason with Eddie in long talks about trust and respect for other people's property and privacy. But he had difficulty making the distinction. Interpersonal boundaries were blurred for him. A young child's impulse to take seemed to outlast the inner mechanism that developed to help one delay such actions.

When Eddie was about thirteen, I purposely walked into the living room while he was having a piano lesson. It was strangely quiet; I had not heard the piano for about ten minutes. I found, spread out on the piano bench the spilled contents of a folder in which I kept my poetry, poetry so primitive and private that I had not shared it with anyone. It contained my innermost thoughts and feelings and had been tucked away in a draw of my desk. Now, there it was, like yesterday's newspaper, being read and discussed by my son and his teacher.

"What are you doing?" I asked.

"Mr. Ansbach is writing a song, and I told him you wrote poetry. We thought you might have some lyrics he could use."

Of course, Mr. Ansbach, red-faced piano teacher extraordinaire, could also have used some boundary lessons.

* * *

At the same time that Eddie was struggling, ever so subtly, alcohol was making its way back into our lives. This time, I didn't see it coming. After Bob attended AA in 1970, I became more trusting. I believed the threat of alcohol had been defeated, eradicated. Since I was now no longer preoccupied with drinking, Bob's having a beer at lunch or at a ballgame escaped my notice. Initially, he drank only when traveling. The corporate benefits business he'd started in 1970 was growing. Accounts were being developed all over the country, and this necessitated travel. Bob did not look forward to leaving home, to being on the road alone. He missed the baseball teams he coached and shooting hoops in the driveway after work with the kids. A few drinks on the plane helped him relax, a few drinks at dinner helped the night go quicker, a few drinks and he did not mind being alone. He reasoned, "I'm not hurting anyone. No one will know," and as is the case with all alcoholics, the disease progresses. As time went on, Bob was no longer able to wait for the next business trip to have a few beers.

By 1978, there were incidents when I thought I smelled beer on Bob's breath or his behavior seemed a little off, more gregarious than usual, and I asked: "Have you been drinking?" He denied it, told me I was imagining things, looking for trouble or just plain wrong. A kind of crazy-making began for me. Without his acknowledgement of what I believed I was seeing, I doubted my own perceptions. I wanted them to be wrong. Denying reality was less upsetting than facing the truth. Life with him started to become a dance of deceit. But by 1979, I knew I was losing Bob to alcohol. A baseball practice scheduled for one of the children was generally an insurance policy guaranteeing his presence home by 6:00 p.m. But if a sudden storm left enough puddles on the field to cancel the game, he might drift into a sports bar and get lost for several hours. For a long time, I concealed this from the children.

"Where's Dad?"

"He's working late," I lied, or "He went to a ballgame with Mr. Crowley."

They all knew about Bob's love of sports and how he prided himself on his ability to calculate and remember any sports-related statistic. Mr. Crowley, in my mind, gave his absence an air of respectability. But Bob and I began to fight. I was unable to reconcile the good father, the smart and savvy businessman with the unpredictable drinking. At times I believed something was wrong with me. I asked myself a variation of the same question he asked me: "Why don't you want me to have fun?" After each of our fights, Bob promised to stop drinking. I believed him. He tried; weeks might go by without an incident. Yet I remained wary about when the next incident might occur. My happiness rose and fell with his drinking. I hated the person Bob became when he drank, slurring his words, secretive, sarcastic. I hated who I became when he drank, angry and mean-spirited. Even on those occasions when he was simply at a ball game or out on a business appointment and there was no drinking involved, I found myself watching and waiting for his car to pull into the driveway. I never knew when one beer could lead to two; two might lead to three, and then—who knew? My heart beat wildly as my mind flooded with images of car accidents and police sirens. I did not know how I would exist without the love I had depended on since I was a teenager. The very walls of the house absorbed the unhappiness that his absence created.

I prayed. Often my prayer was rote and empty and hollow—a last resort when all else had failed, a mere nod to a higher power even if I could not feel that presence. But the commitment to live the questions got me on my knees; to relinquish prayer would be to live without hope.

For a time I sought out a discussion group within the church community thinking I could strengthen my faith and foil the depression that I feared would return by absorbing the echoes of others' belief. Each time I gathered the courage to speak my doubts, I felt tears well in my eyes and my voice begin to falter. My questioning words were met with a silence followed by a sort of pity, as though I had some incurable illness. These people did not know what to say to me. After four or five meetings I stopped attending. I felt as though I didn't belong even as I yearned for the assurances of their faith. At times, I ran into one of the people whom I had revealed myself to and rightly or wrongly, I was filled with shame. Yet I never stopped attending church.

Once again, it was poetry that became the ballast. Each day I recited Denise Levertov's poem "The Fountain," an affirmation that countered my doubt.

Don't say there is no water . . .
to solace the dryness at our hearts
it is still there and always there
with its quiet song and strong power
to spring in us
up and out through the rock.

I begin to notice that I had my most productive thoughts in church. Perhaps it was the only quiet place in my life and thoughts had time to germinate. Sometimes milliseconds of peace entered me. Whether the result of an insightful thought, a letting go or the answer to a prayer, I could never know. So the ultimate value of prayer became one more unanswered question I committed myself to live.

For Eddie, the unpredictability of life at home caused by Bob's drinking added to the burning questions about his roots with which he was already struggling. The petty stealing seemed to be his way of filling not only the void created by the loss of his biological family but also the void that was growing rapidly in our home.

I brought up the idea of a therapist to Eddie. At first he rejected it. "I'm not crazy, I don't need any stupid doctor to figure me out," he said with clenched jaw. But I finally convinced him that I didn't think he was crazy, but I did think he had a lot of sadness and anger and that maybe a therapist could help him feel better. I told him that I had gone to therapy, and explained how I felt better as a result. He agreed to give it a try. Thus began Eddie's relationship with Joe Ryan, a man who would continue to influence him for the next two decades.

After several months of therapy, Eddie came to us and asked for his adoption papers. He told us he had been preparing himself in therapy to initiate a search for his biological parents. I was surprised by the sudden panic that surged through me as I heard his words. He was in the midst of a tumultuous adolescence, and I was afraid of what might be uncovered in Canada, for better or worse. I was familiar with the phenomenon of "the geographic cure," and how, to an adolescent in particular, running away is often looked upon as the best solution to a problem. Stirring deep within me was the fossil of a fear that if things got tough enough for him, he might leave us for Canada, where life was perceived to be slow and easy.

Bob and I procrastinated for a week or two by first giving him his birth certificate and holding off on giving him the actual court order for his and Kurt's adoption. The information about his sister Catherine was in those papers, and we feared that revealing this secret now could plunge Eddie into more turmoil. But when, a few weeks later, he asked again, Bob and I had to reconsider our reluctance. We removed the court order from the file in which it had rested since 1972 and prepared ourselves to help him search for Lucienne and Eric Deveau. Joe Ryan was there to provide additional emotional support for Eddie. Kurt was a willing if not active participant as he agreed to help his brother through a hard time.

However, before we actually gave him the file to make the first inquiry, Eddie changed his mind. As part of the preparation for delving into the past, Joe hypnotized him, and an experience, long stored in his body, slipped into consciousness. He found himself in that attic room of his infancy. He was jolted out of his chair and out of the hypnotized state by a putrid odor that choked him. Foulness was in his mouth and eyes and nose and throat and stomach. It shot through him, like a rocket out of the past, back to the leather chair and book-lined office where he was safe. Eddie refused to ever be hypnotized again. Fear of facing the realities to be found in Canada floated to the surface and filled his therapy sessions. He wasn't ready to face that fear. The idea of a search was aborted.

* * *

KATHLEEN WAS ALSO HAVING HER OWN troubles at this time. As she went through adolescence, the continuous need to balance every morsel of food she ate with the appropriate dose of insulin was causing her to rebel, and she rebelled around food. The extra cookie or handful of potato chips she ate took on enormous proportions for me as her blood sugar reacted, and I worried about both immediate and long-term health repercussions. My attention was never far from her, and she resented my hawkish observations as I tried to control her blood sugar from afar.

Kurt, meanwhile, continued in the private school into high school. The rigorous academic curriculum was hard for him, but music was still the way he fit in, the way he shone, and the way he forged an identity. When his grades plummeted, he received special attention from the music department and even from the principal, who took a genuine interest in him and tutored him, without charge, two afternoons a week. This enabled Kurt to maintain his grades so he could perform in the extravagant school musical productions where each year he won the coveted male lead. Kurt's identity crystallized around his life as a "star" both in school and outside of school where he wrote music and performed as the lead singer and guitarist in his band, Speak Softly.

He was about fifteen years old when he appeared one day with a hole in his ear lobe. Of course, I noticed. "Why do you need an earring?" I asked. "I don't have one," he said as I tried to get a better look under his golden retriever hair, and he pulled away. "It's a freckle, it's always been there."

"No one can see it but you," he said in exasperation, wearing the hole easily, the way a butterfly wears its yellow wings. I wore my righteousness with the incessant noise of a cicada in heat. One day he forgot to remove the earring and ambled into the kitchen with a few books, a Grateful Dead album, and a small gold stud gleaming in the hole. Although it was no larger than a tiny eraser, I saw it as a sign lit up in neon, flashing covert messages across the room—

"I take drugs."

"I renounce all civilized values."

"I don't care what you think."

Armageddon was now. I bought myself an earring, just one. I chose it carefully from the counter at Woolworth's. There was a small clip made of tin. Hanging from the clip was a hoop, and from the hoop hung a veritable aviary of primary colored feathers ranging in length from about two inches to six inches. There was a black feather a crow might have worn in its tail, a chartreuse feather from some tropical parrot drunk on tequila, a yellow one brighter than any canary God ever made. The red one flew down to my shoulder and sat on my white blouse like a cardinal in the snow. The pink and purple were luminous as tropical fish. I put the lasagna on the battlefield of the kitchen table as the gathering troops of the family took their positions at each place setting. One by one they started to laugh at my wordless reprimand of their renegade brother, even as my golden-studded boy protested, "You think you're funny, but you're not!"

It took a while for Kurt to fully appreciate the humor in the incident. But even that night, we could all see the smile he was trying to conceal behind his petulant frown, as he watched me serve dinner with that one ridiculous feathered earring swinging to my shoulder. We reached a truce, a silent accommodation that worked. He wore the gold stud when he performed and probably in school, but kept it in his pocket while at home.

By all outward appearances, Kurt was happy. From the tutoring that kept his grades acceptable, to the music that made him popular, to his apparent lack of concern about his biological family, Kurt seemed to be in a good place. But in his own way, he was having problems. There was less and less of Dad playing basketball in the driveway after work, or tossing a ball while grilling chicken on the backyard barbecue. No more welcoming his band in our basement, when they came over to practice on Saturday afternoons. Most hurtful was the way Bob's old easiness and patience was replaced by sarcasm and blaming, with comments like, "You need to study more, you need to stop watching TV, and you need to clean up your mess . . ." Alcohol was subtly changing Bob's personality. He and I were no longer a team as we dealt with the children, and often found ourselves on opposite sides of their issues when a strong front was what was really needed.

As life changed around him, Kurt's disdain for academics grew, and his turn to music intensified. It was Dennis who found Kurt sitting at his desk making futile attempts to do his homework. When Dennis asked him what was wrong, Kurt could not say. It was Dennis who finally broke through to him with the tears filling his own eyes, and they began to share their sorrow about their father. From that time on, they stuck close together.

Many years later, Kurt told me that during the rough years, Dennis was Switzerland, the neutral state where anyone could go for asylum. He never judged, never betrayed a confidence, and always anticipated Kurt's need to be heard.

๑ 10 ๛

Lost & Found

UP UNTIL THE LATE SEVENTIES WHEN the drinking escalated, life had been good. I could count on Bob to come home in the late afternoon and warm up the meal I had prepared for the kids on the evenings I drove into New York City for a class. Bob's business was prospering, there were summer vacations to the beach, and winter vacations to the Poconos; the kids were happy and healthy and the college tuition fund for five was accumulating.

But the decline from alcohol took on a geometric progression as it spiraled out of control. Denial twisted reality. Trust was destroyed. Happiness was eroded. In time, Bob no longer arrived home early when I needed to go to class. He often arrived ten minutes after I left, his not-so-conspicuous way of avoiding my smelling his breath, or evaluating his demeanor, to satisfy myself that he had or had not been drinking. As the weeks passed, he arrived later and later, until finally all pretenses were dropped, and he came in long after I returned from my class. I considered quitting school. Yet some instinctive act of self-preservation propelled me along.

Things were broken between Bob and me. He left for New York early in the morning, clean-shaven, dressed in a suit and tie and white shirt. The kids saw him as they sleepily grunted through their early morning ablutions, getting ready for school. "I'll call you," he said on his way out the door. By

9:30 we were connected by a telephone wire. With no one else at home to be infected by my anger, I lectured, I cried, I begged him to stop drinking. He promised to come home early that night, so we could talk. I felt some relief, a smidgen of hope for an hour or so before anxiety set in again. A part of me persisted in believing that he would gain insight and stop drinking. Hadn't he done that before? I had gotten through to him in 1970 when he went to AA Why couldn't I get through to him now?

I went to Alanon. Here, for an hour at a time, I experienced some relief as I began to understand my own unhappiness and futile attempt to control Bob's drinking. I learned that alcohol is a progressive disease. It progresses even when active drinking ceases. When Bob resumed drinking in the late seventies, for his body it was as though he'd never stopped. I listened to the stories of others and related to them. I saw myself in their attempts to cope. I witnessed others' return to health. I left those meetings with a determination to take care of myself and my family, to keep things as normal as possible in the constrained atmosphere in which we were living, to live one day at a time because there was no other choice.

I threw myself into stripping wallpaper, painting walls, anything to absorb the energy of my anger. I willed myself to study and continue to advance in graduate school. I cried, mostly at my therapy sessions, where my sadness and anger could not be overheard by my children. Bob reluctantly attended a few therapy sessions with me and became angry and stormed out when the psychologist recommended AA, persevering in his belief that a few nights out with the boys did not make him an alcoholic. I was pre-occupied with myself and the loss of my dreams and barely knew if I was keeping on top of things with the children. Robert and Kathleen were in college, and the three younger boys trod lightly at home. Eddie was still in therapy with Joe Ryan. He bottled up his anger and took it to Joe's little office where he could uncork it safely. Kurt was outwardly keeping his focus on music, talking to Dennis when I was nagging him about grades or attitude and mumbling under his breath when I grilled him about his whereabouts, but inwardly he was hurting. Dennis was trying to be all things to all people. Wary and observant, he never got an attitude toward Bob. He gave me no trouble, plugging along at school, writing his college application essays and watching out for his brothers. But he too was living the pain of our dissolving family.

In the fall of 1981, Bob's business partner, Wil Matura, announced that he wanted to terminate their partnership in the corporate benefits company they had formed in 1975. After reaching a financial agreement, Bob and Wil flipped a coin to determine who was going to buy out whom. Bob won the toss, and with his judgment clouded by the amount he was drinking, opted to be the buyer. On April 1, 1982, using the business as collateral, Bob secured a major loan from one of the insurance companies with whom he dealt. He bought the business and paid Wil a lump sum with the proceeds of the loan. In addition, he signed a contract agreeing to make payments to Wil each month for the next year, from earnings that were expected to flow into the business.

With the added stress of running the business without a partner, Bob's turn to beer worsened. He had fender benders and wound up in hospital emergency rooms. One midnight, Bob called from Connecticut where he had traveled to see a client. He had rented a motel room after disabling the car when he hit a guard-rail. Robert, who was home from college on break, and I drove to Connecticut. Sullen, bruised, and hung-over, Bob was angry with us for coming—for witnessing his shame. He refused to come home with us. Robert and I drove home in silence. Bob was alive. There was nothing more to say.

A few months later, while driving to his office after a late lunch, he got a DWI and lost his license for six months. The court sent him for mandatory alcohol counseling. I drove him. Surely, I thought, this would be the end of his drinking. But no, he refused to acknowledge he had a problem. Counseling was a disaster.

One afternoon, Dennis was home from high school with a case of mononucleosis and pulled himself off the couch to answer the doorbell. "Mom, it's two men. They want to talk to you." I went to the door, still holding the knife I was using to slice a tomato for dinner. They were business-like as they identified themselves as detectives. They handed me a subpoena.

"For what?" I asked them.

"You'll have to talk to your husband," the tall one said as Dennis listened from his nest of blankets on the couch. I tore open the envelope as they walked away. We were being sued, plunged into a web of legal actions brought about by the poor judgment, misplaced trust, and sheer craziness that had taken over Bob's mind as his addiction to beer spiraled.

* * *

MEANWHILE, MY JOB with the hospital gradually increased to three days a week. I was worried about money, and although I was earning very little, it was a help. And I loved the work. It allowed me to immerse myself in another world, freeing me from a personal world that was becoming so painful.

There is a certain intimacy that develops among people entrusted with mending the fragile lives of those who are emotionally wounded. Each patient we encountered came with a very human history that led to their hospitalization and the shattered state of their lives. Masks came off, defenses were dropped, and a kind of beauty emerged in the truth of each person as revealed in their stories. I found that working in this environment of shared concern allowed me to reveal the truth about my own life. I turned to my friends, other therapists at the hospital. Through their combined support and wisdom, I found ways to cope. It was my friend Dena who gave me the most help. She worked full time with the alcohol recovery program and had also gone through a divorce from an alcoholic husband.

"Be your best self," Dena said to me, over and over. "Be your best self." With these four words, she gave me a life-boat in which to ride out the waves of Bob's alcohol abuse. Being my best self took the focus off Bob and put it on me. It took me away from the debilitating anger and thoughts about what he was doing to me, and allowed me to focus on myself and my contribution to the happiness of the family. It gave me a way to take the action I needed to function, and even find happiness in spite of Bob's drinking.

Personal experience is an astute teacher. I took those words from my friend with me into my counseling practice, where I was able to give them back to my clients who found themselves buffeted by the actions of others.

* * *

ON JANUARY I, 1983, EIGHT MONTHS after buying the business, Bob's major account, a Fortune-500 company, left him. With this loss, our major source of income ended. Still under obligation to make payments on the loan, the business fell deeper and deeper into debt. Without telling me, Bob borrowed over $10,000 from each of our five closest friends. Learning about these loans filled me with rage and shame although none of our friends ever spoke to me about them. Unwilling to embarrass me, or perhaps just feeling sorry for the family, they never brought it up. His friends didn't know he was spending his days in a bar. Believing he had cash-flow problems that would resolve, they were there for him. I was invested in keeping his drinking a secret, out of a misguided sense of loyalty and my own sense of shame.

Bob took cash advances on his credit cards to meet his payroll. He didn't have the money to pay the withholding taxes on his employees, and eventually the state of New York came after him for those unpaid taxes. There was no money. The lawsuits multiplied.

By then I had become afraid of the mailman and the notices and letters he left in our mailbox. Each piece of mail I opened relating to our finances or to the increasing number of lawsuits struck me like another blow. These were not small amounts, amounts I could squeeze out of a bank account in order to make it right. There were maxed-out credit cards. Personal loans, taken out without my knowledge, were overdue. There were notices from banks I'd never entered, and, as I investigated, I found my name forged onto loan agreements. Accumulating interest was almost doubling the amount of each loan. Eventually, Bob closed the New York office. Within days, the leasing company filed suit for past and future rents due under the terms of the original contract.

I was most afraid of the certified letters I had to sign for; they were addressed to Bob, and the mailman handed them to me with a pen. If I didn't sign, he couldn't leave them. Those letters became my major source of information. They arrived like foot soldiers warning of an attack, couriers serving notice of the assault being prepared in places I couldn't imagine. Clients kept disappearing from the books. We were drowning in the debt. There was no way to settle it, even if I took every penny we had in savings and sold the house. I needed to protect what little was left. My major concern was college tuition for the children. I was obsessed with keeping it safe.

Each day I lived in a state of anxiety as I anticipated what the evening would bring. Each minute hung like a weight as I made dinner, fielded homework questions, ironed someone's favorite shirt or pretended to Kurt, Eddie, and Dennis that nothing was wrong. Afraid that Bob would get mugged or cause a car accident, I paced the floor in front of the window. I memorized the different closing hours of bars in New York and New Jersey and thought of calling hospitals or the police if he was not home within an hour after closing time. It was only when I heard his car pull into the driveway that my anxiety-riddled heart stopped pounding, and an anger that was as poisonous to me as alcohol was to Bob took its place.

Once again, I thought about ending the marriage. I threatened to end the marriage. Yet I believed it would hurt the children more if I further disrupted their home by selling the house, paying off what I could of the debt and filing for bankruptcy, and trying to make it alone. I believed I had protected them, to some extent, up until that point. They did not know how grave the financial situation was, how their tuition bills were always in jeopardy. There were three meals on the table each day, two cars in the garage, and clothes on their backs, and though their father was rarely present, he still made it, even in the darkest times, to their sports events and graduations and concerts—proof to him that he wasn't like his own father.

As teenagers and young adults: Eddie, Dennis, Kathleen, Kurt, and Robert.

113

I colluded in keeping up a social life. Bob was home every weekend and did not drink at home. Again, proof that he was not like his father. By Sunday afternoon, the two days without alcohol began to affect his body. As the craving for beer increased he became irritable and angry, and by 11:00 a.m. on Monday he was back in the same Manhattan bar.

During these months, I transferred the college savings accounts into my name only. Bob knew and did not try to stop me. I soon realized that this did not protect the accounts since I was in a marriage, filing joint income taxes, and I was as responsible as Bob for our debts. For a period of time, I transferred a savings account into my sister's name to protect it. In my wildest moments, I considered withdrawing the tuition money from the bank and literally burying it under the house. Sanity prevailed, and finally I called a lawyer.

Mike was an acquaintance I knew through Bob's earlier involvement with our parish church. They'd worked together on some educational committees, and Bob once told me that Mike was "fierce about education." I didn't even know what kind of law he practiced, but his office was in town and I could get there easily.

It was a difficult call to make. Revealing this whole sordid mess to someone I hardly knew seemed wrong. I felt like I was breaking some sacred contract I entered with marriage. The words of a friend, another co-worker at Carrier, came back to me. Once, in a casual conversation, when I confessed to feeling guilty for wasting time watching TV, she had rolled her eyes and wisely said, "You need to give yourself permission to do things." At the time, I wanted to laugh at the simplicity of the thought. It was only later that I found the wisdom in its simplicity. Now I gave myself permission to make the call to Mike.

Mike became my staunchest ally. Some chord in him was touched by my plight and seemed to send him reeling back to his own childhood. He told me about his mother with pride. He shared how, during the Depression, his father's career ended, forcing the family to move from their estate on the Hudson, replete with maids, into a small apartment in Jersey City. He told me how his mother got her three boys an education and he told me he would help me do the same for my children. As I handed him our slim bank books tied up in a rubber band, into which I distributed about $100,000, he opened his office safe. "Banks will have to go through me and my safe to get one penny of that money," he said emphatically. I believed him. I trusted him. I left his office giddy with relief. It was as if I had been traveling in some foreign country where I did not know the language and had at last met someone who understood what I was trying to say. Within days Mike had the money invested in five Clifford Trust Funds, one in each child's name. And like loaves and fishes, that money multiplied to cover each tuition bill that came to us.

Mike also told me about a doctor friend of his who was the director of the alcohol rehabilitation program at a local hospital. He offered to put me and Bob in touch with him if ever Bob was willing to accept treatment. It was something to hang onto.

* * *

OFTEN THE BOYS STAYED AWAKE in bed until they heard Bob's key in the door. Sometimes one of them casually got up and said, "Dad home yet?" I quickly collected myself and lied, "Oh, he called. He's on his way. Go to sleep. You have school tomorrow." Unable to read, unable to sleep, unable to watch TV, I tried to pray—"Dear God, bring him home safely," in strident petitions for help, as my fingers slipped over the rosary beads in the pocket of my robe.

There were times when doubt was a weed that grew rampant in my faith. For the previous decade I had been searching for those buds of belief that would blossom into an undeniable faith. I had come through the crisis of my late twenties when questions about the ultimate meaning of life haunted me. Over the years, I had immersed myself in literature and found in the work of William James a solution with which I could live. It related to downplaying the intellectual part of religion and relying on feelings as a way of knowing in one's spiritual life. It was in the inner world of feelings, according to James where "we catch real fact in the making and we directly perceive."

My reading led me again to Emerson and the school of humanistic psychology. Emerson wrote . . . "the highest most trustworthy knowledge consists of intuitive graspings—moments of direct perception . . . free mental acts of cognition and recognition . . ."

These readings led me back to the baby, John. The spiritual presence that grasped me in that sacred moment in the delivery room was as real to me as the gurney on which I lay. It had been a moment of knowing, an intuitive grasping, a direct perception that I return to again and again in attempts to refresh my faith.

I could choose to believe, take a chance that I might meet with ultimate disappointment, or find that, as a consequence of trusting the feelings that flooded me on that occasion when I felt God's presence, I would remain open to another transcendent experience. Or I could choose not to believe.

The choice I made was to not not believe. While falling short of perfect faith, this choosing gave me a conceptual peg on which to hang my yearning. It left the door open to continue to search, even when doubt was most crushing. It allowed me to take action when I was faced with a desperate situation. For me, prayer became action, a way of doing something when faced with my own impotence. As such, it became a constant in my life. Even when I found it difficult to believe, I prayed.

Did I pray Bob home safely all those many nights? Would he have made it home whether I prayed or not? I could not answer those questions. All I knew was that the impetus to pray came without thought or plan in those long, lonely nights of crisis. On some unconscious level, prayer was the branch that I hung onto that kept me from falling over the edge.

Who could understand this turn to prayer? I did not feel God's presence with me, like that night in the delivery room when I lost John. And I did not feel God was counting my prayers, making a choice to answer them . . . or not. But I did believe the residual power of that experience in the delivery room continued to inform my psyche, reminding me that there was more that I did not know about God than I did know. Alone and needing help, I made a conscious decision to pray, and whispered, "Thank you," when each of those harrowing nights ended without tragedy.

* * *

THERE IS, IN EVERY WAR, an escalation. Skirmishes turn to fully engaged battles. Victory or defeat seems inevitable. Such was the summer of 1983. I manipulated a dinner outside the house with Bob in order to insure this would not be the one night he appeared at the dinner table. I knew if he found out about the plan I had set in motion for the children, he would be enraged. Robert had just completed his junior year at college, Kathleen her sophomore year, and Dennis was scheduled to start his freshman year in a few weeks. They were all home for the summer, and I had signed them up for a series of eight ALANON educational meetings at the rehabilitation facility where Bob had been sent after his DWI. Before his alcohol counseling was aborted, a social worker gave me literature about the meetings and suggested I send the children. None of them wanted to go.

In the days that followed, I pieced together the scene that took place when I left the house to meet Bob. There was Eddie running out the back door, defiant as he told the others, "I'm not going to any dumb ALANON meeting, and you can't make me go." There was Robert stampeding after him, the dog, Poo, yelping at his heels, chasing them through the hydrangea bushes, through the holly. Kathleen, gulping apple juice as her blood sugar plummeted with the upheaval, followed Robert and Eddie through the shrubbery. She tried to separate her brothers, "Stop it! Stop fighting. None of us wants to go to the meeting, but Mom made the appointment, and we're going. Get in the car both of you. I'm driving."

"No, you're not," from Robert, as he slid behind the wheel of the old station wagon. "You'll get us killed on the highway. I'm driving."

Somehow, all five of them got to the meeting.

Sitting around a huge table with other families and a group leader, the children listened. Over the eight weeks they learned of each other's suffering through the feelings they were encouraged to reveal in the safety of that ALANON group meeting. They became closer. They learned that they didn't cause their father's alcoholism, they couldn't control it, and they couldn't cure it. It was here that Kathleen spoke of her secret plan to quit college so she could stay home and take care of me and her younger brothers as Dennis left for his freshman year. Thankfully, this wise ALANON group convinced her to return to college.

When Bob found out about the meetings he was furious. In his convoluted thinking, the family was making him an alcoholic; drinking had nothing to do with it.

The summer of 1983 seemed hotter than usual. By the end of August, Bob was sick. He was having trouble breathing. He could not lie down without coughing, so he tried to sleep in a reclining chair in the den. He could not admit how ill he was, and founds all sorts of excuses to minimize his symptoms. It was "a cold," or it was "the asthma I had as a kid," or "I just need to lose a little weight," or "it will go away." I finally persuaded him to go to a doctor, who immediately diagnosed congestive heart failure and put him in the hospital. Over the next three days, twelve pounds of fluid were drained from Bob's lungs. When he was discharged from the hospital it was with a warning—drinking would kill him. I rejoiced in that warning. Surely this was rock bottom; surely this would end his addiction to beer.

It didn't. Within two days he was back at it. "The doctor doesn't know what he is talking about. I feel just fine," he said, even as he strained to breathe. On October 12, 1983, he left the house at 10:00 a.m., supposedly for New York, where he still maintained an office. Craving a beer, he stopped at a local bar for "just one drink" to fortify himself for the mess waiting for him at his office. He could not stop drinking. That one beer evolved into twelve hours in the bar. When Bob came in that night about 10:00 p.m., it was clear to me that he was beaten by this disease. I believed he would die.

The next morning he stayed in bed. After the children left for school, I found him crying. "Let me call Mike and try to get you help," I said for the umpteenth time, and here was the miraculous part. This time he said, "Okay."

Now things moved quickly. I called Mike, who called the medical director at the alcohol recovery program at the hospital.

"They're waiting for your call," Mike told me. I called the hospital, only to be told to put Bob on the phone. "They want to talk to you."

He refused, too ashamed to speak. I handed him the phone, knowing this could all blow up with his refusal to speak. Then I heard him say the words. "I need help to stop drinking."

There were no beds. A bed would be available the next day. Bob was told to call back the next morning. I was worried, knowing that by the next morning anything could happen, including a change of mind.

"I'm going to call the kids," he said. That afternoon, he called each of the three children who were away at college and told them he was going into the hospital for alcohol treatment. He spoke with Kurt and Eddie when they come in from high school. He made five promises, and those promises, more than anything else kept him faithful to his commitment to get help. He entered rehab on October 14.

On October 18, while Bob was in the hospital for treatment, I received notification that a lawsuit against Bob was being brought by the company that loaned him the money to buy the business. The financial situation was overwhelming. I doubted we could ever recover and believed that selling our house was imminent. Yet the major focus had to be on sobriety. Losing our financial stability paled in comparison to losing a life to this disease. Bob was discharged on October 24, having gone ten days without a drink.

That weekend, even though it was early in the college semester, Robert, Kathleen, and Dennis all made their way home. Their father was back. The insanity of denial was broken. By now, they were all educated enough to know how tough it was for him as he choose sobriety minute by minute. They wanted him to know how much his recovery meant to them, and they didn't want to lose him again.

Years later, I found a shoebox full of letters Kathleen had saved from those broken years. As I read them, I was struck anew by the bonds of love recorded on those pages torn from their school notebooks. There was the fourteen-year-old Kurt writing, "Dearest Kathy," as he told her about the decision he had made to study hard and settle for nothing but A's as a freshman in high school. Eddie confided his fear about performing at Carnegie Hall and poured onto the page his confusion about his relationship with Bob. Rugby shirts were the way Robert showed his love as he sent her two team shirts, one for her and one for her college roommate. And a post script at the bottom of Dennis's letter said simply, "I love you so much."

* * *

BOB'S WAS A FRAGILE SOBRIETY, as all sobrieties are in the beginning. Doctors at the hospital convinced him that he would die if he did not stop drinking. The staff gave him the tools he needed to help himself. Other patients, by their very existence, were a mirror that reflected back what was happening to him. Members of Alcoholics Anonymous came into the hospital program to speak of their own recovery and gave him hope. Clichés like "a day at a time," "ninety meetings in ninety days," and "keep it simple," assumed the wisdom of Revelation. Bob clung to them, repeated them over and over in his mind to combat the craving for beer that was constantly present.

We had him back, but it was a tentative reconciliation for all of us. Bob had to focus on sobriety, and his involvement with the family was a second priority. He believed he would never have fun again, never laugh again as he faced the loss of his best friend, beer. Yet he prevailed. He attended AA meetings and became part of a network of people of all races and cultures with whom he shared the deepest shame of his life. While at these meetings, he found pieces of himself in the stories told by convicts and priests, lawyers and bricklayers, doctors and students. The camaraderie he once found around a sports bar was replaced by a new kind of fellowship, one that was deep, honest and sustaining.

He talked to friends who came forward, people he never even suspected had a drinking problem, and they revealed their own recovery stories to him. He found the support that was there for anyone who could break through their denial and ask for help. He attended ninety meetings in ninety days. He wrote to Robert, Kathleen, and Dennis at college, long letters of reassurance. He copied each letter and alternated the originals among them. He told them not to worry if they couldn't reach him at work in the late afternnon. He was leaving the city early to help himself avoid the sports bars that beckoned. They could reach him at home by 4:30 or so.

As Bob became more confident in his ability to stay sober, he was able to re-dedicate himself to business. We worked together. Bob focused on servicing the few clients that remained and on obtaining new business. I worked on collecting income owed him from various companies, income that he had failed to keep track of. I handled the books recording all the debt, culling long meticulous lists of where our obligations lay. I worked out payment arrangements with banks and the insurance company that was suing for repayment of the business loan. Month by month, I wrote endless checks, chipping away at the debt owed to banks, credit cards, the government and friends.

Initially, Bob worked from the house. We bought a copy machine, a fax machine, a computer. He had no employees, no payroll, and no rent. But what he did have was his most precious asset, his brain, capable of taking complicated statistics and turning them into creatively designed medical benefits plans for his clients. He typed his own letters, generated his own reports. All the while, staying active in AA and attending several meetings each week. He was committed to his recovery.

With sobriety, he found new business associates, some of whom were already AA members. They welcomed him like a prodigal son and partnered with him, referring him to new clients. He admitted to former business associates that he was an alcoholic and that he had stopped drinking. Gradually, old business relationships were reestablished. He recognized that there were few families whose lives had never been affected by alcohol. For many, it was only peripherally, but affected nonetheless. Where he anticipated judgments and harshness, he found forgiveness and admiration. With Bob's honesty, friends and associates revealed to him their own families' or friends' conflicts with alcohol and he found himself in a position to help others. The fellowship of AA was truly alive in his life.

Although financial recovery once seemed impossible, hope returned, like bulbs planted long ago that bloomed unexpectedly. I had seen Bob rise to success before. I knew he was born with a good mind and with alcohol no longer poisoning his brain, his mind was back. We put off selling the house. It took a couple of years of hard work, but the business not only got back on its feet, it once again began to flourish.

Yet my fear of Bob having a relapse was never far away. It would be many years before I could pull into the driveway without my heart fluttering, as I looked for a light in the house that let me know he was home and safe.

১৩ 11 ᚑ

Life Goes On

DURING THE FRAGILE HIGH SCHOOL YEARS, music was always there for Eddie. His talent was equal to Kurt's but his demeanor was less flamboyant than his brother's. He never sought star status, but quietly took pleasure in his own creativity and contributions. He was the pianist in the school orchestra, accompanist for the glee club performances and played the piano for any school function that required music, even if it was only the "Star Spangled Banner" at weekly assemblies. With extra help and hard work he was doing okay academically and had a girlfriend, Barbara, a flautist in the school orchestra.

No one disputed that he was musically gifted, but still, when in the spring of 1984 his piano teacher booked Carnegie Recital Hall in New York for a recital, we were all impressed. His teacher, a serious man with crossed eyes and a goatee who wrote and performed chamber music, chose "Rhapsody in Blue" as Eddie's recital piece. Eddie practiced it for months, until he had memorized every note. The rest of the family did homework to "Rhapsody in Blue," brushed our teeth, talked to friends on the telephone, and did the dishes to "Rhapsody in Blue."

The three older children came home from college for the Saturday afternoon performance. I heard them as they tried to ease Eddie's nervousness. Dennis stopped by his room as he was getting ready. "Are you nervous?"

"Yeah, I feel like I'm going to throw up."

"Don't worry. You're so good that no one will know if you make a mistake, and you probably won't. Do you want to wear my good luck belt, the one I wore when I took my SATs?"

Kathleen joined in at the bedroom door. She was pulling rollers out of her hair. "We'll all be there rooting for you, and we'll love you even if you mess up."

"Go to it, bro," Kurt said as he put the gold stud in his ear and gave me a look that said, "Don't make me take it out. I look good."

And so we went, a little army of supporters, proud of the one among us who could play at Carnegie Recital Hall. A hush fell over the audience as Eddie sat down at the magnificent baby grand piano on the stage and readied himself for the *piece de resistance,* the last performance of the recital. His new navy-blue blazer concealed his white shirt turning limp with perspiration. I barely heard the music as I held my breath and prayed to the recital gods throughout the whole piece as it resounded in the perfect acoustics of Carnegie Recital Hall.

Eddie performed without a flaw, and after he played the last note, he stood up as if dazed. We all stood and clapped wildly. Grandpa was crying. Grandma gave him a sideways glance, and I heard her whisper, "Stop it, Joe. He'll think you didn't like it." Neighbors cheered and Kurt yelled, "Yeah, bro." Even Joe Ryan was there, clapping wildly for his young client.

Boisterous as a carnival, we made our way to a restaurant to revel in Eddie's accomplishment. That was when we all heard Robert, who had made the trip down from college, say, "Boy, my brother's good. I knew he had talent, but I didn't know he was *that* good." And I could see Eddie beaming with pride. In a family of five children, it was not easy to earn everyone's attention and admiration and know that you unabashedly, unreservedly deserved it, but that day Eddie knew he was the one.

* * *

By the time Eddie was eighteen, he felt ready once again to search for his biological parents. This time, when he approached Kurt, Kurt was uninterested. Busy developing his band, his guitar, his voice with perfect pitch, Kurt was happy-go-lucky. Each year, another set of huge posters of him in costume for the current school play hung in the gymnasium, the auditorium, the band room. He was Conrad Birdie in "Bye Bye Birdie," and the male lead in both "Bells Are Ringing" and "Pajama Game." His voice was getting better and better with the discipline and training imparted by his beloved music director. He was singing with the glee club and the newly formed barbershop quartet. And he had as many girlfriends as a rock star!

"We have it too good," Kurt said to his big brother. "I don't want to know anything about them." So, Eddie, not willing to "mess with my brother's head," let go of his plan to search.

* * *

A LIFE-CHANGING INCIDENT FOR EDDIE took place during the late summer of 1984. Dennis asked us if his friend Doug could leave his five-year-old Saab at our house for the summer. Doug's home was in Albuquerque, New Mexico, and he did not want to spend the time needed to drive the car home from college, which was in New Hampshire. We said, "Sure, he can leave it in the garage." And so it was arranged.

One morning around the end of August, Bob's car refused to start. "Take the Saab," Dennis said easily. "Doug told me to take it for a spin if we need an extra car during the summer." Bob gratefully grabbed the key from a hook in the back hall, where it had hung all summer. But when he turned the key in the ignition, nothing happened. Not even a cough. Dead.

"We probably should not have let it sit for so many weeks," Bob and I and Dennis all agreed. A call to the local garage produced Larry, the trusted mechanic who had come to the rescue of our cars many times over the years. "I need you to take care of a car we're garaging for a friend," Bob said. "It's in our garage, and I can't get it started. I think it might have a dead battery."

"Oh, you mean that gray Saab, I wondered when you were going to call. I towed it into your garage a couple of weeks ago."

"You towed it into my garage? No. You must be thinking of someone else. This car hasn't been out of the garage all summer."

"I'm pretty sure I've got it right," said Larry. "Your son called one day. He was stuck in town with a friend. The friend had a Triple-A card, and I was

124

the towing company on call." Larry went on to tell Bob how neither of the boys knew how to drive a stick shift and when he got to the car it was smoking and smoldering like a chimney. The boys said they didn't want it fixed just towed back into the garage. Then Larry added, "I'll tell you right now, that car's a goner. I'll take it to the shop and give another look, but I'm betting the motor's stripped."

We were incredulous. Which one of our sons would take the car without asking? It didn't take long to zero in on Eddie.

Of course, Eddie denied it. Finally, with his back against the wall and records from the towing bill confronting him, he caved in and admitted his involvement. There were excuses. They were just going to get ice cream. They were going to bring the car right back. They didn't know it had a stick shift, on and on.

Dennis turned pale at the thought of telling his friend from school. Bob and I were mortified at having to call the boy's parents in Albuquerque. We learned the ruined car was appraised at $5,000. We told Eddie he would have to pay for it. We took out a loan and sent the $5,000 off to Doug. We made a payment plan with Eddie to pay us back. It took years of putting aside a part of his salary, and money earned playing the piano, and accumulated birthday monies and graduation monies—but he finally paid off the debt.

I called Eddie's therapist once or twice during the Saab incident. I was furious when he would not give me the professional courtesy of hearing me out, would not listen to me suggest that "this therapy isn't working." Sometimes it was tempting to end Eddie's therapy, as I ruminated that behaviors like the Saab incident should not be happening. However, Joe made it necessary for Eddie to initiate—or not initiate—his own issues. Thankfully, I never succumbed to my impulse to interrupt the therapy. Eddie's deep trust of Joe made it possible for Joe to shepherd him through adolescence and into manhood.

* * *

AS KURT APPROACHED GRADUATION, he was weary of studying and tutoring. Bob took him to look at several colleges with music programs. When the admissions officer at Emory College asked him what he was looking for in a college program, he answered, in his own inimitable way, "No academic subjects." That was the end of his college career.

Gigs with his band, Speak Softly, brought him a small following of fans and even smaller earnings. He was the lead singer; his stage name was Kurtis Eric, the name given to him by his biological parents. Bob and I, sometimes with our friends, spent long evenings in smoky bars, sipping sodas and waiting for him to perform, while the band tested and retested the sound equipment. A fan club developed and an increasing number of people gathered in the bar wearing purple and white tin buttons with "Speak Softly" imprinted on them. Finally, sometime around 10:30, when the crowd could hardly wait another minute, Kurt approached the microphone, picked up his acoustic guitar, and sang the music he composed. Bob and I loved his voice and really believed he was going to make it to the big time.

Along with his gigs, the smoky bars, and his groupie fan-club there was another aspect to Kurt's performing. Every Christmas Eve, the family quieted as the annual command performance requested by my mother took place. Amid toasters and sweaters and basketballs and the floor strewn with wrapping paper, she asked, "Kurt, will you sing 'Oh Holy Night' for me?"

And my long-haired boy said—"For you, Grandma, anything."

We all gathered in the living room, even his conservative older brother Robert, who never quite approved of Kurt's long hair or studded ear. Eddie rummaged through the piano bench for the music, not seen since the previous Christmas, and took his place at the piano. Kurt cleared his throat and grinned at his Grandma. The room was hushed as the notes of "Oh Holy Night" rang out. Holding our collective breath, we waited for Kurt to hit those gorgeous high notes:

> A thrill of hope
> the weary world rejoices
> for yonder breaks
> a new and glorious morn
> Fall on your knees
> Oh, hear the angel's voices
> Oh, night, Divine
> Oh, night, oh night Divine.

And we heard the angels' voices as Eddie and Kurt, each Christmas Eve, made a cathedral of our home.

* * *

BUT LIVING AT HOME HAD BECOME difficult for Kurt. There were rules. His focus was only music, which took him into bars several nights a week, and the late hours and life style he was falling into concerned us. Bob and I both thought he was vulnerable to alcohol. It was difficult for Kurt to listen to our admonishments, having been through Bob's struggle with alcoholism just a few years earlier. Kurt thought our views were tainted and extreme. Shortly after graduation from high school in 1986, he left home to share an apartment with two other band members. He had watched his four older siblings leave home after high school for college and dorm life. He saw his move to an apartment as no different, although, in my mind, it was enormously different.

The apartment was less than five minutes from home. I found myself driving past early in the morning to see if the car the boys shared was in the driveway or to see some sign of Kurt if I hadn't heard from him for a day or so. Although Robert never said it, his prophesy—"Mom, that kid is headed for trouble and you don't see it"—voiced when Kurt was thirteen years old, seemed to be coming true as I become more and more concerned about the way Kurt was handling his independence.

When the police called late one Friday night, I was stunned. Kurt had borrowed the family station wagon, ostensibly to transport speakers for band practice. However the police stopped him in a nearby town. The big boat of a station wagon looked out of place in the drug-infested neighborhood; it looked to the police like a drug pick-up. It was. After searching the car and finding a gram of cocaine, the police impounded the car and the boys were hand-cuffed and hustled into the police car and driven to the station house.

We got the call on Halloween weekend. My first thought was that someone was playing a joke—a weird trick or treat. Bob was out that night at an AA meeting, and Robert was just going out the door to pick up Erin, his girlfriend. He put off his plans and drove me to the police station. During the drive to the police station, raging mad, I resolved to leave Kurt in jail for the night to "teach him a lesson."

The scene we walked into was straight out of a "B" movie. Kurt was handcuffed to a bench. Touching was not allowed; a distance of three feet had to be maintained between "the prisoner" and others. He was terrified, yet he was surly. A holding pen about ten feet away was crowded with men wearing gold chains, leather jackets, and smirks. Some were asleep or feigning sleep on the floor; some were shouting and cursing, out of control with drugs or alcohol. No one had shoelaces or a belt; both were considered weapons and had been confiscated.

Of course, Kurt insisted he was innocent. "It was the other kids. It was the cops. It was bad luck, and it was only a gram of cocaine." Robert walked away, so angry with his little brother that he couldn't trust himself to utter a word. I knew enough about drugs and about my son to realize it was foolish to assume I would hear any truth from Kurt that night. An officer summoned me to the desk and unlocked a small window in the chain-link cage fence that separated the cops from prisoners and lawyers and mothers. He handed me Kurt's Timex watch, his shoelaces, his belt, and the change that was in his pockets.

As I surveyed the situation, my resolve to leave Kurt in jail for the night evaporated. I did not want to leave him there. But I found I had no choice. He had been booked and was slated to spend the night in that holding pen. Court convened at 9:00 a.m., and a judge would determine what happened next.

Now it was my turn to be terrified. Realizing that Kurt would be bedded down for the night with others in that holding pen, I felt a tiger rise within me. "If anyone touches him, I will sue the police department," I said. "He's only eighteen. I mean it; you will never get rid of me if anyone so much as lays a finger on him."

The police let me go on—they even pacified me. "Look," a cop finally said, pointing to a corner behind the desk, "we have closed circuit TV in the pen and can see everything that's happening right here on our screen." I left Kurt in the hands of the system. At 9:00 a.m. the next morning, Bob and I watched as Kurt, chained to six other prisoners, was escorted by armed guards into the court room. My heart was breaking. The judge put him on probation and released him. The probation officer told us the record would be expunged if Kurt attended a mandatory drug program, reported to probation once a week to have his urine tested and was drug-free in six months.

We took him to our family doctor that same day for a medical evaluation. He told us that Kurt has been snorting coke for about three weeks—enough time for an addiction to take root, but also little enough time so that, with help, he could overcome it. Kurt entered an out-patient drug program under duress, not willing to admit to the seriousness of three weeks' usage. He hated the mandatory probation visits. He hated not being able to use the car. He hated our sending him for counseling with Joe Ryan, and refused to engage in therapy. But the system worked. In those six months, monitored by probation and the medical doctor, and the family, Kurt stayed clean of drugs, his head cleared, and he was able to acknowledge his close call with cocaine. He never went back to drugs.

Things began to get better between us. At least he was gracing us with his presence for a couple of hours each weekend while his laundry whirled away in my washer and dryer. One Saturday, he arrived with his laundry in tow and a new girl, Cath, by his side. Initially, Bob and I thought she was just the latest charm on the bracelet of girls that over the years had hung from his arm. But we were wrong. She did not hang on him. She lived at home and was working at a garden center putting herself through college. She was a steadying influence on Kurt.

By 1990 Kurt was writing music, arranging music, or performing during every waking hour. He was a perfectionist. As time went on, his perfectionism bred anxiety, and the anxiety effected his joy in performing. However, a few drinks enabled him to be on stage with an ease that was winning him an ever-growing following. Along with all of this, there was a fantasy fueling his life. It was based on a scant piece of information we had been given by Heather and had shared long ago with both of the boys. Their biological father, Eric, was a professional musician who played guitar and had his own band prior to 1970, when the boys were remanded to the province.

A dream had taken shape. In it, Kurt was with Eric, "jamming" on their guitars. As they improvised, they sang together, Eric and Kurtis Eric. They were somewhere in Canada and life was slow and easy. The fantasy grew in its own soil as the years progressed. Eric was famous. He was in a famous band. He got his life together somewhere along the years. He could open doors for Speak Softly. He would want his son in his famous band. Who was Eric? Where was Eric?

By the time Kurt was twenty-three, his gigs expanded to New York City. He seemed to have a chance to make it big. He put in his time at the small clubs I sometimes referred to as the "hellholes of the world," where one often had to climb over derelicts sleeping in the street in order to open the door. Huge speakers blasting music dwarfed the rooms in which the band played. His brothers and sister were proud of him and brought their friends to join Bob and me as we sat in a series of dark red vinyl booths, waiting and watching as he performed.

When Kurt was approached by a record producer, the whole family was thrilled. The producer was not interested in the band, but in Kurt performing his original music. With studio space in Nashville, he was in a position to produce an album and showcase my son. Kurt was ecstatic. We agreed to invest what would have been a year's college tuition in the production of a record album. A group of back-up singers was hired, violins and a cello were added to accompany him on his guitar, and a photographer took portrait shots of Kurt and his guitar for the album cover. In a whirlwind week of studio work starting early each morning and ending late at night, Kurt recorded song after song, all pieces for which he had written the music and lyrics. Our hopes were high. We all loved the finished product. However, in spite of the enthusiasm of the producers and the local support, the album did not get played on the radio, and it never made it beyond local exposure. In time, Kurt had to accept that his dream of a career in music was unattainable.

Not knowing about his biological father, Eric, combined with the dawning realization that he was not going to make it in the record business, plunged Kurt into an identity crisis. Without a future in music, who was he? His questions about himself loomed in ever-darkening clouds. Now it was Kurt's turn to gravitate towards his past.

He asked Eddie "What do you think about starting a search for our father?"

But Eddie was enjoying his life and didn't want to jeopardize the peace he was finally experiencing. He was working steadily in a bank, the Saab debt was behind him, and he had his own car. Most significantly he was seriously involved with his high-school sweetheart, Barbara. She was the only child of an adoring mother and father who seemed to love Eddie as much as they loved their daughter. No more than five feet tall and fragile-looking as a piece of lace, Barbara became Eddie's rock. Quiet and shy in her Capezios and pleated skirts, she provided, even in those early years, constancy in Eddie's life. Barbara found endearing those qualities in Eddie which, over the years, had bothered one or the other of us. For example, his tendency to change the stations on her car radio, or eat the half of a sandwich she was saving for the next day's lunch, was greeted with affection and tolerance.

Writing music in his free time and performing occasional piano jobs, Eddie was happy. Each time anger about "being thrown away like a piece of garbage" emerged, and it continued to surface periodically, Eddie talked about it in a session with Joe Ryan. The anger subsided. Interrupting his life to search for his biological parents was not something he wanted to do.

"Can you wait?" he asked Kurt.

Knowing how Eddie had willingly deferred to him in the past, it was now Kurt's turn to accommodate his brother. Kurt said, yes, he could wait, and with that yes, their search was put off yet again. But Kurt's struggles with his past continued.

❧ 12 ☙

Transitions

ALTHOUGH THE CHILDREN WERE ALL NOW LIVING on their own, there was a revolving door at home which they used to propel them through holiday seasons and temporary geographic, monetary or emotional upheavals. No matter how much furniture they carted away to furnish dorms or apartments, they never took the bookcases, shelves, and desks that Grandpa crafted for them in his basement workroom. And they never took their beds, so each one's claim to a space at home was never totally relinquished. But with marriage and the lifelong commitment to someone else, home, the place where they belonged, where each had a room of his own, was changing.

I don't know which one of them came up with the plan, but on a Friday night in December of 1987, three months before Robert's wedding, they started to arrive, one by one. Their suits rumpled from travel, their paisley ties stuffed into attaché cases, they came to deconstruct my casual remark: "I think I'll get an artificial tree for Christmas." Spreading like a holiday heresy among them, those innocent words drove them into a conspiracy, and all five of them descended upon us for the weekend to take matters into their own hands.

On Saturday morning, Bob was ecstatic from his early morning trip to the nursery with Kathleen, Eddie, and Kurt, where he gleefully overpaid for the biggest evergreen on the lot. A trail of pine needles followed him through the back hall as he hauled the evergreen past the hooks where five pair of ice skates once hung on their wet laces. Scrunching the tree through the back door, he pulled it into the family room where brute force and desire combined until the tree's bent trunk was standing straight in the metal stand and he was shouting "It's up. It's up." We gathered with our mugs of coffee and half-eaten bagels and gave the ritual advice—"A little left, a little right, a little more left,"—as he turned the inevitable bald spot to its best advantage.

Dennis rummaged in the basement for the large wire hoop stored away each January. He methodically tied pine branches on it to make the wreath for the front of the house. By 10:00 a.m. his cheeks were as red as they were on those long ago nights when he raided the refrigerator for carrots and, with his frozen mittens sticking out of his pockets, made his way to the rabbit hutch and his Bandito.

Robert went out to help Dennis. I heard them laughing as he reminded his brother of the year he strung blinking lights around their bunk beds and how Robert got up in the middle of the night in exasperation and yanked the plug. Kathleen was in the kitchen; her briefcase bulging with computer printouts was stashed under the hall table. Freckles sprinkled across the bridge of her nose were visible under a dusting of flour as she iced grins onto gingerbread men. Kurt found an audio tape from one of his high-school Christmas concerts. We listened to the carols coming from the school auditorium, where, on a slushy winter night, when he thought he was the next Mick Jagger, Kurt sang the music of the season. Eddie was sitting on the floor amid boxes of decorations and ornaments that had been relayed up the basement stairs. He was untangling the nest of strings of about one thousand lights for the tree.

Christmases past tumbled out of cardboard boxes. The hooked rug with Santa in his sleigh that was Dennis's fourth-grade art project was placed in front of the fireplace. A manger was arranged on the mantle, among boughs of pine. Two dozen stiff burlap ornaments created during a long ago October of chickenpox, were unwrapped. Rudolph, with his brass-button eyes, required a staple to hold his tail together. All the kids claimed ownership of the paper poinsettia, faded to pink, and seemingly held together by a force stronger than glue, as memories merged and re-emerged around the tree.

133

By 8:00 p.m. the tree was ready for tinsel. An impish impulse over-took Robert. He grabbed a handful of tinsel and, with a grin, threw it helter-skelter onto the tree. Kathleen screamed, "He hasn't changed. He hasn't changed. He's still throwing tinsel!" Then everyone was throwing tinsel. There was tinsel in hair and tinsel in eyes and tinsel hanging from sweaters.

All the years of creating memories were given back to Bob and me that weekend. The five children came unbidden. They filled the house; they filled their rooms. Like builders, choosing a cornerstone for the new from the remains of the old, they chose Christmas. This gesture cemented into our lives a memory that became the foundation of the new lives they would build with their own families.

* * *

Grandpa doing a reading at Robert's wedding.

THREE MONTHS LATER, IN MARCH of 1988, Robert married his college sweetheart, Erin. He asked my father to do a reading at the wedding. Grandpa walked to the lectern, tall and handsome in his tuxedo. Midway through the reading, he was overcome by emotion. His face reddened, and tears of love and joy streamed down his cheeks as everyone in the crowded church held their collective breath, willing him through the moment. Yet that spontaneous flood of emotion remained etched in the memories of all who witnessed it. We had already witnessed the brotherly love of Kurt, who willingly went to the barber with Rob to get his hair shorn to an acceptable wedding length. Now my father's tears broadened our experience of love. Here was another love, tried and true, unabashedly passing from generation to generation, endowing and enriching this thing called family.

❊ ❊ ❊

ELEVEN MONTHS LATER, my father was dead.

There was a dull pain in his side that grew throughout the day, a mis-diagnosis in the emergency room, a telephone call at 5:00 a.m., and he was gone.

A great sadness engulfed me, as it must for all who lose a parent—the shocking realization that reality was changed—this was my first day on the earth without a father. They say that death is a layered thing. A new loss opens the wounds of previous losses. Even grief that has healed leaves its mark, a scar on the psyche. The new loss causes that scar to bleed, metaphorically. Old feelings rush to the surface, and are experienced alongside the fresh shock and sadness. And so it was for me. My father's death transported me back to John's death; once again I was catapulted into the questions that plagued me all those years ago. How could I make sense of this? Where was God? Where was my father? Was there a God? Was there an afterlife? Was this all there is?

Amid these feelings, we buried my father.

Three months later, my sister and I began the dreaded job of dis-mantling his workroom. Dreaded because this was where my father's spirit lived, where he was most alive, crafting gifts for all of us, rehearsing the next joke, the "gotcha" that would leave us laughing.

His footprints still etched a trail in the sawdust that covered the base-ment floor. A neighbor's chair, its wobbly dowels glued and fastened, was bal-anced between the clamps of a vice, looking like a modern sculpture defying gravity's impulse to topple. On the workbench were the plans for the bird-house he made for me last Christmas and a carton of mechanical music boxes for his latest foray into woodworking. I pictured him unplugging the radial arm saw, a retirement gift from his co-workers at the bank, the safety precau-tion he always took before taking a soft rag and wiping the blade clean. Then his final check of the chair balanced in the vice before he pulled the cord on the single bulb illuminating the room. He had forty-eight hours left in his life and he was on his way to the kitchen to make a ham sandwich.

Now, I surveyed his workroom. Besides the sheer number of screw-drivers, hammers, drills, wrenches, saws, nails, sandpaper, and paint cans lining the shelves, there were piles and piles of glass. It was stacked against the cinder block foundation of the basement between the furnace and his work table. Rectangles and squares salvaged from old storm windows and plate glass windows lined all the walls. Lugged home from demolition sites and the neighborhood recycling, the glass was all inventoried in his mind, ready to be selected for some future project. I could see that each piece foretold my father's intention by its shape. Some were earmarked for a foyer table that would nestle alongside a stairway, with a rectangle of glass flanked by two squares of glass on either side. Some were destined for end tables or medicine cabinets. Some would go into picture frames he planned to construct with coved molding. Slender pieces would serve as powder room shelves, held up by brass brackets.

Where to start? What to give away? What to discard? The stacks of glass seemed the obvious place to begin. There was no one else who would be building glass-top tables, or painstakingly measuring an obscure corner in someone's dorm room or apartment in order to craft the perfect bookcase or shelf to utilize that wasted space.

The pre-printed instructions for glass disposal as dictated by the town were tucked into my mother's apron pocket. They read: "Each piece of glass is to be individually wrapped in doubled sheets of newspaper and the ends taped securely." Only then could they be stacked at the curb in piles no larger than two feet high. And so we began.

Crawling under the workbench, I gingerly placed a hand on either end of the most accessible piece of glass, a two-foot square. I dragged it to the middle of the room and laid it down on overlapping pieces of newspaper. Pulling each end of the newspaper taut, I folded it over, taped it, and carried it up the stairs and laid it tenderly at the curb. Over and over I wrapped a panel of glass, ran it up the basement stairs, and deposited it at the curb, all the while thinking about my father. As the hours passed, guilt that began as a fumbling of my unsteady hands settled like a dead weight in the pit of my stomach. I hesitated. I sat on the floor in the sawdust, my back leaning against a leg of his workbench. I asked myself if he'd be upset if he were here watching me throw his glass away.

The desire to hold onto my father merged with the objects that I believed were special to him. Part of me felt as though I was discarding him.

Did he know how much I was struggling with the decision to discard his glass? Still another part of me could picture him in his paint-splattered red-flannel shirt, standing in the doorway, a cold Rheingold in his hand, as I tried to maneuver past him with some oversized piece of glass. He would find my indecision funny and tease me—"Put the damn glass out—Let's finish the job. What are you waiting for?"

And so I continued. After a few more hours' work, I came upon a piece of glass buried in the pile. I caught my breath. Cut into a hexagon, it was unlike any other piece of glass in the room. I knew immediately that a lot of work had gone into that shape. It seemed special. My dad had probably taken it to a glass cutter; all six sides were so perfectly angled.

I stopped working, "Do you know what dad planned to do with this?" I asked my sister as I held up the glass.

"No" she answered as she took a break from sorting tools, "but you know how he was, always helping people out. It could have been for anyone in the neighborhood."

We continued to search our memories for some clue to the unusual shape, but neither of us could connect it to any project, person, or place. Finally, with fumbling hands, I wrapped it and carried it to the curb, although a sense of unease preoccupied me. It was as though I had regressed to child-hood, as if I had done something wrong. By the time I finished wrapping the last piece of glass, my unease evolved into an overwhelming impulse to remove the hexagon from the rubbish. I needed it to be my "transitional object," the concrete symbol that would allow me to continue to hold onto my father even though I was turning his workroom into an empty tomb. The impulse sent me scurrying out to the curb to retrieve the piece of glass I had deemed "special."

"What are you doing?" my mother asked from the kitchen as I cart-ed the hexagon back down the basement stairs. I told her. She just shook her practical head.

"That's silly," she said "but if it makes you feel better, leave it in the basement." Within a half hour, influenced by her no-nonsense attitude, I changed my mind and found my way to the curb once again with the hexagon. This went on three times—up the stairs, down the stairs, up the stairs, down the stairs—with the same piece of glass. By now my mother and sister were both laughing at me. Finally my rational mind took over. I placed it at the curb, and, exhausted, drove home.

It was after 10:00 p.m. when I parked the car in my driveway and entered the house. Although I was physically spent from the day's work, I was charged with emotion. I needed to get my mind focused on something else. I needed to cry. I didn't know what I needed. After Bob went up to bed, I stayed up to divert myself with a movie.

Around 1:00 a.m., I was startled by a loud crash from the second floor. Thinking that Bob had fallen, I dashed out of the den, through the living room, through the hallway, and up the stairs, all the while calling, "Are you okay? Are you okay?" There was no answer. I opened the bedroom door. Bob, who had obviously been sleeping, turned over in bed and asked, "What are you shouting about?"

"I thought you fell. I heard a loud crash."

"No, I'm fine, or at least I was until I heard you come bounding into the room. You were probably dreaming." Groggily, he turned over and went back to sleep.

I proceeded to turn on lights all over the house. I even went into the basement and up to the attic to see if something had fallen. Nothing was disturbed. Baffled, I returned to the den and resumed watching the movie. Perhaps I was dreaming.

It was close to 3:00 a.m. when I made my way upstairs for the night. Connected to the far side of the bedroom was another small room that served as a dressing room. It contained two bureaus and two wardrobes. I quietly made my way across the pitch-black bedroom into the dressing room to retrieve my nightgown. I snapped on the wall switch. As the overhead fixture illuminated the room, I gasped. There on the rug, in the middle of the room, lay a shattered piece of glass.

I looked up. The glow from the three one-hundred-watt bulbs projecting from their sockets within the wooden frame of the ceiling fixture was as nothing compared to the illumination filling me. I stared in awe at the shape of the fixture, now without its glass covering—a perfect hexagon.

Suddenly I knew. Time rolled back. It was fifteen years earlier. Changing the all-purpose laundry room next to my bedroom into a dressing room, I bought a new light fixture for the ceiling, one that would give me plenty of light. It had a plastic frame, stained to look like walnut, and its shape was a hexagon. Disappointed after the electrician installed it because the opaque glass inserted over the three bulbs greatly diminished the light, I called my father to solve the problem. He came. Using the opaque glass of the hexagon as a template, he measured and cut a clear piece of glass for my fixture. He installed it. I still was not happy because the inner hardware of the fixture was exposed in all its ugliness, through the clear glass. Choosing beauty over utility, I ask my father to re-install the original piece of opaque glass that came with the fixture.

Now all these years later, I found, tucked away in his basement workroom, exactly what I asked for. I was suddenly laughing and crying at the same time. Flooded with unbounded joy, I felt my father's presence. An indescribable peace came over me for the second time in my life, a knowing without knowing, a direct perception. It was a "gotcha," my father's unique way of communicating with me.

"You certainly got my attention," I heard myself say as tears rolled down my cheeks.

"Who are you talking to now?" Bob, awakened for the second time, mumbled from the bed.

You wouldn't believe, I thought but all I said was, "Everything's fine, everything's just fine." I was savoring this moment for myself, instinctively knowing that an attempt to share it would siphon off some of its power. Like that day in the delivery room when I believed that God's presence informed my psyche, my father's unique presence, unaccounted for by any law of nature or physics, was revealed to me. My belief in the existence of another world that defied understanding in this one swept over me like a perfect wave out of the sea of turmoil in which I had been flailing. The pieces of shattered glass that lay on the soft blue rug became a touchstone for faith, created out of thin air.

There are those who say that faith is a biological as well as a psychological condition. In those sacred moments I felt my faith in my bones. Although the memory would in time become disembodied from the joyous-

139

ness into which it catapulted me, the memory itself was a kind of grace that instinct returned me to, over and over again, like an infant to its mother's milk.

The following day, I told Bob and the children about my unusual experience. They listened to me in varying degrees of astonishment and disbelief. Not wanting to jeopardize my reputation as a sane and grounded person, it would be a long time before I mentioned this to others. But when I finally did, I found my sharing prompted others, many others, to reveal similar experiences associated with the death of a loved one. Like a detective building a case, I accumulated the personal, unaccountable signs received by friends and clients and even strangers. I continued to find evidence of mystery, of something more out there—call it energy, call it a force, call it spirit, call it God—but I had to call it something, and my faith grew strong.

* * *

THE YEARS MOVED SWIFTLY. Kathleen married in 1992. She asked Kurt to sing at her wedding. Throughout the years, they would tease each other about what song he would sing. They joked about his having his New-Wave band back him up in church. His Nashville days over, he was working in a law firm, singing for friends and for Cath and for Grandma, but he still experienced performance anxiety. This time his "yes" to his sister was not so easy, but it was a "yes."

Kurt called his beloved music director from his former high school. Although retired, this man met with Kurt every week for two months and coached him until every note of the song Kathleen chose was perfect.

As the chords of "All I Ask of You" filled the hushed church, Kathleen, who was kneeling at the altar, turned her veiled head around to look at her brother. Kurt never stopped gazing at his sister as he sang the song for her. With their eyes locked, he kept the promise he made when they were barely teenagers. From the front pew, I watched Robert, Dennis, and Eddie watching the two of them, all of us holding our breath as the silence grew around the song. Guests faded into the background, and I was exquisitely aware of the love my children had for each other.

They were as different as flowers in a garden, each with its unique color, each with its own season to bloom. And yet, to Bob and me, in the most important ways, they were all the same—peers and equals. Over the years we had seen each of them through the prism of our own desires for them. As they grew into themselves, a subtle pressure to do well, to achieve potential, was always present. Yet, infused with that pressure was the spoken and unspoken message that potential could only be measured by some internal mechanism, against oneself. Academic, musical, artistic, and sports achievements were all valued—but what really mattered—the overarching value against which all others paled—was our children's overall goodness and generosity to each other and the world. Now some of them were on the fast track to financial success; some were in less competitive jobs. But I knew they were all solid, contributing members of society—good people. That was all we wanted for each of them.

As I looked at them that day, I saw them as they first were, five children, all under ten years old, glimpsing each other across the cavernous airline terminal in Canada when the future was so unknown. Gratitude for my life and my children fell upon me like grace. I thought of John, the baby that came and was gone in a few short hours. I thought of God and his mysterious ways and how I owed this moment to his gift of loss.

Following Kathleen's wedding, there were three more weddings in the next four years. Amid a whirlwind of engagements and bridal showers and rehearsal dinners, Eddie was married in 1993, Dennis in 1995, and Kurt in 1996. With Kurt's wedding came a sense of completeness co-mingled with a sense of loss, as I recognized that all our children were officially settled.

I remembered with fondness the busy years. The tired years. How one or the other of them would amble into my bedroom at night, finding me where I had sought solitude with a book. Ostensibly to say good night, he or she would fling themselves across the foot of the bed—and talk. Sometimes it was a problem, like not making the team or failing a test. Sometimes it was a joy, like having a date or earning an accolade. I could not imagine then how much I would yearn for those ritual visits, the tousled hair, the earnest face struggling with a decision, when they were finally gone from the house. It was a heady experience living at the hub of a growing family.

All but forgotten were those tentative steps taken over the years by Kurt and Eddie to locate their biological family. Questions about their early past were no longer on the radar. A book was closed. Or so I thought.

141

ॐ 13 ⋘

The Appointment

NOVEMBER 6, 1997. THE TELEPHONE RANG. Dinnertime, the calling hour for solicitors. The house was quiet, and the kitchen table was witness to the way this hour had changed for Bob and me. Not too many years ago, there was barely room for another pair of size 10 shoes under the oak boards of the kitchen table. Long gone were the days when lanky teen-agers ate on the run before dashing to basketball practice, or jostled each other for the last piece of chicken that lay like a prize amidst the empty bowls of salad and mashed potatoes.

As I stretched for the phone hanging within easy reach of the kitchen table, I nipped my finger on the knife I was using to peel an apple. My distraction with my bleeding finger abated instantly and my attention was riveted as I heard Eddie at the other end of the line say, "Mom, Kurt and I want to make an appointment to come over and talk to you and Dad."

An appointment?

Never before had the two of them actually made an "appointment" to talk to us. They came with their successes or their sorrows spontaneously. They came together or alone, in jeans and business suits, in new cars and in dented cars with mufflers dragging behind. They came to see one of us or the other. But this was different. Instinct told me, "This is it." The years had flowed, one into the other, in a kaleidoscope of problems and accomplishments. Now our children were settled, with families of their own. Eddie was thirty years old and Kurt was twenty-nine. The prospect of searching for their biological family, which had unnerved me like a dripping faucet when they were younger, had all but vanished. Within the previous two years, both had married. They were among the struggling population of newlyweds trying to furnish apartments—spending Saturday afternoons painting a room or scouting Ikea for a bookshelf or place mats. Now, they were on the phone asking for an "appointment," like a dream re-emerging from the bottom of the night.

We knew—and they knew that we knew—what it was all about, but I asked the question anyway.

"About what?"

"We want to tell you face to face."

"Why don't you come over now? Dad and I are going to be imagining all sorts of things if we have to wait a few days."

"Okay. We'll be over around 9:15, as soon as I get out of work," Eddie said.

"This is it," I said to Bob, as I got off the phone, "they're both coming over to talk to us."

* * *

THEY ARRIVED TOGETHER. We were waiting for them and heard the car rumble up the driveway and come to a halt on the blacktop outside the back door. Eddie took the three back steps in one leap. He was always in a rush, as if time was running out on him. Generally talking while rushing, he always seemed to be ahead of himself, and his presence filled a room before he actually entered it. He rushed when he walked, he rushed when he played, and he rushed when he drove.

As Eddie dashed up the steps, he was folding the tie he wore that day at his job at the Lincoln-Mercury dealership. The jacket of his suit, replete with a buttoned vest, flapped around his hips as he abstractedly patted his tie into the pocket, all the while glancing over his shoulder to talk to Kurt. Eddie's little barrel chest was long gone. Just shy of six feet tall, the top button of his oxford shirt had popped from the bulk of his muscled neck. Even before he came through the back door, it was clear to me—he was wired.

Kurt, on the other hand, rarely if ever wore a watch. He was a dreamer. After his attempt to make it big in Nashville, he had tried working in a bank and then at an insurance company, but he was miserable. He had finally found his niche working as a house painter. He charmed prospective customers with his slow, careful listening and low prices. Digging out cracks and filling them with plaster, sanding them smooth as a "baby's bottom," patiently mixing paints to get the exact color, he was proud of his work. While the paint flowed from his brushes, music flowed inside his head. He discovered notes bursting into melodies, and played them on some internal instrument until a song unfolded. When he took a break to clean his brushes, he stroked the strings of an imaginary guitar, transferring the song to his fingers.

Now, Kurt followed behind Eddie. He hesitated to grind out a cigarette on the black-top. He had already been home, showered, and changed from his painter's overalls and baseball cap into khakis and a black turtleneck. His close-cropped haircut revealed the vee of his high, scrubbed forehead. His eyes, brown with flecks of amber, were thoughtful. He was an inch or two taller than Eddie. When he was a teenager, the orthopedic doctor had prescribed a wire mesh-like brace that he wore to bed each night to straighten the curvature that was growing in his spine. Over the years, a tendency to stoop had resulted in my affectionately knuckling him in the small of his back to remind him to "stand up tall." He would respond with "ouch" or "stop that," but between the brace and the knuckling he achieved his full six feet of height.

Standing under the moon of the doorway light, their faces flushed from rushing, Kurt and Eddie could have been four and five years old rather than two six-foot, hulking guys getting ready to ring the doorbell.

Bob and I give them each a hug, and all four of us headed automatically for the kitchen. Once, years ago, Kathleen had called the kitchen table the "command center" of the house. It was the oval oak table my father and I had refinished in our Brooklyn basement in the early fifties. He had carted it to his lake house, where it weathered the fifties and sixties, and when he sold the lake house he gave it to me for my kitchen. It was the place where our five travel-worn children sat, drank chocolate milk and ate oatmeal cookies that very first night. It was the surface where Eddie worked night after night on his fourth-grade diorama of the French and Indian War, pasting feathers onto cardboard headdresses and fashioning a bow and arrow out of twigs and rubber bands. The place where Kurt, elbows on the table and his chin propped in the palm of his right hand, had plodded through *Lord of the Flies* while the TV beckoned from another room. It was where all serious discussions happened, from what color corsage to get a prom date and what instrument to play in the school band, to how much you drank at the party, and who was responsible for the dent in the fender of the "big maroon boat," that embarrassingly uncool station wagon that was their only means of independent transportation.

Eddie began. His foot and leg still vibrated rapidly whenever he was nervous. Mostly he was unaware it was happening. Hundreds of times, I had placed my hand on his knee and just said, "It's okay." Sometimes this simple act of acknowledgement was enough to make the tremor stop, sometimes it was not. Tonight, it was. After I touched his knee, his leg calmed. He smiled. He took a deep breath. They had both prepared for this moment. Rehearsed.

"Mom and Dad, this has nothing to do with you. You are our real parents. That will never change." Eddie said.

From our places at the kitchen table, Bob and I nodded in acknowledgment, each of us turning those words over in our mind: "Mom and Dad, this has nothing to do with you. You are our real parents. That will never change." We would return to them often in the months that followed, reciting them in our heads like a psalm when we were consumed with fear and doubt. The boys' main goal during the first minutes of that meeting was to reassure us. It was important to them that they said the words directly to both of us, and it was equally important to Bob and me that we heard those words spoken. Once again, we were all moving into uncharted waters.

"You always said you would help us if we decided to look for our biological family, right?" Eddie said.

Bob and I, in unison answered, "Yes."

"And you said it has to be when we both want to do it at the same time."

"Yes," we chimed again.

"Well, Kurt and I and Cath and Barbara have been meeting and talking about it for a couple of weeks. We think we're ready. Will you help us?"

"Of course. Yes," we said separately and together, as we realized this visit was not an impulsive act. All four of them had met and discussed and planned a strategy. They were struggling. Guilt pooled in their eyes as if the idea of finding their biological parents was a betrayal of us. They wanted to reassure us and convince themselves at the same time that they were simply trying to educate themselves about the past, to connect the dots, but of course it was much more that that.

But it did not feel like a betrayal. I had felt betrayal, and this was not it. This was like nothing I ever felt before. It felt dangerous, in an unknown way, like landing on a planet where there was no gravity.

We tried to ease any misgiving about our commitment to help them. Did they want to hire a private detective? We would pay for it.

"Well, maybe," Kurt answered. "But first we want to try the Internet." A recent TV show had told the story of a family reuniting as a result of an Internet search. Kurt's wife, Cath, worked for a law firm. She knew her way around legal subjects and was going to use her computer at work to make the first inquiries.

Bob and I reverted to our parental role of older and wiser and told them not to expect too much too soon. Trying to protect them in advance from disappointment, I said, "These things can take years. Be prepared for a long process."

"We know," they said, nodding. They had already thought of that.

Bob said, "I'll give you the complete file that I've saved since 1972 to help you get started. It contains all the documents and correspondence relating to your adoption, names of agencies and names of the people who worked there."

I told them I had saved all the old letters from Ardis and Allen along with the little wooden puzzles they brought from Canada and the orange plastic lunch pail Eddie used to take with him on a school bus to kindergarten.

"Ah, I remember that school bus," Eddie said. "I used to cry every day when I left Kurt behind, standing on the dirt road. I didn't want to go to school. One day I fell and cut my head. There was blood all over. I remember that like it was yesterday."

We all began to reminisce. Whole scenes unfolded from out of the past, a pageant of memories. We talked about the first time we met in the airport in Canada in 1972.

"Remember how I kept kicking the toy airplane machine in the airport?" Kurt said with a wide grin.

"Yes, you scared me to death when you refused to leave the machine and just kept kicking and kicking," I said. "You were a little wild man."

"And remember how Eddie got sick to his stomach after a few bites of lunch and wouldn't let me help him when we got to the bathroom?" I said.

Eddie blushed. "I was used to throwing up. I didn't need help."

"I remember the long ride in the station wagon with the lady who drove us from Yarmouth to Nova Scotia," Kurt said, as he went to a cabinet and took out some popcorn and put it in the microwave. They were starting to wind down, to relax.

"Yeah, I remember her too," said Eddie. "She was nice. What was her name?"

"Heather," I told them.

"And I remember sitting on the kitchen counter when Ardis put my snow jacket on me. I was crying and she was crying. She told me to be a good boy," Kurt added.

"Mostly, I remember sitting on Daddy's lap in the taxi as we drove from the New York airport to New Jersey. It was very late and very dark. I started to cry, and Dad put me on his lap and said I never had to worry again, and that he would always be there for me. I still remember that," Eddie said emphatically as his eyes filled up with tears. And then it was Bob's turn to be tearful as he heard his own words echoed back all these years later and realized how imprinted Eddie had been by that experience.

We all wanted to go over the story as if by retelling it from the beginning we could insure ourselves that nothing the search would produce could alter its happy ending.

Bob asked them what they expected to find, if they were successful in locating their biological parents. Eddie's answer shocked us both. He told us he expected to find that his father was a banker and his mother some kind of teacher or counselor. He was describing Bob and me! It was as though our explanation, that their parents were sick and did not know how to care for children, had never been absorbed into his thinking. Our words, carefully chosen, and meant to absolve Eddie and Kurt from any feelings of self-blame or shame, had bounced off Eddie like rain on a tin roof. It seemed illogical for Eddie to assume that the same parents who were so damaged that they could not manage the simplest care of their children could have been transformed, twenty-five years later, into "a banker and a teacher." Kurt said nothing.

We were speechless. This was the fantasy that prevailed. We said nothing to challenge it. Confusion gripped us. It wasn't until we spoke with Robert a few days later that we began to understand.

"You're the only parents they know. You're the role models. They expect to find you two again," he told us with a brother's compassion. Ah yes—we were too close to it to see clearly. Of course. Now we understood.

✳ ✳ ✳

IT WOULD TAKE A MIRACLE TO UNDO the disappointment that we felt was in store for them. Then, like smoke finding its way under a doorway, "what if's" seeped into my brain. What if Eddie was right! What if their biological parents had pulled it all together? What if they had been trying to find their sons? What if our assumptions had been wrong? What if, what if, what if . . .

And so that evening came to an end. The search was launched. We arranged to meet the following week, this time with the boys' wives, Barbara and Cath. We would, all six of us, gather again around the kitchen table for spaghetti and meatballs, but the main course would come later when Bob carefully placed the contents of the yellowing files onto the table.

≋ 14 ≋

The Secret

IT WAS AN ORDINARY TUESDAY, NOVEMBER 18, 1997, when we met just a week later. Dinner was filled with animated conversation about everything but the topic we had come together to discuss. It was as though our ideas and feelings about the search were being stored in a box, like sunglasses and bathing suits, to be unpacked when the water had warmed enough to take a plunge. We discussed the classes Cath was taking at the state university, Barbara's new job and the long drive she took to work each day. Eddie talked about his yet-one-more attempt to stop smoking and his desire to try the patch, and Kurt told us about his plans to buy a truck for his painting gear. After eating, the girls helped me clear the table of empty bowls of pasta and sauce. Bob went to his desk to retrieve the adoption file he had carefully gone through and organized during the week, and the boys went into the backyard for a quick, nervous smoke. Within five minutes, we were all back at the table. The unmarked, creamy white file with its yellowing contents lay like an unopened invitation on the white tablecloth.

Bob opened the stiff cardboard cover and began passing pieces of paper around. The previous week he had sorted them into an approximate chronology of events. On top was the newspaper article that had first spurred our interest in adoption. No one read it but rather we scanned it as we passed it around the table. Stubs of airline tickets from the flights to and from Halifax and several pages torn from *National Geographic* with pictures and information about the Canadian coastline and Yarmouth were next. On the back of an envelope, in Bob's handwriting, were the series of hastily written IQ scores, a letter instructing us how to write to the boys via the agency, and another letter from the social welfare department confirming the time and date of our meeting at the airport in Nova Scotia. There were newsletters from Spaulding with dates of bake sales, snapshots of agency picnics, and photos of children along with details of their small lives. There were the letters between Bob and me and our attorney, who guided us without a fee through the legalities of the process.

I had gathered a few precious objects saved in the bottom of a bureau drawer. Among them were the two wooden puzzles we sent to Canada before we met them and which Ardis, their foster mother, sent back with them when they came to New Jersey. There was the orange lunch box belonging to Eddie. For the past twenty-five years it housed all the letters from Ardis written to the boys in the early seventies in the months after their arrival in New Jersey. Now we gave the letters to them. However, they were not interested in reading them, and just put them aside. They were focused on their biological family.

All was prelude.

The centerpiece of the file was two Xeroxed identical court orders. One had Eddie's name highlighted and the other highlighted Kurt. These were the papers containing the secret we had kept from the boys, an omission that would or would not rock them in the next few moments. I instinctively placed my hand over the two documents. They knew something was coming. There was a joke among the five children that every time I said something that I anticipated would be received as critical or disappointing I cleared my throat a few times before I got started. Now I was sitting with my hand over the documents, clearing my throat, clearing my throat.

"What's coming?" said Kurt. They both looked scared. The girls looked baffled.

"There's something about your past that we didn't tell you."

No one spoke. I cleared my throat again. "We thought it would be better for you if we left it out. It's in these papers."

I slid the court order pertaining to Eddie's adoption across the table to him and at the same time passed Kurt's document over to him. They opened them and began to read. The bold lettering on the top of the first page identified the document.

ORDER FOR WARDSHIP AND NOTICE OF SETTLEMENT. There were five clear and simply written sections to the order. Each time the word "child" appeared in the preprinted wording of the document it was underlined, and the word "children" was substituted. It read as follows:

"The matter concerning the children hereinafter named were children in need of protection within the meaning of Sec. I (h)(xI) pf the Child Welfare Act."

Directly following this it read:

Kurtis Eric May 4, 1968
Eddie Robert May 16 1967
Catherine Caroline March 21 1966

They see her name simultaneously. Catherine Caroline.

"Who is Catherine?" Eddie asked.

"Is this a sister?" said Kurt.

We nod and let the information settle before venturing any further.

"Do you remember her?" Kurt quizzed Eddie.

"No, do you?"

"No."

"1966," said Eddie. "She must be older than us."

"She wasn't with us when we lived with Ardis and Allen, was she?" Eddie asked, looking first from me and then to Bob.

"No."

"What happened to her?"

"Why was she separated from us?"

We tell them what had been told to us that morning at Spaulding, when we were as baffled as they are now, as we read the Court Order and came to know that their sister had been separated from them. We were told

Catherine had already been adopted. The explanation passed along the telephone wires from the Canadian agency was reasonable and convincing. We never questioned it.

"A local minister and his wife in Yarmouth knew of your circumstances, how the three of you had been taken into protective custody. They had no children of their own and wanted a little girl. They chose Catherine within a few weeks of her removal, and she was happily settled with them long before you two were put up for adoption, long before Dad and I came into the picture. The case worker told us it was the general consensus of people who had worked with you three children that you were all too young and too traumatized to remember each other."

We told them our understanding of their being considered "hard to place" was related to two factors. One, they were no longer infants, and the request to adopt infants far outnumbered the request for older children. Secondly, the agencies were trying to keep them together. Since couples seeking to adopt generally request one child at a time, this also put them in a "hard to place" category. The case worker had gone on to say that if Spaulding was unsuccessful in placing them together, it was conceivable they would have to separate them.

The enormity of the alternative, sending them to different families, uttered so many years ago, was now unimaginable. It was one of those thoughts, like our own death, that we automatically push aside. A look of foreboding worked its way into each of their faces. Their eyes met above the sepia file and a shudder shook their shoulders. The idea of one without the other was as unthinkable as living without water. There had always been the two of them, Kurt and Eddie, Eddie and Kurt. We all let the anguished thought of that "what if" go, like a foreign word we had no need to learn.

Bob and I went on explaining how Catherine became our secret in that meeting, like a little jewel shining in someone else's ring. "It seemed best that we not volunteer any information about you to Catherine because we did not know how her adoptive family was handling the fact of your existence. We felt we did not have the right to disrupt the foundation already laid down by Catherine's new family. We reasoned that we were protecting you from the reality of additional loss. Dad and I agreed that if at any time either of you showed any signs of remembering Catherine, we would reveal what we knew."

"Holy shit," Kurt said, as he and Eddie found each other's eyes across the table.

"However, that never happened," Bob quickly added. "No one from Canada has contacted us in the twenty-five years since we brought you home."

"There was one time when I thought we might be close to telling you," I said, looking at Kurt for some sign of recognition. He stared back blankly.

"Do you remember the time you were in the eighth grade and a new little boy was brought into the school for a day, to see how he liked it?

Kurt's eyes lit up in recognition.

"I remember," Kurt said. "It was weird, he looked so much like me, I actually thought I might have another brother. The boy never came back. At least, I never saw him again, and I forgot all about it. But what does that have to do with Catherine Caroline?"

"Probably nothing," I said. "But that day my mind started working overtime. I asked myself, could this possibly be another child from the same parents? Could he also have been placed in New Jersey through Spaulding for Children?"

Kurt looked at me with raised eyebrows, waiting for more.

I took a deep breath, and told them about a piece of information given to Bob and me during those early months of waiting to adopt them. "Your mother was pregnant with a fourth child at the time you two and Catherine were taken into protective custody. She had gone into labor and somehow gotten herself to the hospital. When the authorities entered the house, they found your father, Eric, unconscious in a downstairs bedroom."

Both Kurt and Eddie's eyes were riveted on me as I spoke, and now, once again, they found each other's eyes. "Do you know anything about that baby?" Kurt asked.

"Not really. We were told that, after the birth, the infant was going to be placed for adoption. We assume that's what happened.

I paused, waiting for another question, but everyone was silent.

"When you came home from eighth grade and told me about the visiting student," I went on, "I couldn't help wondering if he might be the infant with whom your biological mother was pregnant all those years ago. I thought about calling the principal and trying to get information."

"Did you?" questioned Kurt.

"No, I periodically asked you about him, but you never saw him again, and the incident passed. I have thought about the child every once in a while, and a sense of mystery is attached to the whole incident for me. I really don't think there is any connection—but, still, I have wondered."

I continued, "the main reason for reminiscing about this is to prepare you for what I am sure you are putting together at this very moment. In all likelihood, you have a fourth sibling someplace, someone who had not yet been born when you were taken into protective custody."

Eddie slowly pushed his chair away from the table and stood up, as though he needed to stretch to his full height and use every inch of his body to absorb the information. There were beads of perspiration on his lip. Kurt, at first startled by Eddie's move, took a deep breath. He gently patted the empty kitchen chair. "Come and sit down, big bro. We've got more reading to do."

Their wives sat quietly, listening, as if mesmerized. Each reached for her husband's hand. The shock of these discoveries passed through the kitchen like a two-headed man in the circus parade, unbelievable, but a part of the circus, not a part of the life you are living. It's interesting in the moment, but then disappears into the circus tent. Leaving Catherine Caroline on the page, they scanned the remainder of the Court Order.

Following the children's names on the ORDER OF WARDSHIP AND NOTICE OF SETTLEMENT was a second section of two columns. One for Father of Children and one for Mother of Children. There was a line for each name, address and occupation.

Father Eric Charles Augustus Deveau - Yarmouth.
Mother Lucienne Alvanise (Moffett) Deveau - Yarmouth.

Eric and Lucienne, real people, with histories and problems and three children that they were losing; beneath their name, the document read:

I am satisfied that the proper parties have been given notice of the hearing under said Act or that every reasonable effort has been made to cause them to be so notified.

As agent of the Administrator of Family and Child Welfare consenting in writing, I order that the said children be committed to the care and custody of the Children's Aid society.

To the Mayor, Warden, of the Municipality of Yarmouth.

The matter concerning the children hereinafter named were before me for examination and I find the children were in need of protection within the meaning of Section I(h) ( ) of the Child Welfare Act.

Bob and I watched them as they read.

I remembered the day I first pored over the order. I remembered the questions I had. What happened in that house? What did the children go through that culminated in such drastic action? "Protection"—from what? No one at Spaulding could answer those questions for us at the time, and Kurt and Eddie knew, in those moments at the kitchen table, that we were powerless to tell them what we didn't know.

Over the years I had wanted to hate Lucienne, but I couldn't. I somehow held her more responsible than Eric. Sins of this woman, committed in ignorance or illness or evilness, had become my blessing. My brain refused to wrap itself around the notion of evil, and I was left with ignorance and illness. I could not judge this woman. In a convoluted way, I was thankful for her. She had given birth to my boys! In ways that could never have been predicted, the losses of this woman had become the gifts that fulfilled my life. I was predisposed to look kindly upon her, and I often wondered what circumstances conspired to cause her children to be taken from her.

This was perhaps my earliest realization of how connected we all are. Not only connected, but entangled. The physicist says that particles influence each other light years apart; the poet helps us understand when he speaks of "a butterfly flapping its wings in Tokyo causing the wind to blow in New York City." My life was intimately entangled with this woman, but what was more important, I felt myself part of a larger plan, one I was incapable of orchestrating, a plan orchestrated by God.

Had Eddie and Kurt picked up on these feelings of mine over the years, feelings that they were part of a larger plan and meant to be with us? I hoped so. But a new feeling was emerging and entering my consciousness: jealousy. For the first time, I heard Eddie say "my mother" and he was not referring to me.

* * *

THE NEXT SECTION OF THE COURT ORDER referred to the religious affiliation of the boys and "Catholic" was noted. The section read:

> Commencing the 2nd day of September A.D. 1971.
>
> I find the settlement of the said children to be in the City of Yarmouth in the County of Yarmouth Province of Nova Scotia.
>
> I order the said place of settlement to pay to the Administrator of Family and Child Welfare Children's Aid Society of Yarmouth, the expenses of apprehension and detention of the said children made up as follows:
>
> Medical Examination _____
> Clothing $65.87
> Traveling Expenses & Witness Fee $50.80
> Temporary Care (Board) $549.60
> Fees (witness) $15.00
> Total $681.27
>
> I further order under Section 47 that . . .

This area was left blank. Inconceivably, it seemed there was nothing more to say.

Finally, the order was signed by Judge Black, Judge of the Juvenile Court Province of Nova Scotia.

* * *

WATCHING KURT AND EDDIE READ, engrossed as I had never seen them before, I could only imagine what they were thinking. I remembered poring over the order in the tiny third-floor office at Spaulding twenty-five years ago, reading it as if it were some kind of hieroglyphic, with the power to reveal hidden information if only we could find the key. We had read and re-read each word, trying to decipher the larger context of these few official sentences, looking for clues that would feed us more knowledge.

We had asked ourselves, "Were the parents in court? The order states that the parents were notified. Did they fight for their children? Were the children actually in court? It was unclear from the wording in the second section. Was the "matter before the court" examined, or were "the children examined?" Who were the witnesses? What was the testimony in that court room?

Now the boys had to be be asking themselves the same questions. There were no other official documents. Notes taken by the social worker during telephone calls to Canada at the time of the adoption, revealed the answer to only one of our questions. Regarding the biological parents, she had said, "It's my understanding the mother fought for them."

This had been ominous information at the time. We knew it took extraordinary circumstances for a court to sever ties with biological parents. Would their mother continue to try to get them back?

It was likely, we were told. Was this the main reason the boys were being placed in the United States and not in Canada? We had deduced that this was why Ardis and Allen hid them under a blanket in the back of their pick-up truck when they drove into Yarmouth. Was this why Ardis never broke her silence to reveal our address in New Jersey, which we in all innocence had freely given to her? Even though it was unlikely that their biological mother, in her "mental condition" (which remained unnamed), could sustain the effort required to search for them, Ardis and Allen continued to protect them.

Bob and I had learned to live with the unanswered questions. The reality was, whatever had happened was over and could not be changed. The spontaneous flood of questions that erupted after we read the court order probably had more to do with a yearning that accompanies falling in love, and we had been falling in love that summer. It was a yearning to know the loved one more fully in order to love more deeply. It was the hunger that exists in each of us to discover details about a loved one—"the way you got the little scar on your finger" or "the first time you rode a bike" or the countless other bits of information we accumulate when falling in love. We counted them like beads on an abacus and then we multiplied our love.

Now Kurt and Eddie were facing the same hieroglyphics, the legalese of the court order. Yet their motives were much more complicated than ours had been. Theirs were a search for self, a need to fill a hole existing in each of them that had culminated in their sitting at this particular kitchen table in Montclair, New Jersey, on a cold November night, wondering at events that happened in a fishing village before they could remember.

That Tuesday night, November 18, 1997, as we hugged each other good-bye in the kitchen, snow started to fall. The fat flakes, backlit by the spotlight attached to the garage, glowed and dissipated above the blacktop. None of us could know as the boys ducked into their cars, that due to a mail strike in Canada, a thin white envelope addressed by their biological mother would lie for days among thousands of other envelopes stacked in the back of a mail truck. Eventually it would reach its destination, and when it did, the last link in a chain of events that had its beginning twenty-six years before would be complete.

℘ 15 ℂ

Searching

WITHIN THE NEXT TWO DAYS, the world changed for Eddie and Kurt. On Thursday evening, November 20, 1997, both of them, with Cath and Barbara, were once again gathered around our kitchen table, pale with excitement. With trembling voices they began to braid together for Bob and me the incredible events of the previous forty-eight hours. This was what they told us.

On Wednesday morning, November 19, 1997, the day after we all met for dinner, Kurt's wife, Cath, sat down at her computer in the law firm where she worked as a paralegal. She typed "Children's Services of Yarmouth County Canada" in the search window and clicked "Go." The screen filled. A website listing children's agencies in the Province of Nova Scotia, complete with general information and contact telephone numbers appeared. Scrolling down the list, Cath read each agency's description and stopped at Adoption and Foster Care. A telephone number was listed; the agency was in Halifax, the capital of Nova Scotia. With the website still posted on her screen, she picked up the telephone and dialed the number. The phone was answered on the second ring. "Children's Services, Margaret Clack speaking." Cath told us she took a deep breath and began to speak the words she had rehearsed while she was driving to work. She gave Margaret Clack her name and told her she was calling for her husband, Kurt Goldstein. "Kurt was adopted twenty-five years ago by a family in New Jersey in the United States. His adoption papers indicate that it was your agency that handled the adoption, and now he would like to locate his birth family. Can you help me?"

"I don't know," said Margaret Clack, "I will try. What was your husband's family name prior to his adoption?"

"It was Deveau."

"That's a very common name up here in the provinces in Canada. Do you know the year and date that Kurt was released to his adoptive parents?"

"Yes, it was November of 1972."

"Do you know the name of the agency in the United States that placed him?"

"Yes, said Cath. "It's called Spaulding for Children, and it's in New Jersey."

"Yes, I know of it."

"You do?" Cath said excitedly. "Were you involved in my husband's adoption?"

Margaret explained that she wasn't at the agency twenty-five years ago. She told Cath that Spaulding closed its doors around 1989. She knew this because others had called in recent years. Through her work on their behalf, she had learned that Spaulding's records had been turned over to an agency called the Division of Youth and Family Services in New Jersey and were being stored in a warehouse somewhere in Trenton.

"Oh," Cath said with disappointment. It was no secret that DYFS was one of the states's most understaffed and criticized agencies.

"What about your records in Canada? Can you give me any information about my husband's birth family from those records?"

"Unfortunately, I can't." Margaret explained that the adoption laws were written in such a way that once a child was released to a private agency in another country, the records were all forwarded to that country. "It's one of the ways we protect the privacy of children and the families who adopt them." Margaret went on to explain that in order to have a file opened, the search must be initiated by the adopted child through the agency that placed him. "The laws are written to safeguard the procedure," she said.

Cath told Bob and me that she didn't want to hang up the phone. She couldn't believe she had gotten to the right people but she was at a dead end.

"Are you sure there are no files in your agency?" Cath pushed. "We do know the name of the social worker who coordinated the adoption in Halifax. She's Heather McDonald—perhaps she would remember my husband. Is she still there?"

"No, but even if she were still working here and happened to remember this case, the law would prevent her from revealing anything to your husband."

Cath was silent. There seemed to be nothing more to say.

Margaret broke the silence. Sympathetically, she said, "The most I can do for you is get the appropriate telephone number at the Division of Youth and Family Services. You and your husband can start there, but I can't promise you anything. Let me have your phone number so I can call you back."

"That's okay," said Cath. "I can get the number off the Internet. You don't have to call me back."

"No, I don't mind," said Margaret. "Let me also see if I can get you the name of someone at the Division of Youth and Family Services in New Jersey. Having a name might help you and your husband get through some of the bureaucracy. I'll call you back within a few days."

"Thank you," said Cath, after leaving her number.

They were all disappointed. The expectations of the previous twenty-four hours had slowly risen like the first hill on a roller coaster, only to plummet them into the valley that preceded the next hill. They would wait for Margaret Clack to call with the DYFS number and contact name, and then begin the next climb—this time in Trenton, New Jersey.

* * *

THE FOLLOWING MORNING, Thursday, November 20, Cath heard her phone ringing as she entered her office. Unwrapping a scarf from her head as she ran past cubicles of computers, she picked it up on the fourth or fifth ring. An operator told her she had a person-to-person call from Halifax, Nova Scotia. It was Margaret Clack. Margaret was so excited she could barely speak.

"I'm so glad I got you," she said to Cath. "I think I have some unbelievable news for you and your husband."

"Really?"

"You'd better sit down."

"Okay, I'm sitting."

"The most extraordinary thing happened yesterday a few hours after we spoke. Another phone call came in from a young woman with whom we have been working since 1987. While I was speaking with her, I suddenly realized I was on to something."

"What do you mean?" asked a confused Cath. "Who is she?"

"Her name's Catherine Newell but her maiden name is Deveau!"

"Oh, my God," said Cath.

"As I told you, Deveau's a fairly common name up here in Canada, probably as common as Smith or Brown in your country."

Cath broke in excitedly, "Yes, yes! But I'm with you. I've seen Kurt's wardship papers. They list a sister named Catherine."

"Yes, and I have Catherine Newell's wardship papers in front of me. They list a brother Kurt and a brother Eddie," Margaret said.

"Did you say she called you yesterday?" Cath asked in awe.

"Yes," Margaret continued, tripping over her words as she spoke breathlessly. She went on to tell Cath that it was not the first time Catherine Newell had called. Catherine had made her first call to the agency ten years earlier, in 1987, when she was twenty-one years old and pregnant with her first child. She was trying to find her two little brothers, whom she had not seen since a day in 1971 when the three of them were picked up by a state agency and taken to a shelter. She wasn't searching for her parents per se, but she was interested in their whereabouts only to the extent they might lead her to her two brothers.

Cath told Bob and me that a chill beginning in the soles of her feet slowly climbed through her body as she realized Kurt and Eddie might be about to find their sister. Margaret had gone on to explain that the agency's work back in 1987 on Catherine's behalf produced very little information. They could not locate her family. All they could find was a birth record of another child, Deborah, born in 1971. Most devastating to Catherine was information that each of her two brothers had been placed for adoption in 1972, through a private agency in the United States and this out-of-country placement made it impossible for anyone to trace them. Her only chance of being reunited with each of her brothers would depend on one of the boys initiating a search for her. There was nothing more the agency could do. It was very sad for Catherine.

Margaret told Cath that Catherine had not given up. The records indicated that at least once a year, for the last ten years, she called and talked to one of the caseworkers about any inquiries that might have come in about her. Faith that her brothers would search for her never wavered. Each year, the same disappointing answer, "Sorry, but no one's looking for you." In 1994, since Catherine was so driven and disappointed, it was suggested she write what was called a non-disclosing letter and send it to the agency.

"What's a non-disclosing letter?" asked Cath.

Margaret explained that it was a letter written by the adoptee that contained personal information and could even include pictures but did not reveal an address. The letter was kept in the file. If the agency was notified that a search had been generated on behalf of the adopted person they could act quickly because they had the non-disclosing letter ready to send on.

Margaret had continued, "Catherine's non-disclosing letter had been sitting in her file for four years. And then two weeks ago, around November 7, we received a letter, the first contact in twenty-six years, from Lucienne Deveau. The letter was mailed from her home in St. John in the province of Newfoundland. She stated she was looking for her three children whom she had not seen since 1971.

"We had a match! Of course, we had information on only one of her children, Catherine. We already knew Kurt and Eddie's files were irretrievable in the United States. We immediately placed a call to Catherine to alert her to the fact that her biological mother had contacted the agency. However, Catherine's phone had been disconnected, and there was no forwarding number. Now it seemed Catherine was lost, so we sent the non-disclosing letter from her file, written in 1994, on to Lucienne Deveau., her biological mother. Lucienne responded to it immediately and wrote another letter to Catherine that we received on November 14. We have been holding both letters as we tried to locate Catherine.

"Here is the incredible part," said Margaret Clack. "Yesterday, November 19, just hours after I spoke with you, totally out of the blue, Catherine called this agency to notify us that she was moving. She wanted us to have her new address and to advise us she would shortly have a new telephone number. She had no idea we had been trying to reach her."

An eerie feeling gripped me as Cath, with the boys at her side, recounted this sequence of events. Dates stood out in my mind as if in bold relief. On November 6, 1997, the boys met with Bob and me to initiate a search. November 7, a letter from Lucienne arrived at the agency in Canada. On November 18, we revealed the adoption file to Kurt and Eddie. On November 19, the same day Cath made telephone contact with the agency, Catherine also made contact. After a quarter of a century, some unseen force had motivated all three segments of that family, connected by blood and separated by circumstances and miles, to seek each other out. What was the energy behind this confluence of events? My sense of wonder and awe was exceeded only by my need to know more. I urged Cath on. What happened next?

Margaret told Catherine about her mother's letters.

"What did Catherine say?" Cath asked Margaret.

"Well, remember, it wasn't her mother she was yearning for. It was her two brothers. Her thoughts jumped to them. Catherine immediately asked, 'Do you have any information about my brothers?' I said no. 'Does my biological mother know where they are?' Catherine asked. No, I told her she's looking for them also."

The call ended after Margaret arranged for Catherine to notify her of the new telephone number when it was assigned the following week.

Then Margaret said to Cath, "As I finished updating Catherine's file a few minutes later, my conversation with you yesterday morning flashed through my mind. Up until that moment, your call and my work with Catherine were totally unrelated. Suddenly, it hit me! Kurt Goldstein nee Deveau, Catherine Newell nee Deveau, Lucienne Deveau. My God, I thought, could it be possible that Kurt and Catherine are both Lucienne's children, that they're siblings? And if so, then we have not only found Catherine's mother; we've also found Kurt's mother!"

164

"Did you tell Catherine?" Cath asked, reeling.

"No, it was premature. I had to be sure. I went into our files and reread the court orders and verified all the names and dates. Now I am sure."

"Oh, my God, this is unbelievable," said Cath, "I can't wait to tell Kurt."

"I know how you feel," said Margaret breathlessly. "I can't wait to tell Catherine. She's going to be ecstatic. She's supposed to call me with her new phone number as soon as she gets it. I expect that'll be next Monday or Tuesday. She's already given me her new address in Yarmouth, and I'll send her birth mother's letters on to that address. However, because there's a huge mail strike in Canada, I don't know when she'll receive them."

"One more thing before you go," said Margaret Clack. "I know Catherine will ask: you wouldn't happen to know anything about the other brother, Eddie, would you?"

Cath was stunned at the question. She recovered in a moment, realizing she had never specifically mentioned Eddie's name.

"Yes, yes, I do," said Cath. "He's my brother-in-law. The boys were adopted together. I see Eddie all the time. They're in this search together."

Margaret gasped. There were no words. Then, finally, "Oh, I've found both of Catherine's brothers for her."

A shock of reverence poured into me as I tried to reconcile these stunning events. Were the stars aligned, as the astronomer might say, in such a way that all the forces of nature were in harmony to produce this outcome?

Of course, I had prayed around this subject. Vague amorphous prayers—let it turn out all right; let my boys find what they need; let nothing change between us; let our family survive intact. And in the not-too-distant future, I would learn that their biological mother had prayed the same universal prayer of mothers.

There are no coincidences. This was a phrase I heard many times in many contexts and never really attended to, but now I was brimming with wonder at the chain of events in which my boys—and by extension, myself and my whole family—were embroiled. If not a coincidence, then what? How to explain a synchroneity that seemed to defy the boundaries of normal expectations? It felt miraculous! I asked myself, "Could this epiphany of strangeness be the result of divine intervention?" There was no intelligence known to man that could answer that question. Yet an overpowering transcendence filled me and seemed to answer it for me.

I asked myself—What is divine intervention? Who among us has not asked for it in our darkest moments? Does this three dimensional world of ours that grounds us to the earth hide from our limited intelligence a realm of possibilities that we cannot begin to comprehend? A miraculous event is one whose cause cannot be found in any natural law, either known or unknown. Yet we are learning that there are undreamed and unimagined natural laws that exist outside our awareness.

A kaleidoscope of thoughts emerged in the wheel of my mind. Scientists postulated ten dimensions. I could not help wondering if we were destined to find God in another dimension. In the forty-first century, would sentient beings find our twenty-first-century culture and beliefs primitive, the way modern man now views ancient civilizations? Would undiscovered natural law bring us face to face with our God? Could desire and prayer and will alter reality? Was this astonishing convergence of events in my life the result of unknown natural laws accessed through the desire and intention of five people connected by biology and blood? Did our minds, blossoming with prayer, waft across the boundaries of natural law into the realm of the divine, where in the aftermath of its effects on our earthly experience we both knew and could never know?

A desire for the miraculous seems to be a part of the human condition. A yearning to confirm that there is more than meets the eye is a theme infused in the art, literature, and religions of the ages. Have we not all wondered at the mystery that surrounds us? We yearn for the veil to part; we yearn to glimpse the divine.

I remembered how one night I drove into a fog so thick it frightened me. One moment I was cruising over the crest of a hill, my windshield filled with the lights of Manhattan twinkling fifteen miles away. As I descended the hill, a fog, white and creamy as mushroom soup, enveloped the car, forcing me to stop. Length and width and depth no longer existed for me. I tried my fog lights and then the high beams, but no light penetrated the fog. Disoriented, I could not find my way. The veil that separated me from my senses was as real to me as the veil shrouding the miraculous.

Like a lost pilgrim, I could not help playing with these ideas, pushing to the limit the paucity of knowledge lodged in my mind. Perhaps some millennium, a scientist would penetrate the fog that envelopes mystery and we would know coincidence from Divine Intervention. But for now I was that pilgrim. I was in awe. I chose miracles.

✼ ✼ ✼

HOW QUICKLY THINGS MOVED! Yet as my awe settled in, I began to realize that for me the reality of the situation was as sweet as it was sour; as pure and fresh as the white silk of a wedding gown and as rough and blotched as a bolt of denim. Everything was as it should be and everything was wrong. Even as we talked, I could hear papers from Canada coming through the fax machine in the other room—Release of Information papers that would change our lives. As I listened I heard the sound of my own thumping heart.

The boys signed the Release of Information forms. Bob faxed the signed copies back to Margaret Clack. The originals were Fed-Exed to Halifax the next morning, Friday, November 21. In the meantime, Kurt called the contact person that Margaret had provided, a man named Jerry at DYFS, to formally open the adoption file. While Jerry was sympathetic to the speed with which things were moving, he explained he had thousands of locked files to go through, and it could take days, if not weeks. He promised to make Kurt's request a priority. He came through. Within twenty-four hours, he wrote and mailed to Kurt a summary of the court order he had located, plus the necessary papers to be signed and sent to Canada so Margaret Clack could proceed.

Margaret Clack received the signed Consent to Release Information forms Monday afternoon, November 24, but not before Catherine called with her new telephone number on Monday morning. "I went out on a limb here," Margaret said, "and did something I've never done before. I gave Kurt and Ed's home telephone numbers to Catherine before I had the original copies of the signed Consent to Release Information forms on my desk. I just couldn't hold back."

That night, Monday, November 24, barely one week after the first tentative call to Canada, both Kurt and Eddie found identical messages on their answering machines when they get home from work.

"Hi, this is your big sister Catherine calling from Yarmouth!"

Kurt rushed over to Eddie's apartment so they could be together when they called her back. They talked long into the night, and the connectedness that was established all those years ago, among three babies who survived together in a cold attic room was rekindled from the embers of their long separation.

Catherine, their sister, loved them both. She had carried within her the indelible residue of their presence in her life like a relic buried in the sanctuary of her heart.

Eddie and Kurt did not remember Catherine. Perhaps they were too young when it all happened and had not yet developed the cognitive ability to bank those memories. Perhaps they were too traumatized by the wrenching separation that had left Catherine alone and bereft. What was present in each of them was the ability to recognize and treasure her love. Finding her brothers had cracked it open; her pure, unadulterated affection poured through the phone. To be loved could only enhance existence. They recognized this. They received her love, and, awed by it, began that night to love her back.

ɞ 16 ʗ

Catherine Speaks

T HE FOLLOWING DAY, TUESDAY, KURT AND EDDIE came by the house after work to tell Bob and me about their telephone conversation with their sister Catherine. Sitting at the kitchen table amid brown paper grocery bags bursting with the fixings for Thanksgiving dinner, we listened. The long-held fantasy Bob and I had of Catherine as the chosen child, thriving with her adoptive family, exploded like shrapnel in our faces.

From the words that tumbled from their mouths and the emotions evident in their faces, we learned about Catherine. She was the desert flower who had somehow survived in the arid soil of rejection. Now, at long last, she was experiencing happiness like never before. She had found her brothers.

Catherine told them she had been pacing in front of the telephone, willing it to ring since early afternoon when she placed the two calls, one to each of "my brothers." Those two simple words represented a lost world to her. Both Kurt and Eddie understood. These words were huge, as solid as rocks to Catherine. They gave her something of substance to hold onto. The joy in her voice spilled over, like spring water cascading over a fall, as she absorbed the reality: the three of them were connected on one call. She wanted to know everything about their lives. She asked them questions—

169

"Did you always live together? Were you ever separated?"

"When did you leave Canada?"

"What is it like in the states? I have never been out of Yarmouth," she told them.

"When did you get married?"

"Who got married first?"

She told them about her husband, George, and their three children. They had just moved into their first home. It was flooded from the recent rains, and they had been mopping up for two days. It was disappointing, but she and George were dealing with it. She told them that all her front teeth had fallen out, and she was self-conscious about the way she looked, and how she hoped to have new teeth before meeting them.

Kurt told her he had two teeth pulled when he was seventeen. He knew it was no fun. He was afraid of dentists, but that went back, he told her, to when he was five years old and the dentist told him if he didn't stop sucking his thumb his teeth would all stick out of his mouth forever. Catherine laughed, and Eddie added, "It was after that that he let Mom paint this foul tasting stuff on his thumb to help him remember to keep it out of his mouth."

"I sucked my thumb, too," said Catherine. "So we have one thing in common."

"Do you remember me?" she asked.

"No," they answered truthfully.

"Do you remember us?" Eddie asked.

"Yes," she said, "but it's all mixed-up."

She did not have the words to explain those mixed-up feelings. "One thing is for sure, I always knew I had two brothers. Sometimes I see pictures in my mind," she said. "I think they are of you two, but the harder I try to remember, the more the pictures disappear. It's like a dream that slips away. It makes me feel all weepy and sad." She told them of the fleeting images that had surfaced over the years, in and out of her dreams: the thin blue blanket, damp and rank with soil, the curve of her own wrist reaching through the bars of the crib, the soft skin of a twitching leg beneath her fingers, the rhythmic sound of a thumb being sucked, the whimpering. These images, tied for all the years in a knot of affection, were unraveling now, breaching the miles to her brothers, the living, breathing embodiment of her dreams.

Kurt and Eddie listened to their sister. This was heavy, hard to absorb. Kurt tried to relate. "I know what you mean. Some of my memories are mixed up too, like fishing."

"What do you mean?"

"I love to fish, from as far back as I can remember. No one else in our family even wants to try. Sometimes I think I remember baiting a hook with a live worm back in Canada, but then the memory goes away."

"Well, there sure is a lot of fishing up here in Yarmouth," said Catherine. "It's the main source of work hereabouts. I work in a fish market right here in town, cleaning and cutting up the fish that come in every day with the fishing boats."

Catherine proudly told them she'd been told by her third-grade teacher that she had a good voice. She loved to sing. Eddie told her he played the piano, bragging a little to his big sister. "I played 'Rhapsody in Blue' at Carnegie Recital Hall when I was in high school."

She wanted to understand. "What's Carnegie Recital Hall?"

He put trying to impress her on hold—"Oh, just a nice place in New York."

Kurt chimed in, telling Catherine he played the guitar and wrote music. He told her he made a recording of his own music in Nashville. Catherine knew Nashville. She squealed, "No way. Are you famous?"

"No," he told her, "I sure tried, but it never happened. Now I just write music and sing for myself."

Catherine brought up their biological father, Eric. She had vague memories of him as being a musician—with his own band. All three of them were now aware that their adoption papers identified his occupation as "musician."

"I guess we can thank him for passing music on to us," said Catherine.

"Was he famous?" Kurt, for the first time, asked the question burning inside him for years.

"Could be, but I really don't know. I remember seeing a picture of me standing next to him in front of a big band when I was little. Everyone was clapping," Catherine said. "But music sure saved my life many a time."

Kurt and Eddie agreed with her about music. Eddie asked Catherine if she played any instruments. She did not—although she could "coax a tune out of a piano and a fiddle, I never had an instrument of my own," she said.

"Someday, let's all three of us get together and perform," said Catherine. "I'll sing, and you two can back me up. Won't that be great?"

"Yeah," said Kurt. "We can call ourselves 'Two Bothers and a Sister.'"

"I like that" said Catherine. "But it'll have to be after I get my teeth."

"We can wait," said Kurt.

She asked them about their family, and they told her about Bob and me, and Robert, Kathleen, and Dennis. And then she asked them when they were adopted.

"1972," Eddie answered.

"Oh, you were lucky," Catherine said.

"Yes," they agreed, "we had a good life. What about you? Tell us about the family that adopted you."

"Not much to tell," Catherine said.

"Well, tell us anyway," they said in unison.

"I don't know where to begin," she said.

"Tell us about your adoption."

Her first sentence whizzed by them like a stray bullet discharged from an unexpected weapon. "I was adopted in 1976 by a minister and his wife when I was ten years old. It was—"

"Wait a minute," Eddie interrupted.

He was confused. Kurt was also confused. The minister and his wife were right, but the date was five years off. It didn't match the information Bob and I had given them about Catherine just days before, when we handed the court order over to them. Each of them played over that conversation in their minds. We had told them Catherine was adopted months before they were. She was chosen first, before them. The minister and his wife wanted a girl and took Catherine, leaving her brothers behind. Eddie knew and Kurt knew their adoption took place in November of 1972, so her placement had to be prior to that.

Kurt asked her, "Don't you mean you were adopted by a minister and his wife when you were four or five years old?"

"No, that didn't work out," Catherine said matter of factly.

"What do you mean?"

"There was this minister who took me when I was five. The reverend and his wife had two boys of their own and wanted a girl. It just didn't work out. I was always fighting with those two boys. They didn't like me, and I didn't like them. I guess I must have been a bad kid because they gave me back after less than a year."

"They gave you back?" It was inconceivable to Kurt and Eddie. It was inconceivable to Bob and me as we absorbed what the boys were telling us. I felt as though the reality I had been living dissolved in a nano-second. My thoughts leapt wildly as I mentally re-envisioned alternative histories for my family. "No one told us," I protested. Even as those thoughts swirled in my mind, I felt tears welling up in my eyes. Bob was shaking his head in disbelief. "We never knew, we never knew," he said.

The boys acknowledged our feelings with a knowing look. They continued with Catherine's story, recounting the many families she told them she lived with for the following five years.

"There were so many families, I can't even remember their names. It was bad." Catherine told them.

Kurt sighed as he added that Catherine had been talking rapidly by then. They could hardly follow her words. This tendency was familiar to me. I had experienced similar phenomena with clients, who rushed through their history as if they were reading it from a book or talking about someone else, all in an attempt to diminish the experience, and distance themselves from feelings of sadness and hurt. Neither Eddie nor Kurt interrupted Catherine as the chronicle unraveled like a sweater into which all her pain had been knit.

"I guess I was a bad kid," she repeated. "No one wanted to keep me, so they kept sending me back."

Kurt and Eddie did not know what to say. Their hearts were breaking as they listened.

Catherine continued, "The last family I lived with were parishioners of another minister, Jon Eichorn and his wife, Femme." She told Kurt and Eddie that the Eichorns had seven children of their own. A few of the older ones were married and had moved away, so they had room for her. Jon had sold his dairy farm to become a minister when he was about fifty years old. "When he and Femme heard that my last foster parents were going to send me back again, they decided to adopt me. I was ten years old, nearly eleven."

"Were you happy when you were finally adopted?" Kurt asked.

"I gave them a lot of trouble, too. I was bad. They told me I nearly ruined their family, but they kept trying to help me. I never felt like I belonged. But when I met George I changed, and I'm not bad anymore. I think it was having my own kids that changed me. That and George."

"It must have been hard." Eddie said.

"Yeah, but I'm okay now," she continued. "I've got my own kids, and one thing I learned is how not to treat them."

"I bet you're a really good mother," said Kurt

"I am, and I don't mind if I say so myself."

*　*　*

THE LAST THING THEY TALKED ABOUT was Lucienne. While Catherine had been in a fever of excitement anticipating speaking with Kurt and Eddie, she was uninterested in speaking to Lucienne. Months later she would tell me how her hurt had hardened into a red-hot anger. Memories had wedged themselves into corners of her mind and over the years would come slithering out of the dark to taunt her. Sometimes she would concentrate hard and try to catch a memory—the pale faces of two babies—the echo of their cries trailing off into a hungry sleep—the thin bony shoulder blade—the matted hair. Nausea would fill the back of her throat, tears collect behind her eyes, and rage would grow.

Other times she thrust a memory from her like a heavy stone, using every ounce of energy she could muster to obliterate the shrill voices that had hung in the rancid air of that house—the liquored breath—a door slamming shut—the pitiful wail of a dog. Thoughts came unbidden. Often when she was stroking the fevered forehead of one of her three children, or fixing them breakfast or changing a diaper, she was transported to a time when she and her

174

brothers were trying to survive on their own. She had learned to quiet these memories with a feeling of revenge that kept them at bay, a revenge that now frightened her as she told Eddie and Kurt, "I don't know what I'll do if I see her. I'm afraid."

Kurt and Eddie understood. They would make the call to Lucienne; Catherine didn't have to be involved. She gave them Lucienne's telephone number. They would be there for her, their big sister, in whatever decision she made. But for them, there was no getting off the roller coaster. There was no turning back. They were also afraid. Afraid of the answers to questions they needed to ask, afraid of the unknown. Eddie had, over the years, continued in the therapy he began in high school with Joe Ryan. Part of their work together was to prepare for the eventuality of a search for his mother and father. No one knew it then, but Kurt was totally unprepared, and the next few months would thrust him into confusion and crisis.

It was near midnight when the three siblings said good-bye to each other and hung up the phone, feeling a bond they had not known before, a richness born out of the void.

* * *

UPON HEARING THIS STORY, BOB AND I were beyond upset. In righteous indignation, we asked ourselves and each other, "Why did no one tell us in the early seventies that Catherine was alone, an only child, orphaned and sent back into a system of revolving doors? Why did no one bother to ask us if we would take her when she was rejected by that first family at five years old?" She obviously always held memories of her brothers somewhere in her mind or body. Surely the five-year-old must have given some sign to the adults in her world of the loss she was experiencing. Perhaps her whole early life was a re-enactment of that loss as it manifested itself in behaviors the first adoptive parents found too intolerable to work through.

Eddie asked us directly, "If you knew in 1973 that Catherine was given back to the social welfare agency, would you have gone up to Yarmouth and brought her back to live with us?"

How to answer that question? "Yes—maybe—of course—probably—yes." What would we have done? We would never know. The question lay in that ghostly mountain range of what-ifs that was part of the emotional geography of our lives.

This unexpected gift of a sister, whom they didn't even know existed until a week ago was just the prologue. It was almost noon when Kurt and Eddie left the kitchen to return to their jobs. It started to rain. The day lay ahead of them, hours they had to wade through until that night, Thanksgiving eve, the anniversary of their arrival in the United States. It was then they would carefully dial a number in St. John, Canada, and place a call to their mother, the mother of their nightmares, the mother of their dreams.

❧ 17 ☙

Lucienne's Story

WEDNESDAY NIGHT WAS ENDLESS. We knew Kurt and Eddie were scheduled to call Lucienne that evening, and we expected them to call and let us know how it went. Busying myself, I sat down at the kitchen table and peeled dozens of tiny pearl onions for Thanksgiving dinner, explaining to Bob as he paced back and forth between the den and the kitchen, "I always cry when cutting an onion." Preoccupied, I lost the milk and found it in a cabinet with the flour. I chopped mushrooms and sauteed celery for the stuffing as thoughts broke furiously into my waiting like the transparent bubbles in a pan of water finally reaching its boil.

My mind flew back to another Thanksgiving eve—that night in 1972 when, after the months of anticipation onto which were grafted our fears about retardation, we were finally home with our new family. It had felt enormous. I saw us in my mind's eye as we were back then. It was past 11:00 p.m. and no call from Eddie or Kurt. Could they possibly still be on the phone?

"Should I call one of them?" I asked Bob.

"No, wait, they'll call," he said.

The call never came that Wednesday night.

* * *

177

Thanksgiving was the one holiday when, as the years went by, Kurt and Eddie always found their way back home. Claiming it as their anniversary day, there was no negotiating with new mothers-in-law or friends for their presence elsewhere. Christmas or Easter or any other holiday might be negotiated away, but never Thanksgiving. Each year the ritual reminiscing about "the year you first came to us" warmed and strengthened us all. And now, twenty-five years later, Thanksgiving was the day we would hear of Kurt and Eddie's first conversation with their birth mother. She was on everyone's mind, as present as the bowl of chrysanthemums in the center of the table. The family arrived: Robert and his wife and baby; Kathleen and her husband; Dennis and his wife; Grandma, my two sisters and a brother-in-law, and of course Kurt and Eddie with their wives. A lifetime had transpired, and now those two little boys, first glimpsed by Grandma as they kneeled in the snow at the rabbit hutch, were towering over her as each of them kissed her on the top of her head.

Spellbound, we gathered around the Thanksgiving table and listened as the boys recounted to the whole family their recent conversation with their "big sister Catherine." Joyous, we reveled in the reunion of these three. Toasting Catherine with wine and water and apple cider, everyone marveled at the tenacity of this extraordinary young woman whom we had never met and who, but for a simple notification twenty-five years ago, might have been sitting with us at our Thanksgiving table that very day.

Bob and I waited nervously to hear the details of Eddie and Kurt's phone call to Lucienne that we knew had taken place the night before. We were saving her for dessert. Everyone helped clear the table; the leftover platters of turkey and stuffing were left on the kitchen counter. Fumbling in my anticipation, I dropped a plate and just let it lie there, not wanting to take the time to sweep it up. Apple pies and ice cream were flown to the dining room, someone poured coffee, someone else took care of the tea, and we once again settled around the table, too enthralled to eat. Lucienne was next.

"Okay, go," Bob said to the boys. "Tell us about Lucienne."

Kurt began with a slow smile. "She likes to talk" he said.

"She sure does," echoed Eddie.

"Tell us from the beginning," I said. "Did she answer the phone?"

"No, actually Deborah answered it."

"Who is Deborah?" asked Grandma.

"Well, Grandma, looks like we have another sister named Deborah," Eddie said.

"So, there *was* another child," I said, a question more that a statement.

"Yes, she's still with her mother. She's our younger sister."

"What did you say to her?"

"Well, they knew to expect the call. Margaret Clack had called and told them she was giving us their phone number," said Kurt.

"Deborah sounded really happy," said Eddie. "She told us Lucienne wasn't well, and had been hospitalized a few times recently. She was laughing and said our mother was weak but feisty, and we would soon come to know just how feisty she is." (There it is again, I thought, "our mother." How strange it sounded. Now there were really two of us. The boys had gone from calling her birthmother, to biological mother, to Lucienne, and now our mother. I tucked it away. There was no time to dwell on it now, but I knew even then, from the knot in my stomach, I was not prepared to share my name.)

Kurt said, "When she got on the phone, she started to talk and didn't stop for a long, long time."

"We just let her talk."

"What was she saying?"

"She wanted to tell us none of what happened was her fault."

Eddie said, "I told her we didn't want to rehash the past. We weren't angry with her, but she didn't pay any attention to what I was saying."

"What do you mean?"

"Well, she just kept telling us the same story. She seemed to need to say it over and over."

"What was the story?" Bob asked.

Eddie took a long drink of water before responding. "She told us there was a huge international kidnapping ring operating in Canada during the 1970s. Babies were being stolen and sold for money to people in the United States."

"Oh, my God, what a thing to say," I gasped, feeling my heart start to beat rapidly—as if I had walked into my home and found it ransacked.

"I know. It sounds weird, but she really believes it, and so does Deborah, our youngest sister. She says her mother has proof."

"Proof? What kind of proof?" Bob asked.

"Papers or something," Eddie said as tension filled the room like a foul odor. Kurt and Eddie's eyes met across the table.

"That's all she wanted to talk about," said Kurt. "It's as if she was waiting all the years to tell us that one thing, and once she started, it was like a stuck phonograph record, playing itself over and over. She couldn't stop talking about it."

"Did she ask you anything about yourselves?"

"Not really," they said in unison.

"Did she ask if you've been happy or have had a good life?"

"No, not really."

"Did she ask you about us?"

"No, she just kept talking about the kidnapping and all the people who were involved in it."

"You don't believe her, do you?" I asked in quiet horror.

Eddie hesitated, "I don't know what to believe."

Kurt said nothing. I was stunned. This was crazy. Did the hesitation and silence contain an accusation? Could they be starting to believe we had conspired with kidnappers to take them from their parent's home? My mind reinterpreted years of family dialogue, my oft repeated statements—"I can't imagine what our family would have been like without you two. We are so lucky to have found you."

I grasped the table covered with the white linen tablecloth to steady my shaking hands, spilling my cold cup of tea in the process. The brown stain that blotted the white linen would never be fully erased.

"Eddie, how could you even think we'd be involved in something like that?"

"I don't think you were, Mom, but it's possible you didn't know what was going on in Canada. Maybe you and Dad were duped."

The Thanksgiving table filled with an awkward silence. Finally Robert pushed his chair away from the table and stood up. "That's a load of crap," he said. Kathleen shot a warning look across the table to her brother that said, "This is bad enough. Don't make it worse." Dennis just held Bob and me with his eyes.

Confusion spread like a retrovirus throughout my body. I tried to look at it from Kurt and Eddie's perspective. Here was a woman, their mother, who was now claiming she had been looking for them all their lives. They wanted to believe her. They wanted to find goodness and beauty and love. Hadn't we taught them to look for the good? There had been other shocks in the last few days. Only weeks ago, we revealed the secret of Catherine's existence, and they had been stunned. In addition, our long-held beliefs about Catherine's adoption, our belief that she had been safely ensconced in a loving family when she was five years old, turned out to be all wrong. Who could blame them for thinking we might be wrong again? For one wild moment, even I doubted part of the foundation on which our family had been built.

"Don't get upset, Mom and Dad," Kurt said. "It doesn't really matter. If it makes her happy to believe that story, we'll just give it to her."

"It was so long ago. What's the difference?" Eddie added to soften the moment.

But it did matter, and I could not get beyond it. I was reeling with anger and shock. I felt personally attacked. My hands shook and the china rattled as I cleared the dessert plates. Lucienne, the woman whom I felt I had protected in vagaries of language, "sick" and "unable to take care of children," had suddenly become "that woman" to me, and I wanted to tear her eyes out.

* * *

LUCIENNE HAD ASKED THEM TO CALL HER again that evening, and they had promised to do so. Shortly after dinner, they left Thanksgiving early for the first time, to place another call to Canada.

I went into the kitchen and cleared a spot on the table. I felt the cool oak boards on my forehead as I lowered my head into the cradle created by my folded arms. The residue of the Thanksgiving meal that lay strewn on the table and the countertops, turning itself into garbage, was as nothing compared to the emotional residue Lucienne's story left in my heart. A strange feeling of loss now permeated Thanksgiving Day. By virtue of biology and blood,

Lucienne had power over my boys. I was suddenly afraid that I would lose them.

* * *

EARLY IN DECEMBER, CATHERINE called Kurt and Eddie and told them she had finally received the letter from Lucienne that Margaret Clack told her about weeks earlier, and which was held up in the mail strike. Catherine sent a copy of it to Kurt and Eddie. Written on November 11, 1997, it had taken almost a month to find its way to her in Yarmouth. While the letter languished in the mail, Eddie and Kurt and Catherine had had several contacts with Lucienne. So, in a sense, the letter was anticlimactic for the three of them. However, it was, for me, a window into the life and mind of a woman who was now living rent-free in my head.

> Dear Daughter:-
> Hi, my name is Lucienne. I am now fifty-seven years old. Please excuse my typing, as my writing is like hen scratches. I was born in Kirkland Lake, Ontario, on September 10th, 1940. Your 1994 letter states that you have been married seven years, that you have three children, two boys, one girl. I am elated that you have found me. I cannot find the words to express my innermost feelings. All I can tell you is that for many, many years I have tried so very hard to find you. I never gave up, I prayed and prayed and never gave up hope that one day in God's Grace that He would lead the way back to the road that brings us together.
> After twenty-six year, God did hear my plea and the miracle has finally happened. I cannot describe the feelings or the joy that swept me up, when I received a letter from Halifax, N.S.
> I have received your photos. I presume they are from 1994, you cannot imagine how happy that made me.
> As for hobbies, I used to knit, but can't anymore. I had many hobbies when I was younger, but now I like to play Nintendo, watch TV, and study the Holy Bible, not necessarily in that order. I love the piano, but I do not have one.
> You do have a baby sister, she is now twenty-six years old. Her name is Deborah, and she is single, so I am still a mother as you will see by the photos, their not recent, the guy in the photo is an ex boyfriend. I am looking to hear from you real soon.

May God keep you all safely and bless you all.

P.S. The man you see in the photo of me was Deborah's ex boyfriend.

(It was signed) Lucienne

I read and reread the letter like a detective looking for clues. Clues to what? Probably for some sign of craziness that would support my already formed opinion of Lucienne based on the "baby scam" story. I was looking for evidence that would make her less threatening to me. However, my detective work failed to confirm my suspicions. I could tell from the grammar and spelling she had limited education, but so did many fine and good people. I could deduce that her life was sparse and that she lived in a small world of TV and Nintendo, but again, so do many others.

I knew from conversations with Kurt and Eddie about Lucienne's self-proclaimed ability to "know things," that she was infused with a generous dose of religious preoccupation. I was expecting to find clues to a kind of religious grandiosity that I had witnessed during my work with some psychotic or schizophrenic patients. Yet this letter did not speak to a religious extreme—rather it revealed a woman who prayed—just as I was a woman who prayed.

Above all, her words: "I cannot find the words to express my innermost feelings. All I can tell you is for years I have tried so very very hard to find you. I never gave up. I prayed and prayed . . . I cannot describe the feeling or the joy that swept me up when I read a letter from Halifax, Nova Scotia."

I knew I could have written those words. They were the universal language of motherhood. Here was a mother who, after twenty-five years, had found her first-born child. How "normal" her response. How frightening her normalcy was for me.

183

The Rift

THE DAYS FOLLOWING THANKSGIVING FLEW from the calendar in bunches. On November 29, Eddie stopped by and innocently asked me to preview a letter he had written to Lucienne. As I read, I willed the tears collecting behind my eyes to cease. In part, this was what he wrote—

Re: Lucienne/Catherine/Little Sister

Dear new found family:

My God!!! It is truly a miracle. Kurtis and I are very excited to have found you so fast. We only started looking for you 48 hours ago. Many emotions are rolling around. First let me say there has not been a day that has gone by where I haven't thought about you mom#2. . . . It has taken years of therapy to accept what has happened. . . . I am grateful for you bringing me into the world. Even though I haven't met you, I love you very much, you are the person who gave me life.

[Twenty-six] years, 9,490 days, 227,761 hours, 13,665,6000 seconds is how often I have thought about you. There has never been a moment that has gone by in a given day that I haven't thought about you. Some days have been filled with anger, some days sadness. Knowing you are alive, I anticipate many joyous days thinking of you. My feelings about the past and what happened are very strong. I still need to know how and why. I am not even sure you want to answer those questions. I can't blame you and I certainly don't hold myself responsible. My adoptive mother has always said, "You can't change the past, so don't try to. You can only live in the here and now." This is how I live. The "now" tells me I have a biological mother, younger sister, and older sister. What a wonderful feeling. To have a family you didn't even know you had is a lot to absorb.

I waited until he had happily bounded down the back steps and jumped into his car before I allowed my own sobs to fill the still and empty kitchen.

Phone contact between Canada and the boys became a daily ritual. Twenty-five years before, as Bob and I anxiously waited for the Canadian courts to release the boys to us, we hung on every anecdote and image of their small lives that we could glean from the Yarmouth letters. Now they were cherishing every conversation that took place with their sisters and mother. Every clue of the past, every aspect of personality was fitted into the empty space carried within each of them. Like a puzzle being constructed, one piece at a time, a picture was emerging. By Christmas, Kurt and Eddie were caught in a riptide of emotions.

Their calls to us, reporting on the news from Canada, became less frequent, dwindling to about once a week rather than after every conversation. What seemed like a paucity of information during those December days was hard for Bob and me to live with. Fantasies of losing my boys emotionally to their real mother preoccupied my waking hours and infiltrated my dreams. I analyzed their words when they did call, wary of Lucienne sabotaging their affection. As the weeks went on, however, a more complete and complicated picture of Lucienne emerged.

* * *

KURT AND EDDIE TOLD BOB AND ME that one of the first things they asked Lucienne about was their father, Eric. He had been hit by a car and killed in 1986, she told them. He had gone to an AA meeting to pick up Deborah, who at age fourteen had an alcohol problem but wasn't old enough to drive herself to meetings. "Damn bad luck, hit right smack in front of an AA meeting," Lucienne continued, in what they came to know as her own inimitable way. "He wasn't even there for himself. He was sober, been sober for years. Deborah still loves him—he was the greatest—just ask her and she'll tell you—she misses him every goddamn day."

Kurt and Eddie each felt a deep stab of pain as they heard and echoed her words. "Eric is dead?"

"Yeah, killed instantly, over ten years ago. I still can't get it through my head. Talk to him every day," she said.

Kurt could feel his heart, an iron weight in his chest. The palms of his hands dampened with perspiration. In an instant, his dream of playing guitar with his father was exploded. Eddie could hear Kurt's voice crack and knew that the duel fantasies of a "famous musician father" and of jamming with his "dad" were dissolving.

"What was he like?" Eddie asked.

Lucienne warmed to the question and dreamily told her sons, "The best. He was the best. We were some pair. All the girls were crazy for him and when he strummed that guitar, heaven came to visit."

"Did he have his own band?" asked Kurt.

"Yes," she told them. "He was known all over Nova Scotia. People came from far and wide to hear him play that guitar and sing. Most nights you couldn't get another person through the door." She told them how she was always right there with him from the first night they met. "It was *bam*. We were always together." And then, casually, she dropped a bomb that would reverberate down the years. "He had a wife in Yarmouth and four kids, but once me and your father got together, he left his wife and those other kids, and it was me and him all the way."

"He had four other children?" Kurt and Eddie asked with caution.

"Yeah, so you have four more half-brothers and sisters," she said with a laugh. "But don't ask me where they are, 'cause I don't care to know nothing about any of Eric's relatives."

"Why is that?" asked Kurt.

"Busybodies." She began to rant as she told Kurt and Eddie that all Eric's sisters and brothers, especially his oldest brother, Wilfred, thought they were so high and mighty, but in fact they were busybodies. Angrily, she tried to explain how it was "them that called and told lies about me, and that's how I come to lose my children."

"Lies? Why would they do that?"

"Never liked me, that's why. They liked that other one he married and her kids."

She told Kurt and Eddie, "Those government people took you two and Catherine right out of your beds when my false pains came the first time. I couldn't stop them 'cause I wasn't present. I took myself to the hospital. Well, my pains stopped, and when I got home the next morning the house was all quiet 'cept for the dog. Never did see any of you again."

Kurt and Eddie didn't know what to say. I didn't know what to say when they told me. I knew the bare facts; the children were taken when Lucienne went into the hospital with false labor, but hearing it from her perspective added a dimension for which I was not prepared.

Later, when they were off the phone, they discussed this new revelation. More family. Aunts and uncles. Why didn't they intervene? Why did they not stay involved, try to help them? Neither Kurt not Eddie wanted to pursue these relatives. However, the fact of their existence was distressing; especially the four other children. Relegated to a footnote in the margin of their father's life was another whole family he had deserted. It was hard to reconcile the great dad that Lucienne had described with the man who walked out on four older children. It was too much. As for the other relatives, aunts and uncles, whatever part they might have played at one time in Lucienne being reported to authorities, they were, in reality, strangers who never took a personal interest in either of them or Catherine.

Lucienne continued. "I've got your daddy's picture right here next to my chair, and he's holding his guitar. I talk to him all the time."

"Do you still have his guitar?" asked Kurt

"I had to sell that particular guitar. Needed the money. Bought a Nintendo to pass the time. He was the best, but he got killed anyway. But I don't blame God. God gave me special gifts, and my gifts are what pulled me through."

"What do you mean?"

"Oh, you'll find out. I know things."

"You know things? What kind of things?" from Eddie.

"Yeah, that's all I'm gonna say now, but you'll see when you get to know me a little better," she told them with an air of mystery. She went on, enumerating her health problems. "Asthma, and pressure and heart things. I have to use this oxygen tank to breathe. Almost died three times just last year. But I'm a fighter, and I keep praising the Lord, and I'm still here," she said with a wheezy laugh.

* * *

THE TELEPHONE CALLS WOULD LAST LATE into the night. The boys were speaking to her separately now. Sometimes Eddie would call; sometimes Kurt, then they would talk over their respective conversations with each other.

Lucienne told them about Deborah's birth. "There are things I know," she said enticingly, as she narrated how some primal instinct warned her after she gave birth to Deborah about the likelihood of the newborn being taken from her by the courts. On the baby's second day of life, the infant girl was rolled, in her plastic bassinet, down the hospital corridor into Lucienne's room. After lifting the infant, swaddled in a little pink blanket, from its bed, the nurse handed Lucienne a bottle of formula and placed the baby in her arms. When the nurse returned forty-five minutes later, the room was empty. Lucienne had received a message from God to "get the hell away from the damn hospital," and she did.

Lucienne was proud of her cunning in outsmarting the hospital bureaucracy. She proudly told the boys she simply walked out of the hospital with Deborah. No one saw her stuff the pockets of her coat with baby lotion and extra diapers, then throw her coat over the blue-and-white hospital gown that barely covered her body. No one saw her shuffle into the elevator and press the lobby button. Passing through the glass door that served as the entrance to the hospital, no one noticed her bare legs or the scuffs she wore on her feet. Deborah was hidden beneath the ripped lining of the coat that covered her swelling body through four pregnancies. The baby was quiet, locked on her breast, sucking for milk that most likely had not yet begun to flow. As Kurt and Eddie became more and more exposed to the symbiotic relationship between Deborah and her mother, that simple act of the infant sucking an empty breast seemed like a foreshadowing of what would become their sustaining relationship, one that would keep Deborah fiercely attached to her mother in the years that followed.

Lucienne had simply eloped from the hospital with her infant. The court order to place the child named Deborah in protective custody was never acted upon, and Deborah's fate was sealed with her mother's. Deborah became her mother's protector and advocate. As gatekeeper, she would warn Kurt and Eddie to be careful about upsetting Lucienne because of her poor health. That included disagreeing with or questioning the kidnapping theory. Now twenty-six years old, she was trying to pull her life together. It was not easy, but "she managed," Deborah told them proudly.

"I had trouble with the law when I was a kid, around thirteen. Got mixed up with drugs and alcohol. Our dad was still alive then. But I'm clean now," she told them.

A job babysitting for a local family earned her $50.00 a week for four twelve-hour days. This supplemented the government check that came to Lucienne for $375.00 a month. Deborah quit school at fifteen and now had aspirations of joining the army. However, "Mom needs me," she said, so her plans for the military were on hold. Her knowledge about her three abducted siblings was as old as she was, and her belief in their kidnapping was as real as her mother's.

She told them she had been "Miss Halifax Teen-Ager" when she was seventeen, and mailed Kurt and Eddie a picture that once appeared in a magazine. It was a portrait of her head and shoulders. Masses of deep brown waves framed her face and covered her shoulders. Her skin was flawless or air-brushed, but it was her eyes that were outstanding—large brown orbs emitting amber light. I looked for Kurt or Eddie in her features—perhaps Eddie's cheeks or Kurt's nose, but could not find either of them. There was a certain attitude behind those eyes staring straight into the camera, a fearlessness that seemed to meet the world head-on that I did not recognize in either of her brothers.

(Months later, when I finally spoke with her on the telephone, it was those eyes, with their intimations of self-assurance, staring back at me from the glossy photo that I would remember as I sat trembling with fear at my kitchen table, trying to determine whether to ask this stranger sister to help me.)

In the days and weeks that followed, Lucienne was dogmatic as she persisted in her view of the kidnapping. She drowned out Eddie's questions with the assurance of a revivalist preacher. She embellished the original facts. She added that there were about fifty other families whose kids had been stolen and sent to work farms where they were forced to help out with chores until sold to someone in the United States. She claimed to have heard it directly from one of the kids who had been recovered.

The "damn kidnapping story," as it came to be known, was the Damocles sword hanging over my head, threatening every conversation that took place after Thanksgiving Day. However, there were moments when even I found myself questioning reality. Duped, Kurt and Eddie had inferred. Complicity without intention. I asked myself—could we have been duped? Anything was possible. However, the more embellished Lucienne's recollections, the more ludicrous the claims became.

"You were three and four years old. Do you really think a three-year-old can do forced labor?" I asked them after hearing that flourish to her story. Each answered with a thoughtful silence.

But what I did know unreservedly was that the triple bureaucracy of health, social services, and immigration could not have missed an international kidnapping ring.

"Just think," I found myself saying to the boy. "Two governments, the United States and Canada, would have had to be involved and conspiring."

And so, initially shaken by Lucienne's accusations and half believing that Bob and I could have been "duped" all those years ago, Kurt and Eddie gradually came to reject Lucienne's theories. Their own emotional conflict had kept them confused. It was as though the storm of events had churned up the silt at the bottom of a river. Now Eddie was bent on proving the truth to Lucienne. Kurt was ambivalent. He didn't need to prove Lucienne wrong.

"What is, is," the old philosopher in him mumbled. He was content to let "the whole damn kidnapping story" fall from the table like crumbs to be swept away. It was Lucienne's fantasy, no longer a piece of reality that had to be woven into their history.

* * *

AS CHRISTMAS APPROACHED, I could sense frustration from Eddie as he reprised the Canada conversations. Communication with Lucienne remained difficult. She refused to entertain another view on her kidnapping theory. There was her Canadian dialect that took some getting used to. This was further complicated by the fact that Lucienne had lost her dentures and had difficulty pronouncing certain sounds. Her speech was slurred, and some of the words drowned in the steady, unrelenting stream of her sentences.

They were well into their second week of calls before Lucienne finally began to show interest in their lives. She asked if they graduated from high school. But it was the questions Lucienne didn't ask that gnawed at Eddie. As though avoiding an ancient taboo, she never brought up their adoptive family, never a question about the kidnappers. Nor did she ask if they had been happy, if they had been treated well, or how they felt about anything. Each of them had carefully prepared responses to questions never asked.

They wanted their mother to know they were special, to be as proud of their accomplishments as the rest of us were. When they finally initiated a conversation with her about their music, she was not surprised. Seems she had taken it for granted they would be "like Eric." She wanted to hear them for herself, and they happily packed off audio cassettes of their best performances. Kurt sent the recording of his own music that he had cut in Nashville when he was in his early twenties. Eddie sent tapes of his performances at Carnegie Recital Hall and tapes of songs he had written and performed on his keyboard. After mailing them off, special delivery, they waited anxiously for her to listen to them and respond.

She liked the tapes. She was impressed. "You're good," she said, "real good."

But when she added that their talent was the "God-given gift from Eric and me," it threw some cold water on their own achievements.

191

"Yes," they agreed with her, "music is in our genes." It was the one thing in their background of which they were proud.

* * *

THEY SAY THE HEART IS THE REPOSITORY of broken things, and the desire to be made whole is never far away. In spite of Lucienne's fractured communication, each of the boys was lifted to joy by one constant message that permeated the victim motif that Lucienne subscribed to. That message was a perfect fossil preserved in the amber of her memory and pinned down into an eight-word sentence, making irrelevant all the contradictions they had to sift through to unearth it. "I always loved you, and I fought for you." These words stood alone. Nothing else mattered. They had been and still were loved by their mother. Doubts about their own lovableness that for years had nibbled away at their insides like insidious worms were suddenly dispelled. Those words validated each of them in a way that nothing and no one else ever could.

* * *

EARLY IN DECEMBER, KURT TOLD LUCIENNE and Deborah he had taken a part-time job selling Christmas trees every night, and he would not have as much time for evening telephone calls. As a result, both the joy and burden of the telephone calls fell upon Eddie. Subtly, the tenor of the calls was changing. From a welcomed surprise that caused delight in Lucienne, they evolved to an expected "checking in." Pressure was building. Lucienne wanted to know when they were coming to St. John for a proper reunion. Missing a night's telephone call left Eddie vulnerable to criticism and sarcasm.

"Too busy with your life to remember your mother, eh?" was the greeting he got after a two-day hiatus from calling. This was followed by a reprimand: "It costs money to call you, you know." Slowly sadness engulfed Eddie. Although he knew that Lucienne and Deborah lived on government assistance and food stamps, he longed to feel worthy of the cost to call him.

An incident the week before Christmas brought his feelings to a head. It was well after midnight when the phone rang. Eddie had been asleep, and let the answering machine pick it up. It was Deborah, frantic and crying. "Mom's in the hospital, and she wants to hear from you right away. Call her." *Click.*

It was the middle of the night. From the slurring of Deborah's speech, together with his knowledge of recent "incidents" involving bars that had been revealed in previous telephone conversations, Eddie suspected she was drinking. He wasn't sure from the message if he was supposed to call their apartment or the hospital. He was unnerved. The midnight SOS angered and annoyed him. Like a horse carrying on its back the tools and provisions needed for a long journey, he had been trying to pace himself in his interactions with Lucienne and Deborah. Now, with this call, he felt an extra burden of responsibility was being strapped to his back, one for which he was unprepared. He reared, he bolted. He did not call back until the following day. The price imposed for his failure to respond immediately would be forthcoming.

* * *

MEANWHILE, THE BOYS' CALLS BACK and forth to their older sister, Catherine, were lovely in their progress. Catherine's delight in her brothers enhanced their delight in her. Her oldest child, George, who was nine years old, caught his mother's excitement. Letters, written in pencil in the boy's tiny print, began to arrive. "Dear Uncle Eddie," "Dear Uncle Kurt"—and each of them swelled with pride at having a niece and two nephews of their very own, up in Canada. A circle was being completed for them. It was as if the blood flowing through their veins connected them not only to a past but to a future, represented for now in Catherine's children.

As the weeks progressed, Catherine was no longer ambivalent about meeting Lucienne. She was adamant in her opposition. Lucienne's continued insistence regarding a kidnapping infuriated Catherine, for Catherine, unlike Kurt and Eddie, did have memories of the early years. She remembered the attic room, the shuffling from one foster home to another, the rejections. Catherine knew the pain she lived through had nothing to do with a kidnapping. Refusing to listen to what she now called "Lucienne's ramblings," Catherine said good-bye and politely hung up the phone when the conversation with her mother became too difficult for her to tolerate. Fear of her own anger was not extinguished by contact. It was now clear to her that she could not trust herself to meet with her mother.

"I'll blow," she told her brothers.

＊ ＊ ＊

EDDIE DID NOT HEAR FROM CANADA for a few days after that midnight SOS, but Lucienne and Deborah resumed calls to Kurt, leaving messages on his machine. Eddie was hurt and needed some time to calm down. By the time he called them, Lucienne had been released from the hospital, but she refused to get on the phone and speak with him. She was "mad at him" for not calling back that midnight, Deborah told him. Cutting him off, rejecting his phone call was pay back. He tried again.

"This is Edward," he said as Lucienne picked up the phone.

When nervous or unsure of himself, Eddie had a tendency to speak very formally on the telephone, thus the "Edward" instead of "Eddie." If he was going to leave a message, he bought time to collect his thoughts by giving the hour and date, including the day of the week and the year. He was often teased by his siblings for his slow-starting messages. They'd tell him, "We know what year it is. We know the month."

He took the teasing with good humor, but it was the mechanism he had come up with to prepare what he was about to say.

"Edward—what kind of shit is that?" Lucienne snapped. "I don't know no damn Edward. My son is Eddie, and I don't appreciate your changing it to Edward. I don't want to hear that again. You are Eddie."

He was taken-aback and shaking with anger. At first speechless, he gradually regrouped and defended himself. "My name *is* Edward, and that's it."

"Shit it is," he heard as the line went dead.

Later on that night, Deborah called Eddie back. She left a cryptic message from Lucienne: "Mom does not appreciate either yours or Catherine's attitude."

＊ ＊ ＊

NOW KURT WAS EMERGING as the favored child; Eddie and Catherine were the bad children. In four weeks, using jealousy as her weapon, Lucienne had begun to turn brother against brother. Rather than encourage them to share themselves with each other and her, she was vying for one-hundred percent of one of them and threatening to discard the others. This newest rejection was killing Eddie.

Things came to a head on Christmas Day. After the yearly marathon of gift-giving took place around our tree, Eddie followed me into the kitchen and offered to help with dinner. As he started to whip the potatoes, I heard him say over the whirr of the machine, "I think Kurt's going to drive up to Canada by himself."

I stopped in my tracks. "No, he wouldn't do that."

Before Eddie could respond, Kurt's voice came from in the doorway. "Well, you don't seem to want to go anymore—you and Catherine are being mean to Lucienne and Deborah, and I don't know why."

Eddie was angry. "Catherine has nothing to do with how I feel. I'm just sick of the lies and pressure, and that crazy kidnapping story. Half the time she's not lucid."

"So what?" said Kurt, "Sometimes she is okay."

"Now I think they want money, and I don't have it to send to them."

"Why do you say they want money?"

"Well, first it was hints to pay their telephone bill, and now Lucienne lost her dentures and they're hinting I should pay for them."

"Well, no one said anything like that to me," said Kurt

"Just wait."

Eddie, his face red with anger and looking as though he was going to cry, said to Kurt, "Let's go out back and have a smoke." Then he turned off the mixer and left the bowl of lumpy potatoes on the counter. The air was thick with tension as they stomped out together.

Over the past few weeks, as I watched the boys struggle with some aspect of their past, I would become enraged at Lucienne. However, my rage was always diluted when I considered how unthinkable circumstances could destroy the good in people.

Now, here it was, Christmas Day and I was as close to hate as I would ever get. Subjectively, "evil" was the only word I could think of that would allow a mother to turn one of her sons against the other. I could not remember the last time the boys had been this angry with each other, and it hurt me to witness it. Objectively, I knew from my professional work that this splitting of the boys was a primitive defense of a very fragile ego, the behavior of a sick woman. However, I no longer cared.

I did not know what Lucienne was attempting to accomplish, but I did know my boys. I had always been confident that these two, who had been through so much together, were too bonded for their relationship to be severed by any unhealthy ploy that might emanate from Lucienne's loose mind. Now my confidence was shaken as I watched the door slam shut behind them. Through the windows, I saw the glow of two cigarettes in the dark. I watched as the curls of smoke billowed upward in the cold air. Every once in a while one of them turned his back on the other and walked away, then found his way back. They kept talking. Kicking the snow, Eddie's black wingtips grew halos of white stains, and Kurt's heavy work boots imprinted a circle of giant feet into the snow. After a while Dennis came into the kitchen.

"Where are Kurt and Eddie? What's going on?"

I nodded and turned my head toward the yard just in time to see them hug each other, a big bear hug with pats on the back, and I knew it would be all right. When they came back into the kitchen, they were smiling; they had a plan.

"We want to pick a date to go to Canada to meet Lucienne. Will you and Dad come with us? We don't want to leave you out. You've been with us for every important event of our lives, and we want you there with us for this one."

And so it was decided.

৪০ 19 ল

Death Watch

URING A SERIES OF WINTER MEETINGS around our old oak kitchen table,
a plan to meet Lucienne, referred to by the boys as "The Reunion," crystallized. The six of us, Kurt and Cath, Eddie and Barbara, and Bob and I, met
every Tuesday night for dinner starting in early January. The first thing on Kurt
and Eddie's agenda was the question, "Do you think Robert, Kathleen and
Dennis would want to come to Canada with us?" It was a complicated question: for Kurt and Eddie it was first of all, a matter of inclusion. Major events
in the family had always been undertaken together, and for them this compet-
ed for one of the most meaningful events of their lives. They did not know if
it was as significant for their three siblings. What they did know was that
Robert, Kathleen, and Dennis would most likely choose to come if they
thought Bob or I or either of them might be vulnerable to some sort of hurt,
and in need of support.

They reached out to each of their brothers and sister, asking the question, "Do you want to come to Canada with us for the reunion?"

Each sibling hesitated and asked both Kurt and Eddie if it mattered
to them. The boys said, "No," they just didn't want them to feel left out.
Robert, Kathleen, and Dennis each said, "Let me think about it and get back
to you." Within hours, Bob and I got separate calls from each of them.

"Do you need us there with you?"

"No," we said.

"Are you sure? Are you going to be okay with this woman and her tales of kidnappers?"

"Yes," we assured each of them, and meant it.

"Do you think Kurt or Eddie needs us to be there to get through this?"

"No," we said. "They need your moral support, but we honestly don't think you need to be physically present."

Truth was, Robert, Kathleen, and Dennis did not really want to meet Lucienne, but each was willing to make the trip if it would make it easier for their brothers.

* * *

PLANNING OUR TRIP, EDDIE WAS the detail man. He arrived each Tuesday night with file folders bulging with weather forecasts, airline schedules, road maps, hotel accommodations in St. John, and copious notes needed to construct the itinerary. He told us snowfall could be massive during a Canadian winter, and roads were often impassable for days. He learned that the first thaw in St. John could not be relied upon until early April. To insure good traveling weather, we planned the trip for late April. The six of us—each of the boys, their wives, and Bob and I—would fly to Montreal and then take a short commuter hop across the Bay of Fundy to St. John.

After we met each Tuesday night, either Eddie or Kurt called Catherine and coordinated the developing plans with her. The timing was planned so that we would all arrive within an hour of each other. Catherine's parents, Jon and Femme were driving her 300-miles from Yarmouth to St. John and they would meet us in the lobby of the hotel late Friday afternoon. Catherine had chosen to travel without her three children in order to conserve all her energy for the reunion with Kurt and Eddie and for dealing with the decision she still had to make about actually meeting Lucienne face-to-face. Catherine was coming to meet the brothers she had been longing for since she was five years old. Holding in abeyance any meeting with Lucienne gave her a needed feeling of safety.

Towards the end of January, Kurt received a letter from Deborah. He brought it with him to the next dinner. Eddie had already read it. Unlike Eddie, with his organized files and meticulous agenda, Kurt had the letter folded into a square and stuffed in his shirt pocket.

Jan. 1998

Greeti ngs To bo th of you: -
I must say I t was such a great pleasure to hear from you, Wed. the 7th of Jan. Unfortunately I missed not talking to your wife Cath because she was working. But all in all I was so happy that you called.

Have to tell you that Mom wasn't feeling too well, but she did not want me to tell you that, so you wouldn't worry about her, that's the way Mom is. She can be head-strong at times, she doesn't want you, Eddie or Katherine to worry. She is sicker that she lets on. I hope we can keep this subject between us.

Could have lost her 3 times last yr. May, July & Sept 1996.

She told me by the Grace of God, I will live to see the yr. 2000, she would be 60 by then. Shes a fighter when it comes to her health, but she keeps praising God and so do I, to keep her fighting for her health & knowing Mom like I do, shes determined and believes in God that's the way its going to be. Shes is a very strong believer in God, and so am i.

You all have to understand one thing, all of you, she cannot handle too much pressure & or stress, because of her health.

Shes determined to find a way to get the "Family Court Transcripts" from Yarmouth Family Court. She knows and feels things were not forthright about what happened, and wether you know it or not, her God given gift of these knowledge are never wrong.

We have not heard anything from Margaret Clack from Halifax, N.S., nor from Eddie or Katherine, as of yet since we talked on the ph. The last time Mom & I talked to Kate was Nov. 29th/97. the one and only time we heard from her, and we did the calling. I called Eddie once when Mom was in the hospital, he sounded very different than you.

I believe you & I have a lot in common, our looks our way of thinking, music and lot of other things in general. I believe you truly love Mom and she told me so. She said its all in the sound of your voice, the way you speak, the way you talk to her, however she doesn't get that feeling from Kate or Eddie, and nor do I, but I know you love me as your sister, but I feel like Mom when it comes down to it about Eddie and Kate, its not there (the love). They want to meet me and Mom but??? Well enough of that.

How are you and Cath, your Mom & Dad & Eddie & Barbara????. Hope you are all in good health. Me & Mom are managing o.k. Its probably non of my business, but I dare ask, just what do you do for a living?? From my talking to you on the ph. its part time this and part time that, like xmas trees, that's not a steady job, so what do you do for a living. You told me Eddie was a financial wizard. What does that mean? Mom said to me (I feel Eddie works "Stock market Exange", Wall ST. New Yor) could she be right? No

You already know about me (severe anxiety) its in the genes, lucky me, Dad had it very bad. I take medication and am trying to ween myself off, I'm not taking as many as I used to, I also have pressure and stress, but I'm doing fine.

Can't wait till April-May comes to see you all. Word of warning, with Moms health, she can't take too much pressure or stress so when we do all meet, she may be quiet like a wall flower for a while, after all 26 yrs is a long time, but when she lets off, then, watch out, she'll sing like a bird, she kind of shy to meet your parents, Mr. & Mrs. Goldstein, but I know with the help of God she'll handle it. Liked promised a photo of me when I was on the front cover of *Singles Mag*, 93 Hope you like it.

The letter was signed, Your sister Deborah

I listened as Kurt read it aloud. I didn't miss his upward glance towards me from under his dark "uni-brow," the thick unbroken road of eyebrow that both he and Robert had across their foreheads. The quick glance warned me something unpleasant was coming. He read from the letter, "you have to understand one thing all of you."

Kurt knew me well enough to anticipate my reaction. He had endured his share of mother-son disagreements over the years, and knew I had tolerated the mumblings from under his breath and even the anger erupting when he or one of the others defended themselves. But an outright admonishment from one of the kids, like "you have to," was like the thunder clap preceding lightening.

My mind was racing with *I don't have to do anything and who are you to tell me what I have to do?* but I said nothing. He read on:

"She's determined to find a way to the Family Court Transcripts from the Yarmouth Family Court. She knows and feels things were not forthright about what happened and whether you know it or not, her God given gift of these knowledge are never wrong."

Anger filled me. It was the "damn kidnapping story" again. Following that—a reference to Kate. Who was Kate? Of course I knew the answer to that question. Kate was Lucienne's moniker for her first daughter, Catherine. She would call her what she pleased just as she let Eddie know she refused to acknowledge his name was Edward.

I watched from across the table as Eddie sighed and began to fidget. Having already read the letter with Kurt, he knew what was coming next.

"Get this," he said, in sad anticipation as the letter exploded with criticism of Eddie and Catherine, followed by words of affection and endearment towards Kurt.

"I believe you truly love Mom and she told me so. She told me it's all in the sound of your voice, the way you speak, the way you talk to her, however she doesn't get that feeling from Kate or Eddie, and nor do i . . ."

There it was. The letter validated Eddie's feelings of rejection. I saw it as one more attempt to split and spoil the relationship between my boys, who had never wavered in their loyalty to each other. I had witnessed it for the first time when they argued in the backyard on Christmas Day. Now this letter was written confirmation of the attempt to designate a good son and a bad son.

Then, like a yellow bird flying out of the thicket, the words— "Lucienne was kind of shy to meet your parents." I softened, wondering for the first time if maybe somewhere deep within the recesses of her pain, Lucienne knew that Kurt and Eddie's parents were not the kidnapping outlaws that thrived in her mind.

The last paragraph began, "Can't wait till April-May comes, to see you all." Lucienne and Deborah were obviously excited about the reunion. They had been kept abreast of the evolving plans, and had agreed with them before anything was finalized. Eddie had made reservations for all nine of us at a local hotel. He also reserved a private meeting room at the hotel for the actual reunion, which would commence at ten o'clock on Saturday morning. Sunday and Monday were open, and the boys hoped to spend some additional time alone with Lucienne.

* * *

FUELED BY LUCIENNE'S AND DEBORAH'S determination to produce court transcripts shoring up their "things were not forthright" agenda, Eddie decided to follow through with his plan to get records released from DYFS in New Jersey. He was nervous. Delving into the details of the court record might tarnish their ability to leave the past in the past. Perhaps it contained things the boys didn't want to know, things that would adversely influence the blank slate with which they were trying to approach Lucienne. But with Lucienne threatening to produce papers validating her baby scam story, Eddie finally sat down and wrote to DYFS. He was determined to gather evidence to refute what he feared would be false accusations coming from Lucienne at the reunion, accusations that could blow it all to pieces.

With the logistics for our trip to St. John all worked out, the plane tickets were purchased. Everything was "go" for April twenty-fourth through the twenty-seventh, when the plans came tumbling down around us like a house of cards.

* * *

BY THIS TIME I HAD LEFT MY JOB at the hospital and had a private counseling practice in town. Shortly after noon on Wednesday, February 18, I was getting ready to leave the house for my office. It would be a busy afternoon and evening, with seven clients scheduled, starting at 3:00 p.m. The phone rang. It was Eddie. He was sobbing.

"Lucienne's in the hospital, in intensive care. She probably won't survive the night. Deborah just called. She's hysterical. Kurt and I don't know what to do," he choked between sobs.

"When did this all happen? Do you know what's wrong with her?"

"Deborah said she just went in for a check up, and then took a turn for the worse. She said if we want to see her alive, we have to go to Canada now."

I was wary. Thinking about the midnight SOS from the hospital that had gotten Eddie into so much trouble weeks earlier, I asked, "Do you think it's true, or just a ruse to get you up there quicker?"

"It sounds true, but Deborah's practically hysterical and can barely speak. It's hard to understand her. She said they have Lucienne hooked up to machines that are breathing for her. She said they removed three liters of fluid from her lungs, and she's on a mask. Do you know what that means?" he asked. "Deborah also said Lucienne is combative and is ripping tubes out of her arm."

I listened to the language Eddie was repeating from Deborah. Three liters of fluid, intensive care, combative—it sounded legitimate, the kind of words you would find on hospital charts, precise, informative.

"I think it's probably true," I said.

"What should we do? I've already talked to Kurt."

"I think you have to go right away," I said. "You're so close to meeting her that if something happens to her now you'll always have regrets."

"Okay, I'll call Kurt and tell him. Mom, can you and Dad come with us?"

My refusal surprised me.

"I don't think I can. I have clients scheduled for this afternoon and evening, starting in about two hours. I can't just leave them high and dry."

This was true, but what was also true was that, in that moment, I did not want to leave. I did not want to disrupt my life for this latest drama that might or might not be real. I was angry at Lucienne for being sick. My mind was working like the computer at NASA, running a hundred programs simultaneously. Everything about Lucienne seemed dangerous to me. Maybe she was not really sick. Suppose one of the hastily booked flights crashed? Her drama would be my drama. My children would be orphans. Talk about drama—that's irrational. The plane wasn't going to crash. Your children were all adults. They would survive. Just deal with the facts.

"I'll call Dad and ask him to start working on tickets for the next flight to St. John."

* * *

"Do you think we should go with them?" Bob said to me through one phone line while the travel agent, Peter, was trying to book tickets on another line.

"I don't know. What do you think?"

"I think they need us more in these circumstances than they will when we're scheduled to travel with them in April," Bob said.

I was wavering. In my heart, I felt we should go, but I really did not want to.

"I'm going to call the other kids and tell them what's going on. They can help us decide." I hung up and started dialing Robert, then Kathleen, then Dennis. Miraculously, everyone was reachable in those minutes of decision making.

"Here's what's going on," I said to each of them, ending with, "What do you think we should do?"

The three of them had the same response, even as I was still speaking. "Oh, my God," and then, "You have got to go with them. This is huge. They'll need you."

I got back to Bob. "Tell Peter to book two more tickets."

Since there were no direct flights to St. John, Peter had scheduled the boys on an Air Canada flight to Montreal, leaving Newark Airport at 5:00 p.m. It connected with a hop to St. John leaving at 9:00 p.m. that evening. Bob called Peter for the two additional tickets. With Bob still on the line, Peter went into his computer to access the flight information.

"No good" he said within seconds. "I can get you as far as Montreal, but the flight to St. John is full. There is one seat left. You or your wife?"

"I don't know," said Bob. "I'll call you right back."

He called me. I quickly called each of the boys. "Who do you want with you? We can't both get on the plane. There's only one ticket available."

Kurt said, "Dad, he knows how to travel. You're not as sure of yourself in airports and hotels."

Eddie said, "Mom, you should come. You'll be good for Deborah and us if Lucienne dies."

They were both right in their evaluations. Finally, I decided to be the deciding vote. "You go," I said to Bob. No more than three minutes had passed when Bob told Peter, "Book the ticket in my name." Peter typed the order into his computer. The screen refused. In those three minutes of indecision, the ticket had been purchased by someone else. There were no seats left on the plane.

Human nature being what it is, the inability to go was like adding tinder to a smoldering fire, bursting it into flames of desire. Now we both clearly wanted and needed to be on those flights. Bob told Peter to keep trying. "I'll get us on something. It might not be Air Canada, but I'll find some airline to get us there tonight," Bob said to me in his most "positive thinking" voice.

Bob left his office and picked up the tickets. Kurt and Eddie threw clothes into a knapsack. Passports, thankfully were already in order in preparation for the April trip. The boys drove to the house. Bob and I got our passports out and packed bags. My associate canceled my clients for me. It was nearly four o'clock. We called a taxi so we would not have to spend time parking the car.

We got to the airport minutes before flight time and checked the departure screen. The plane was boarding. "Run," we told them. "We'll try to get tickets. We might be right behind you."

We kissed them quickly and watched them disappear, Kurt's blue overcoat, and then Eddie's green parka diminishing to streaks of color swallowed up by the crowded terminal. Bob and I ran to the ticket counter. He had his American Express Airlines schedule book open, checking every flight entering Canada. At the ticket counter we begged—telling the sympathetic ticket agent our story. It couldn't be done. No matter how we got to Montreal, there were no seats available on the one and only plane to St. John. Defeated, we looked at each other and were finally forced to acknowledge we were not going. By now I was crying. Images of Kurt and Eddie's backs disappearing into the crowd took on an ominous hue. This was big. Even though physically they were mature and self-sufficient, inside each of them at that moment was a four-year-old looking for his mother.

We stood beneath the departure screen. It was five o'clock. The flight lit up in blue. "DEPARTED" flashed. Standing there in the middle of the airport, staring at the screen while the real travelers tripped over us, we were heartsick.

205

"There's got to be a reason," I said. "We aren't meant to be on that flight." Bob looked at me with doubt. "We'll just have to trust that there is a reason. I don't know what it is, but my intuition tells me there is a reason we are not on that flight."

I remembered thinking this once before, that night in 1960 when we lost John. Now, an exquisite awareness of the gifts my dead child had led us to wafted into my mind like an echo of faith, a scent of hope. How desperately I wanted to believe.

ᔥ 20 ᔥ

Kurt's Crisis

L UCIENNE WAS INDEED VERY ILL. "IT IS PITIFUL to see her," Eddie told us when he called. She could not speak. Monitors beeped and blinked with every labored breath. She was as little and pale as the sea of white linens in which she was immersed. The side of the bed was cribbed with metal bars to keep her safely confined. Her index finger was fitted with a red emergency light with which to call for help. Intravenous drips, hanging from tall poles were inserted in each of her arms and left almost no space for anyone to approach the bed. Nurses were hovering. She looked like she was dying.

The hospital staff was kind to Kurt and Eddie, treating them like celebrities of a sort—for they had never experienced exactly these circumstances before, reunion and death, compressed into a day. Familiar with death, each nurse had witnessed families' good-byes—even those terminal acts of forgiveness over long-held grudges, forgiveness that soothed like salve on a wound, allowing the dying to slip more easily out of their bodies. But this was different. Never before had they watched two sons gaze for the first time in twenty-five years at the woman who gave them life, the woman who was struggling to both stay alive and to meet her past in the men who now stood at the foot of her bed.

Conflicted emotions washed over Eddie, not only because Lucienne was so ill, lying in the crib of her hospital bed, but also because she was so unknown. Anger erupted from some ancient fissure, even as she squeezed his hand and smiled her toothless smile. It stained the moment like a red dye. And surely as the anger came, it disappeared on some undertow of love that pulled him toward her. He wanted to hold her responsible for the loss he had felt, and he wanted to love her. Yet how could he continue to hold onto his present life and wish it otherwise at the same time?

"It is so confusing, Mom," he said to me.

They stayed at the hospital all day, crowded into the tiny hospital room or pacing the hallway outside the thick wooden door. Deborah, Kurt, and Eddie kept a death watch. Lucienne understood who they were. She smiled. She held their hands. Now she could die in peace, she said as she coughed into the pillow and slipped in and out of consciousness.

But she did not die. As the hours dragged across the day and the slush turned metallic in the streets, the blackness that surrounded her began to lift. Her eyes brightened, she motioned for water, there was talk of removing the breathing tube, and the monitors purred quietly. Still they stayed. Night descended, and the hospital grew quiet as a cloister. Here in the silence, Eddie at last felt the slight stirring of empathy for his waif of a mother lying benignly in her hospital bed. It washed over him, and for a moment he was free.

Lately, a new terror had burst into his thoughts. Married and thinking of having children of his own, self-doubt and fear haunted him. Over and over, it played inside his head. What if I fail my children the way my biological parents failed me? What if I am genetically wired in such a way that I cannot care for my children? Battling these demons, he would break into a cold sweat. Hope that meeting his mother would help put these fears to rest was part of the driving force that had prompted the search. Eddie wanted some explanation to tip the balance for him, an understanding that would lift him to an even playing field where his potential for fatherhood was safe. Deborah provided him with a ray of hope. She had been with Lucienne since birth and obviously loved her very much. Her protectiveness and solicitude toward her mother seemed to imply that some good parenting must have gone on.

Eddie called us at home every few hours with an update. By late Thursday night the crisis was over. His relief was palpable. Since he had a longstanding obligation with his in-laws for the weekend, he was going ahead with his plans to return to New Jersey Friday evening. Kurt was going to stay on till Sunday.

"How's Kurt doing?" I asked Eddie during what was about his seventh phone call to us since getting on the plane. I had not spoken to Kurt since leaving them at the airport. Since Eddie was the one with a cell phone, I assumed he was speaking for both of them each time he called.

Eddie hesitated. "He's okay. More upset than I am."

"Is he all right?"

"Yeah, he's okay."

"Put him on the phone."

"He's not here."

"He's not? Where is he?" I was surprised they were not together.

"He's out with Deborah."

"Out? Out where?"

"I don't know."

The short responses, the hesitation, the edge of irritation in his tone of voice all told me that Eddie was struggling with anger towards Kurt. Something was going on that was driving a wedge between them. I couldn't imagine what it was.

"Tell him to call me when he comes in, no matter what time it is."

"Okay."

It was well after midnight when the call finally came from Kurt. His voice was barely audible. I could hear his shallow breathing over the phone. He was crying. He told me he couldn't stop shaking and hadn't slept at all since boarding the plane at Newark Airport. Nauseous and unable to eat, he still believed Lucienne was going to die. He had really wanted to meet Eric, and it was just hitting him how final death really is, how they would never, ever, play guitar together.

I become alarmed. My mind flew in those few seconds, to a recent family wedding where I had watched Kurt drink beer after beer until, bleary eyed, he gave up his keys, and Cath drove him home. "Are you drinking?" I asked.

"Just socially."

209

"Socially, what does that mean?"

"I've had a few beers."

"Kurt, don't drink anything else." I said. "Alcohol will make it worse."

"Okay," he said easily and flatly, accommodating me.

"I don't want Eddie to leave, I'm scared." His voice sounded different and very far away.

"Why don't you come home with Eddie? It sounds like Lucienne's going to be all right, and you can still go back in April, like we planned."

"No, I need to stay. I want to stay. I belong here, and so does Eddie," he said combatively. "I just wish I could sleep."

He was not changing his mind.

"Take some deep breaths," I said. I breathed with him over the phone, had him match his breathing to mine in a slow rhythm. "Smell the roses, blow out the candles," I chanted. I inhaled and exhaled with him, just as I had over the years with any number of anxiety-riddled patients, hoping to give each a way to overcome the racing thoughts and speeding hearts that were immobilizing them.

A litany of tools to fight anxiety poured out of me. "Try to relax. Take a hot bath. Order warm milk from room service. Don't drink any more beer. Keep breathing slowly. Say some prayers." We continued to take deep breaths in unison over the phone wires, my flimsy connection to his troubled self.

He seemed to calm a bit. "Will you call me tomorrow morning and let me know how things are going?" I asked.

"Yes," he said. And the call ended.

Oh, how I wished he were getting on that plane tomorrow and coming home with his brother.

The following morning, Kurt did not call. He did not call in the afternoon. I finally reached him at about 7:00 p.m. He told me Eddie left on an afternoon flight. With Eddie gone, his anxiety had escalated.

"I don't want to be here alone," he said. "I may have to plan a funeral."

"A funeral! What happened? I thought the crisis was over. Is Lucienne worse?"

"Yes, I think she's going to die. She took another turn for the worse after Eddie left."

I could hardly believe what I was hearing and I was filled with compassion for Kurt, for all three of them. "Do you want Dad and me to fly up? Would that make you feel better?" I asked.

"Would you? Yes, I can't handle this anymore."

"Are you drinking?"

"No," he said, and I believed him.

"Okay, we'll come. I'll get tickets for the next available flight. Keep in touch."

Bob called the airlines and found there were seats available on Saturday morning. He reserved two tickets.

* * *

EDDIE CALLED FROM THE AIRPORT ABOUT 9:00 P.M. that same night, minutes after his plane landed. "I'm back" he said. "I've been thinking all the way home, and I have to tell you something. It's about Kurt, and he may never speak to me again, but I have to tell you. It's not good, but I don't want to talk from here. I'll call you from home in a half hour."

"What is it?" I said, frightened. I could hear the roar of planes taking off and landing in the background. The signal on his cell phone was weak and full of static.

"I can't talk from here. I'll call you as soon as I get home." He hung up.

My mind went to the worst possible scenario.

Oh, my God, Kurt's not coming back! I thought wildly. Hadn't he said he belonged there?

I waited for what seemed like forever, but in reality was less than an hour. I lunged for the phone before it completed its first ring. Eddie was upset. "Mom, Kurt's going to be mad at me, but I don't know what else to do. I think he has a serious drinking problem."

"Well, he told me he had a few beers last night. Is that what you mean?"

"Mom, he started drinking the moment the doors to the plane closed in New Jersey when it was clear you and Dad were not going to be on it. He drank

211

constantly on the flight. When we arrived in Montreal he headed straight for an airport bar for the two-hour layover. At one point I left him alone to check the flight. When I came back there was a large group of people gathered around him like some street-corner preacher, and he was telling them personal information about why we were going to St. John. It was so embarrassing."

Eddie continued. "It was almost midnight when we arrived at our hotel on Wednesday. He insisted on calling Deborah, and then insisted on leaving the hotel to go to another bar and meet her. I didn't want to leave him because he was so drunk. I went, although all I wanted to do was sleep. After an hour or so, I went back to the room, but he stayed out for a couple of hours more. He was acting crazy. I had to book another hotel room for Deborah because he brought her to our room and told her she could spend the night with us. My God, they were both drunk, and we had just met her hours earlier. I told him I didn't care, even if she was supposed to be my sister, I was not ready to share my bedroom with her. Kurt wouldn't have either, if he were not drunk.

"It was the same thing yesterday. He was weird when he saw Lucienne. He had a dream on the plane about a flashing red light, and when he saw the red call light on her finger he freaked out. Thought he was clairvoyant. He's a mess. He had already drank everything in the mini-bar in the hotel room."

Strangely, relief flooded me. This was bad, but it would be so much worse if Kurt had decided to stay in Canada. It was as though I had ridden some enormous wave into the shore where I could feel the hard wet sand of the beach grounding me. I sank for a timeless moment into my relief, and then the next thunderous wave rolled out of my thoughts and engulfed me. I was not losing my son to Canada or to his biological mother, but nonetheless he was lost in a most profound and dangerous way.

The poet Josephine Jacobson wrote about "the moment of knowing," that instant when the heart recognizes and is inflamed by something it didn't know it knew. Suddenly, I knew why Bob and I were not on that plane to Canada. Two sets of parental eyes observing him would have been enough to constrain Kurt. His out-of-control drinking would have remained unknown to us. I wondered how long he and Cath had been struggling with this, keeping it a secret, much the way I had hidden Bob's drinking from my family and friends. Now he was exposed. Knowing the truth made it possible for Bob and me and the rest of the family to intervene and try to help him. Yes, we were losing him, but in a way we had failed to recognize.

Later, Bob and I talked. Each of us reconsidered that fully booked flight that left us crying in Newark Airport, totally unaware of the drama unfolding with our son. Once again I wondered, was this coincidence or divine intervention; was it synchronicity or grace? Our inability to board the plane could be explained simply enough—there were no seats. Yet my intuition was that of a deeper involvement of forces that, in their unfolding, produced events that once again, were part of a larger design. I silently prayed that we could use this incredible and unanticipated experience to help Kurt overcome his demons.

Eddie had one more thing to tell me about the trip. Just days before he learned of Lucienne's illness, he had received the long-awaited papers that he had requested from DYFS. Summarizing the case history of his biological family from 1967 to 1971, they had been a vital part of the court proceedings that resulted in the three children being made wards of the province.

Eddie told me that, although it was painful, he read the report over and over, absorbing every last detail. The effect was to strengthen him. It was as though the sinkhole at the beginning of his life was being sealed, and with it the nothingness that had swallowed him.

I understood. My own experience had taught me that it was the unknown that infiltrated the imagination with fear and fantasies. Truth, on the other hand, dissipated endless imaginings; there was power in knowing, for what was known could be confronted; what was known could be overcome.

Eddie offered the documents to Kurt to read on the plane, but Kurt refused.

"I do not need to know the gory details," he said.

Now Eddie asked me if Bob and I had seen these papers at the time of the adoption. I told him no. The case worker at Spaulding had made no mention of their existence, and they were never revealed to us.

Like Kurt, I was ambivalent about reading the documents. Although a part of me wanted to know details from the past, at that moment I was preoccupied with the present, with the crisis surrounding Kurt. I trusted Eddie's evaluation when he told me, "The papers absolutely prove that Lucienne is wrong about the kidnapping theory." That was enough.

Eddie proceeded to tell me that, before returning from Canada, he wanted to set the record straight with Deborah, to debunk the kidnapping fable and the belief that court papers existed supporting Lucienne's story. The report from DYFS confirmed another reality and he had stuffed it into his knapsack and carried it with him to Canada. He asked Deborah if she would be willing to read it. With trepidation, she said, "Yes." While Kurt slept in another room and snow pelted the side of the hotel with great sheets of ice and the radiator hissed, brother and sister sat on the worn carpet of a hotel room and deconstructed history. Eddie helped her read the words that were beyond her eighth-grade education. When they were finished reading, Deborah was quiet. She seemed neither shocked nor unbelieving nor argumentative. She simply gathered the facts like so much colored thread that she put away to embroider onto her own story some time in the future.

As I listened, a sense of relief fed the hope that slowly arose in me as I heard of Deborah's evident capitulation.

Finally, I told Eddie of my conversation with Kurt that had taken place while he was in flight, of Kurt's belief in Lucienne's impending death and our newly reserved airline tickets for Saturday morning.

"He's nuts," Eddie said, with renewed agitation. "I don't believe it. He's exaggerating, probably drinking again tonight. I'm going to call the hospital right now. I know the nurses and have the direct line to the desk. They'll tell me what's going on."

Eddie was back to me within fifteen minutes. Lucienne was not dying. He had, in fact, been able to speak with her; the nurse had transferred his call to her room. He had also called Kurt's room at the hotel and spoke with Deborah. Kurt was asleep. Deborah confirmed Lucienne's improvement and shared with Eddie her concerns about Kurt's drinking.

"He must be pretty bad tonight, Mom, if Deborah's concerned because while I was with them she drank as much as he did," Eddie said.

Upon hearing this, I knew I would be canceling our Saturday morning flight to St. John. What I did not know was whether Kurt would agree to come home.

"I'm going to call Canada now and tell Kurt we changed our minds about coming up to St. John, and tell him to come home." It was well past midnight when Eddie and I finished talking and said good-night. I still had one more call to make—to Kurt.

❧ 21 ☙

History Revealed

I WAS NERVOUS AS I DIALED THE PHONE. Kurt answered on the first ring, a muffled "Hullo."

"It's me, Mom. Kurt. You need to come home."

Silence.

"Eddie called the hospital tonight. Lucienne's recovering and there's no need for Dad or me or you to be there."

Another long silence ensued during which my mind unhinged itself and took a slide into panic. Then like a Japanese fan, Kurt folded—no resistance, no argument, perhaps relief.

"Okay, I'll come home tomorrow."

"Good. Are you drinking?"

"A little."

"Are you alone?"

"No, Deborah's still with me."

"Will she speak to me?" I asked.

He handed her the phone. Although I had never spoken to Deborah before, I felt that the seeds of a relationship with her had been sown within the last twenty-four hours. On our trip to the airport on Wednesday, the four of us talked about how totally alone Deborah would be if and when Lucienne died. We told the boys they could tell her we would be there for her and help her should that happen. I knew from my earlier conversation with Eddie of Deborah's happy reaction when they conveyed this message to her. This gave me the courage to contemplate asking for her help in getting Kurt on a plane and back to New Jersey the following day. However, I soon learned our offer to help her had developed a life of its own in its many translations. We started with the usual formalities, "Hello. It's nice to finally talk to you," we each said in turn.

And then she began to thank me profusely for inviting her to live with us in New Jersey when Lucienne died. I took a deep breath as I realized the disparity between my offer and Deborah's perception of it. Live with us—could it come to that? Help in its original offer meant guidance, support, tuition for education or vocational training, money to get by on when Lucienne's disability checks stopped. But give up my privacy; give up my quiet house to the revolving door that taking in this stranger/sister would entail—could I do that?

My clinical training clicked in. Although I felt blindsided, I tried to remain objective and redirect the conversation. Of course, Deborah was concerned about her own future. She had no way of knowing that, at that moment, I was consumed with Kurt.

"This must be a very difficult time for you," I said.

"Yes," she answered, "but I'm glad I'm not alone anymore, and that I have my brothers." She was talkative, evidently like her mother, and she sounded sober. I told her about my conversation with Eddie minutes earlier—his call to the hospital, his belief that Kurt was out of control with his drinking, and his exaggeration of Lucienne's condition.

Deborah agreed with Eddie's evaluation of Kurt. She went on to tell me how Kurt reminded her of Eric, their father. Tall and lean, they had the same lanky body, the same high forehead and hairline that formed a perfect vee. "He's the spitting image of Eric," she said.

She told me she had a professional photograph of Eric taken when he had his band that she kept with her professional photograph of Kurt, taken when he was with his band. In the two separate photos, each of them were about the same age, sitting with one leg folded over the other while strumming the guitar that lay easy in each of their laps. "Kurt not only looks like Eric but even sounds like him, that's what scares me," she said. It was then that she told me how Eric's drunkenness ruled and ruined her life as constant seizures from alcoholism left him incapacitated and ugly.

Deborah had opened the door to alcohol. Here was my opportunity to enter with my own consuming preoccupation. "Is Kurt's drinking upsetting you?"

"Yes," she said cautiously.

I continued to listen as she told me she could not go through it again, not even with her brother. Similarities between Kurt and Eric were causing her to re-enter the trauma of the past with her alcoholic father.

"I told Kurt I won't be around him if he drinks. In fact, I told him not to come back in April if he's still drinking," Deborah said.

She told me she was sorry about the kidnapping mix-up, acknowledging the Children's Services report she and Eddie had read the previous night. Now she knew there was no baby scam. She would try to convince her mother.

Sitting in my kitchen, dark except for the lemony slice of moonlight on the kitchen table, I confided to this stranger/sister my fears about my son. Could she help me? I asked. I was relying on this young woman, so far away and troubled more than I could know, to see my son through the night and onto a plane back home the following day.

* * *

KURT'S ACTIVE BATTLE WITH ALCOHOLISM began the night he returned from Canada. Like Bob before him, there had been previous incidents around drinking. The most serious was in early 1996 when, after leaving a Super Bowl party, he was issued a DWI. Kurt had gone with Cath to watch the Super Bowl at a friend's house. He was not feeling well and left the party at around 7:00 p.m. to go home. He no sooner left the party than he was stopped. The local police had announced that they would be out en masse that Sunday, and Kurt came to Bob and me to balk about the perceived unfairness of his having been stopped. We took it seriously. The mandatory penalty, as it had been for Bob, was loss of his license for six months and attendance at Alcoholics Anonymous. Bob went to AA meetings with Kurt. He spoke to him from his own experience, from knowledge gained in his own battle with alcohol. Kurt listened politely, he engaged with those who reached out to him at meetings, but he could not find it in himself to call himself an alcoholic. He truly believed he could drink normally, and this DWI was an aberration caused by an overzealous police campaign.

Perhaps he was right, we eventually thought. This seemed to be an isolated incident. In all other areas, his life was going smoothly. His wedding had taken place three months later. His painting business was steady if not flourishing. Cath and he were very much in love, and Cath gave no indication that drinking was interfering with their lives. She also believed his DWI was bad luck. We tried to watch him from afar—and in time bought into his belief about overzealous cops. He got his license back, and there were no more incidents. And now this telephone call from Eddie, as distraught as he had ever been about his brother, reporting Kurt's three-day drinking binge while traveling in Canada.

The following night, we all breathed a collective sigh of relief when Kurt safely disembarked at Kennedy airport. Bob met with Kurt and Cath the following day, in what Kurt had since come to refer to as "the sit-down." With carefully chosen words, Bob painted a graphic picture for Kurt, showing him how he had missed out on one of the most significant events of his life, meeting his mother for the first time. Bob tried to illustrate for Kurt that, by being drunk, he was not truly present those days in Canada, but floating through time on the fumes of alcohol.

Kurt said nothing, but his clenched jaw and avoidance of eye contact spoke for him. He was not buying it.

I wrote him a long letter, detailing why I believed he had a problem, referencing his brush with drugs at eighteen. I met him for lunch a few days later, the letter in my pocket. I talked and talked while our hamburgers turned cold on the plate. I never gave him the letter. I could tell by his responses to me that he was steeped in denial, and I was afraid my giving him a written history of his mistakes might alienate him further.

I went to lunch with Cath the following week. She was bewildered by Bob's and my strong reactions. She believed Kurt could control his drinking. I recognized myself in her. I told her how once I had been just like her, believing that Bob was not powerless over alcohol. I told her about the mistakes I made, long before she and Kurt married, and about what I had learned about addiction since then. I gave her literature to read and kissed her and told her to call us anytime she needed support.

Determined to prove us all wrong, Kurt didn't drink for three weeks. And then it happened, an event that changed his life.

It was an ordinary night, February 28, 1998. Kurt was invited to a friend's house to watch a hockey game on TV. He had no intention of drinking. He could control his drinking. He brought a case of soda. Yet without plan or intent, he drank. He could not remember picking up the first one, nor could he remember the subsequent drinks. He could not remember most of the night; the memory was gone. But the next morning he was, for the first time, afraid. His lack of control suddenly became apparent to him. That night became the last time he drank alcohol. Like his father before him, he could not account for that moment of knowing.

Years later, Kurt would tell me, "Maybe it was divine inspiration or an epiphany, but something inside me was going nuts. It was as though an internal choice pushed its way outward. Something snapped. I'd had enough."

Over the next few days, he sought out his brothers and his sister and asked for their help. During meetings with them he opened his heart. Each in turn loved him and supported his efforts to help himself. But it was Bob who was able to help him the most. It was Bob who dropped everything to go to him. For the following three months, they talked and talked. Sometimes they met early in the morning, before work, and went to an AA meeting, other times they met in the early evening for a hamburger before going on to a meeting together. Sobriety was hard. Kurt told his friends that he was no longer drinking, but being with them, being with others who could enjoy a beer without incident, took tremendous effort. His friends didn't really understand. "Just have one," he heard more than once. He began to isolate himself, withdrawing from others to avoid the temptation to drink. A strain started to show in his marriage. Eventually, even AA meetings got to be too much for him. The anxiety of his early twenties that had clustered around performing came back full force in the form of a generalized anxiety disorder.

One desperate winter morning, after a sleepless, anguish-filled night, he pulled himself out of the house and instead of going to his job made his way to Robert's office. It was a risk. It was well known in the family that Robert was pretty much uncompromising in his standards and less inclined to empathize than to urge a "just do it" stance. Yet it was this quality that drew Kurt to his big brother.

Robert turned off his phone, closed his office door and listened for a couple of hours. He didn't judge Kurt, but rather offered him respect for overcoming his denial that, like an iron weight, had kept him anchored to alcohol. Something within Kurt shifted. "Go see Mom," Robert finally said. "She'll know what to do at this point."

Twenty minutes later, Kurt, his eyes red and his face covered by his big paint-splattered hands, crumpled like an empty bag at my kitchen table. Symptoms of a full-blown panic attack infiltrated his body. Beads of perspiration broke out across his lip and forehead. The shaking started somewhere in his chest, and spread into his limbs until his whole body was trembling. He placed his right hand over his left and squeezed it in an attempt to quiet the violent shaking. I put my arms around him and held him tight. The panic ran its course and finally abated. I snapped into clinical mode. He needed medication. I asked his permission, and called the best psychiatrist I knew and referred my son. So began his treatment for anxiety disorder, with a psychiatrist who, for the next several months, monitored the anti-anxiety medication that allowed him to function.

Kurt also began seeing a therapist to address the underlying feelings he could no longer self-medicate with alcohol. All the pain around his early life had burst like a boil, saturating his body and mind with its poison. He talked about his past in therapy. He practiced deep breathing and thought-stopping techniques. He took his medication and he persisted. Gradually he improved. Every once in a while he stopped by the house for lunch and what he called a "kitchen-table therapy session." In time, we talked about the DYFS report that neither of us had read. Kurt called Eddie, and Eddie gave him the report. And so it happened. After our lunch of tuna sandwiches was finished, Kurt went out to his truck and got the manila envelope containing the report written almost thirty years before. He and I sat next to each other at the kitchen table and finally had the courage to confront those pages from the past.

Prepared by the Children's Aid Society of Yarmouth County in 1972, it was a legal-sized document, six pages long. It was separated into two sections, the initial contact and the final disposition.

According to the report, Eric Deveau had initiated the first contact with the agency on April 24, 1968, when he called the office for financial help. Excerpts from that first interview in a section of the report labeled FAMILY HISTORY provided a window into the background that culminated in the court order to apprehend the children on February 17,1971.

The final report, as transcribed below, summarizes interventions that took place between 1968 and 1971.

CHILDREN'S AID SOCIETY OF YARMOUTH COUNTY
PROVINCE OF NOVA SCOTIA
PROTECTION CASE FOR: MR. & MRS. ERIC DEVEAU
SOCIAL REFERRAL:
On April 24, 1968 Mr. Deveau called the office and wanted me to come up to see him as he was in difficulties.

Following this were several paragraphs which included personal background information on Lucienne and Eric and which described the living conditions that the family were enduring between 1968 and 1970. It read partially as follows:

At the present time they are paying $8.00 a week rent at _____. The house is very much in need of repairs; in fact it is certainly not worth $8.00 a week. They have six rooms; several of them way up on the third floor which they do not use. The rooms are certainly not suitable to live in.

CASE HISTORY

This case has been periodically before the Children's Aid Society since 1968.

Prior to 1970, workers had attempted to work with this family, mainly to provide financial help and supply material needs for the home.

Mr. & Mrs. Deveau had managed to present a decent picture to the community, and the only complaints received were about the children appearing naked in front of the attic window. During this period Mr. Deveau was not working.

In September 1970, this case was given to me when additional complaints about child neglect arose.

At first, Mr. & Mrs. Deveau were uncooperative, mainly Mrs. Deveau. She claimed persecution and meddling on the social worker's part. The home conditions were poor and by helping financially to provide cleaning aids and by being patient, worker was able to visit weekly without much conflict from Mrs. Deveau.

During the first two months, obvious problems in child rearing were discussed and the children became less confined. Case work was given; however, the Deveaus were extremely defensive and an excuse could be found for every problem. If the house was dirty or cold, it was because they couldn't get help from Municipal Welfare, and this became a common complaint. No one was willing to help them. Worker arranged many case conferences with all agencies involved and it was learned that the Deveaus drained what they could and went on to the next agency.

When the agencies were informed, we received co-operation and worker continued to work with the family. In order that the children could learn from peer groups, worker arranged for the three children to spend two days a week with a foster mother who had small children in her home. This went on from November 1970 until February 1971.

Clothes were provided by Municipal Welfare: bedding by Catholic Social Services; however, progress was intense for a few days and then dropped off completely.

Mrs. Deveau was taken on food shopping trips to learn the best buys for their limited budget.

Several arrangements were made so that the children, and particularly Catherine, could be observed and assessed by professional people.

_____, Psychologist, saw these children prior to apprehension. Catherine was admitted to the Isaac Walton Killam Children's Hospital for neurological assessment. Medical help was also offered, re: inoculations, examinations. Worker assisted in getting these children to a doctor frequently as possible. The reasons were twofold (a) to keep their medical health good (b) attempt to localize some form of neglect, i.e. speech, teeth etc.

Surprisingly, the parents cooperated with worker in this, although they did not originate the visits themselves.

The Public Health Nurse came in to deal with lice and their treatment and later for pre-natal care.

Between November 25th, 1970, and February 15, 1971, worker made 52 calls on the Deveau home, as well as related visits to collateral.

During an interview, Mr. Deveau would be very amiable but he lived in a land of illusion. He had a different plan each day to make a living, always tomorrow; he would look up a job offer. These never materialized.

Mrs. Deveau was always prompt with an excuse or answer "why not" and case work became impossible as the Deveaus would not admit the difficulties were caused by them and could be solved by them.

In February, Mr. Deveau was drinking heavily. Mrs. Deveau was expecting and delivery was expected soon. Mrs. Deveau and her husband had not made a small amount of permanent progress toward looking after their children properly.

By this time, I had been looking for legal grounds for which I could apprehend the children, and these came when Mr. Deveau got drunk and left the children unattended while he was unconscious, and Mrs. Deveau was in the Hospital with a false labor.

Home conditions had become terrible and neither parent would correct the situation.

The children were apprehended in February, 1971.

DESCRIPTION OF HOME AND NEIGHBORHOOD

Prior to apprehension, the Deveaus lived in an upstairs apartment, located on the outskirts of Yarmouth. It was an older home consisting of two apartments.

There were three bedrooms, a bathroom, a living room, and kitchen on one level, and two rooms in the attic.

The apartment was heated by an oil pot burner in the kitchen, a hot plate in the living room, and a coal stove (kitchen type) in the hall between the living room and bedrooms. Although the apartment was small in size, there was not adequate heat. The attic was only heated by what seeped upstairs.

Thirty percent of the windows were broken and covered by cardboard or boards, and it was a usual occurrence for the pipes to freeze and the hot water to disappear. The landlord refused to fix the apartment because it had been in very good shape when the Deveaus moved in.

Mr. & Mrs. Deveau used the bedroom across from the living room. There was also a crib there for Kurtis. Catherine slept in the next room to them and Eddie across the hall, next to the living room.

Each room was sparsely furnished and very dirty. Catherine's room had only a single bed and the same with Eddy's room. Mr. & Mrs. Deveau had a couple bed, the crib and a dresser. At no time did I see the beds made with sheets, pillow cases, etc. They were always being washed, or on the line, Mrs. Deveau claimed. There was insufficient bedding and what there was, was soiled.

The living room had an old TV, not working, an old pedal organ, a sofa and chair that was once blue, but now was discolored with dirt. The floor was once carpeted but had been worn down and had become thin and soiled and stuck to the floor.

The kitchen had only a sink, an old wringer washer, a round table and two chairs.

HISTORY OF NEGLECT

The Deveau children are apparently healthy, although Catherine has severely decayed teeth and Strobismus in her eyes. No attention had been given these conditions prior to apprehension of the children.

The two boys were also healthy in spite of home conditions. However, all three children exhibited strange behavior when worker visited, behavior which lead one to believe they seldom saw outsiders. The two oldest children could not speak coherently. Both were afflicted with Echolalia whereby they repeated whatever was spoken to them.

Neglect was observed in the following manner:

The three children were required to play in the attic, and were never seen playing outside or with other children. The home was usually very dirty, with poor sleeping materials, which were frequently wet or soiled.

If the children were misbehaving or just underfoot, they were often locked in bedrooms alone. From this, the children suffered many emotional problems which accounted for their bizarre behavior. (see Psychologist's Report) (Not included)

Mr. Deveau received financial help but could not refrain from drinking excessively to provide decently for his family. Kurtis would be kept in his highchair continually when not locked in a room. They couldn't cope with the children making a noise or getting underfoot.

Also, in the home was a full-grown German Shepherd, which used any part of the home for its functions. Mr. & Mrs. Deveau would close the door to a room if the dog had messed there.

It was an indication to me of what the children might be going through when the dog would fall over from terror if you moved towards it. It was starved for affection and would literally be all over you if you indicated no harm to it.

The Deveau home was indeed in an area on the Main road and with no children around to play with, but this is no excuse for the children not to have been seen out playing since the Deveaus came here over four years ago.

Neither parents were friends with neighbors, and were on a poor relationship basis with those close by the home.

COURT HISTORY

After apprehension took place on February 17th, 1971, the case first came to Court on March 3rd, 1971. It was adjourned at this time for two reasons—Mrs. Deveau was expecting, and they were also represented by the Agency Council through Legal Aid Services.

It again appeared before Judge Black on March 31st, 1971, but was adjourned pending new evidence until May 12th, 1971.

On this date, evidence was heard, and an adjournment was granted in order to allow Mr. & Mrs. Deveau an opportunity to improve their circumstances.

Court was slated for June 23rd, however, it again convened on July 7th, 1971. On this date additional evidence was heard and His Honor Judge Black adjourned for consideration of the evidence, and to read the evidence in its entirety at one time. Worker and client's counsel were instructed to submit a brief, if desired, within ten days of receipt of Court evidence.

On September 2nd, 1971, Court again convened and on this date, after due deliberation, the children were made Wards of the Children's Aid Society of Yarmouth County.

The report was signed by the protection officer, and the administrator of the court and was dated September 15, 1971.

We read in stunned silence. We both sighed audibly upon finishing the final section. I was crying. Kurt was surprisingly calm as he stood and stretched his cramped back to his full height. He smiled his slow smile. "The truth is hard, but not knowing is harder," he said, and when he added with a mischievous grin, "Well, I guess we're all lucky I'm not feral," I knew everything was going to be all right.

"Oh, Kurt," was all I could said as I reached up and hugged him.

ജ 22 ര

The Spring Trip

THE ORIGINAL PLANS FOR ALL OF US to go to St. John for the reunion at
the end of April were resumed. Events surrounding Lucienne's illness
had unfolded so rapidly that no one had thought to call Catherine, in
Yarmouth, the day of Kurt and Eddie's hastily put-together January trip to
Canada. Upon learning of it the following weekend, she was upset. She rightfully felt left out, not so much because she missed an opportunity to see her
mother, but because her brothers were in Canada a mere three hundred miles
away and had not gotten in touch with her. When they told her they were still
planning to go ahead with the April trip, she was appeased.

On April 24, 1998, Kurt and Eddie, Eddie's wife, Barbara, and
Kurt's wife, Cath, and Bob and I made our way to the airport to board a
plane for the "reunion." As we waited in the boarding area, Bob and Kurt
went to get coffee, and Cath and Barbara were chatting with each other.
Eddie and I were sitting together on one of the banks of blue plastic chairs
bolted to the floor. Eddie had evidently been waiting for a chance to be
alone with me. Half sitting on the edge of his chair, he pulled a wrapped
package out of his knapsack and handed it to me with a nervous smile.

"Mom," Eddie said, "I want you to have this before we meet
Lucienne."

Oh, what's coming? I thought. "Do you want me to open it now?"
"Yes."

Inside the package was a slim volume of inspirational poems with watercolor illustrations entitled, *Forty-Two Gifts I'd Like to Give You.* Inside the book was an envelope containing a card. Underlined on the card was a line of verse that read "There's no other mom like you." Inside the card was a letter.

"Should I read it now?" I asked.

"Yes, read the card and letter. I want to be with you when you read it."

And so I read—

Dear Mom,

For a long time I have been trying to come up with the one word or phrase that best suits my unyielding love for you and Dad. When I was younger, I used to think we were like the Brady Bunch, but that was too sappy. Then for a while, I used to relate us to Kennedy's Camelot theme. You the Queen and Dad the King, but they had too many tragedies. Anyway, it seemed fitting when I was a teenager. Since that time, however, I have come to realize that the only word that I can say that epitomizes my true feelings for you and dad is that you are my heroes. Thank you for saving me from a life of poverty and giving me a chance to live a productive life.

Talking to other people who were adopted has made me realize how fortunate and blessed I am. Other adopted people who have brothers and sisters who are biological to their parents tell me that they felt they were treated differently than the biological children. That saddens me because I can truly say that neither you nor Dad ever made me feel any less loved or not a part of this family ever. From the first day I met you till now, you have made me feel like your own.

Remember the first night? The first thing we saw was a poster on the front door in French welcoming Kurt and I to the U.S. It was late but still I managed to play a few keys on the piano that night. For the next several years life was grand. Everything was a big deal. I remember Dad letting me choose the very first family trip. We pulled out a map and drove to Pennsylvania to the coal caves. What fun we had. It was a perfect Norman Rockwell kind of life. We still had the milk delivered in bottles on the back porch. You could leave the door unlocked and not worry about being robbed or murdered. Times sure have changed since then. Then the 1980s happened. Things were moving fast. New cars, new house, new schools, dad was drinking and things were getting bad. I was stealing money and was wrecking cars. Ah, the memories. What strength you had in protecting your children for so long from the alcohol abuse. Things could have gone differently if it wasn't for your faith in God. Thank God for Dad's strength and his ability to change so dramatically.

Defining a mother has been a challenge in recent months. I wanted you to know how I separate the two. As far as I am concerned, Lucienne was my birth mother. It's as simple as that. I believe with the knowledge of my past out in the open, it will benefit me in the future. The limited and irrational conversations with Lucienne have proven to me that she couldn't and shouldn't be a parent to anyone. This includes Deborah. My only hope is that Deborah can be saved after Lucienne is gone.

I chose this card because it represents the words I've never been able to find to show how thankful I am to be your son. They say 'blood is thicker than water." I'm glad to be the exception. This will always be a part of me and Kurt. We can only live day by day. You are my mother by choice. I feel special being chosen by you and Dad.

Thus, on an early spring morning, in a crowded Newark airport, amid the chatter of travelers, my son orchestrated this symphony of love and validation that echoes still. Within hours, we would all be in St. John. The reunion was really going to happen. Eddie was to call Deborah when the plane touched down in St. John, and she was to make her way to the hotel to meet Catherine and her parents and us. Lucienne might or might not be with Deborah. She had made no promises for Friday. The meeting with Lucienne that was set in stone, the centerpiece of the trip, was to take place at 10:00 a.m. on Saturday.

* * *

THE LOBBY OF THE HOTEL FLOATED in fluorescent lights and vinyl columns masquerading as marble. Disco music thrumming from an open bar shook even the plastic leaves and the lights strung on the potted plants. Revolving

230

glass doors swished as people pushed their way into the lobby. Teenagers milled around the lobby as a teacher with a placard that read "Science Club" desperately tried to corral them. A girl in a flowing orange robe, trying to sell roses, was being escorted to the door by a security guard. It was bedlam.

Scanning the crowd, each of us was looking for Catherine and Deborah. The boys knew what Deborah looked like from their earlier visit, and Catherine had sent her picture. We were standing near the front desk, inching our way forward in line to register for rooms. My eyes were burning from the combination of cigarette smoke and staring intensely into every face in the lobby. And then, as if drawn into the orbit of a sudden flood of light, I saw Eddie and Kurt seeing Catherine seeing them. She was there, rushing ahead of her parents, who trailed behind her.

"Are you–?" she said.

"Are you–?" they said.

Their eyes locked, and suddenly all three were in each other's arms, rocking back and forth, holding each other, as tears of joy streamed from their eyes. They were an island unto themselves in the sea of people rushing around the hotel lobby. Parents and wives stood aside, receding into the background like brush strokes on a painting. The air was charged. Strangers stopped.

"What's going on?" someone asked.

We told them.

"How many years have they been separated?"

"Twenty-five."

Total strangers welled up with tears.

What is there in human nature that draws us into such moments of reconciliation? Is there not in each of us the residue of a yearning to be whole, to capture what we have abandoned or what has abandoned us? It is like grasping something under water. It floats before us, always just out of reach. When we witness those rare moments when others recover their loss, we recognize our own obscure longings and desire floods to fill the cup of our own emptiness.

Bob and I, with Jon and Femme, moved to the side. We introduced ourselves to each other and sank into the upholstery of the wingback chairs

231

clustered next to the smoky glass window serving as the wall of the hotel. We began to talk tentatively about our experiences as adoptive parents while keeping an eye out for Deborah's arrival.

Jon and Femme had been dairy farmers. Married as teenagers in Norway, they had immigrated to Canada some time during World War II. They spent the next thirty-five years raising their family of seven children and working their farm. Each morning they, along with their children, were up before dawn to milk the cows. After the milking, Jon climbed into his truck to deliver the milk in huge tin cans to customers in neighboring towns. As the children grew up and left the farm and the milk industry became more regulated and mechanized, Jon decided it was time to make a change. He had long been drawn to another calling, the ministry. In his mid-fifties, he and Femme sold the farm, and Jon began a course of study to become a reverend. It was shortly after his ordination that he and Femme became acutely aware of Catherine's situation. The foster parents, with whom Catherine was living, were members of Jon's new congregation in Yarmouth. They were getting ready to return Catherine to Children's Services. Upon hearing this, Jon and Femme were moved by Catherine's plight and her history. Believing they now had the time and means to offer her a stable home, they applied to adopt her.

It would be a difficult decision to live with. At eleven years old, Catherine had been hurt over and over again. Trusting was almost impossible for her. She rebelled in all sorts of ways. "There were whole years when we could not manage her, and it nearly ripped our family apart," Femme told us as we sat across the lobby from our excited children. "We almost lost our other children."

"She seems so docile," I said. "It's hard to picture the behavior you're describing."

"When she was eighteen, she met George, her husband, and she changed."

"We were surprised that she asked us to make this trip with her," said Jon, "surprised and happy."

Not five feet away, at a dime-sized cocktail table, Catherine was telling her version of her life to her brothers. I could hear her short clipped sentences

as she glided past details of her childhood and adolescence like a skier coming down the mountain. She'd learned to survive by leaving the past in the past.

"It was all bad until I met George," she told her brothers from behind
a sudden blush that worked its way from her neck to her forehead whenever
she talked about herself.

At last Deborah arrived, pushing her way through the revolving doors,
her girlfriend, Trina, at her side. Later, we would learn Deborah had been
scared about this meeting, scared to meet Catherine, scared to meet Barbara
and Cath, scared to meet both sets of parents. She and her friend walked past
the hotel twice before venturing in. Each had "taken something" to blunt the
edge of nervousness. Its effect had made them spacey and giddy. Deborah
stayed no more than thirty minutes and left hastily, but not before exploding
her homemade bomb.

"Hi, bros," she said in a husky voice when she walked up to the three
of them seated at the little cocktail table. Kurt and Eddie sprang from their
chairs to greet her. Then Eddie reached out for Catherine, to bring her into
the circle. The city girl and the country girl, sisters were facing each other
for the first time. Each hung back, as if to size up the moment before entering it.

Catherine's face was flushed with excitement. Her mouth was a taut
pink ribbon that she had to concentrate on so as not to reveal the pink gums
where her front teeth should have been. Her dark hair, parted near the center,
hung in soft curls to her shoulders. Shorter hair on either side of her forehead
created a fringe over the sides of her large horn-rimmed glasses. The whole
effect reminded me of an owl, all eyes, observing quietly. Later she showed us
how each day she swept her hair under the hair net she must wear while working in the local fish market. Her black jeans and white cotton blouse were
spotless and functional, as was the vinyl jacket she never zipped, even when the
wind blew hard. Slung over her shoulder and across her chest was the thin
strap of the pocketbook that held pictures of George and her three children.
It rested on her left hip all weekend.

Deborah, on the other hand, was all attitude and sparkle. She was a presence. The whites of her eyes were headlights framing the dilated pupils.

Glistening auburn hair framed her face in a thick gleaming cloud. She and her friend Trina wore matching jeans and black leather jackets with matching logos embossed on the back. Trina stayed as close to Deborah as Catherine's pocketbook stayed to her. She was a thin girl with so much hair that her face got lost under its multiple blonde tiers. She said little.

The sisters shook hands and embraced tentatively. Kurt pulled two more chairs up to the cocktail table. It was a short time after this that I saw from across the lobby the stricken look on Kurt and Eddie's faces as Deborah spoke. It was a look of pure disbelief. Deborah was telling them that Lucienne would not be coming to meet us on Saturday as planned.

"Why? Each of them asked in panic.

"Well, she isn't feeling that well. Besides she's angry because she was not more included in picking the dates."

Kurt and Eddie were speechless with shock and disappointment. Lucienne had known of the dates for weeks. Catherine could no longer be disappointed. She expected nothing from her mother, and in fact had still not committed herself to meet with Lucienne. But Kurt and Eddie were devastated. Deborah told them she would go home and try to convince her mother to come to lunch on Saturday, but she could promise nothing.

"You don't know how stubborn Mom is," she said laughingly.

Deborah promised to call Eddie early the following morning with an update on her progress in convincing Lucienne to meet her three children. We all agreed to meet early the next morning for breakfast. Catherine, Kurt, and Eddie stayed up and talked into the wee hours.

None of us were able to sleep that night. We tossed and turned, wondering if the purpose of our trip was in the process of being aborted. We were all at Lucienne's disposal.

* * *

EDDIE KEPT HIS CELL PHONE ON THE TABLE as we ate our breakfast and lingered over coffee, waiting to hear from Deborah. But when the phone rang, it was to torture her children once more with her ambivalence. Lucienne was not coming. We were puppets dangling on the end of strings she controlled. Deborah promised to call again, and the nine members of our caravan took to the streets to pass the time with sightseeing.

The streets of St. John were narrow and tired looking. Abandoned stores, their windows cracked and boarded up, gave testimony to the wrecked economy that had driven prices to unfathomable heights. We visited a farmers' market where the vegetables were displayed alongside tee shirts and pocketknives. Willing the cell phone to ring again, all nine of us walked and walked. Somewhere in those measured steps a moment transpired that sent me reeling.

Catherine and I happened to be walking together. I could hear Eddie and Barbara and Cath several yards behind us as they walked with Jon and Femme. Bob and Kurt had paused to take pictures of a huge wooden Indian, a totem pole of sorts, which stood in what served as the town square, welcoming visitors. Wind was blowing up the cobblestone street from the harbor carved into the jutting edge of St. John that butted into the Bay of Fundy. Catherine and I were chatting, with our heads down and buttressed against the wind coming off the bay. Catherine had relaxed, I could tell by the spontaneous way she now spoke, no longer guarding the embarrassing space between her lips. She was telling me about her children, how "little George" wanted to come on the trip to meet his uncles, how her little girl needed stitches in her chin last week after she fell, how her new house flooded each time it rained. Then I heard it—as though the wind whispered it casually into my ear. Catherine called me "Mom."

At first I thought I made it up, an auditory hallucination related to the question that had glued itself onto my thoughts and grown into a fantasy during the last two days. What would life have been like had we known of Catherine's plight all those years ago? Would we have returned to Canada and tried to adopt her? How would her life have been different if she had remained with her brothers? Evidently, she and I were having similar thoughts, only her fantasy spilled into her vocabulary.

Around two o'clock, exhausted from tension and walking, we returned to the hotel. We tried to convince ourselves that the cell phone had not been transmitting during our trek around St. John. Or perhaps Deborah lost the number and left a message in one of our rooms. Eddie checked the room—there was no message, and it was 3:00 p.m. We had all been in St. John for twenty-four hours. The hour for the reunion had come and gone.

Tired, all nine of us crammed into Bob's and my hotel room to discuss what to do next. Eddie called Deborah, and Deborah put Lucienne on the phone. Using every ounce of salesmanship he possessed, Eddie begged and then he begged some more.

"Okay," Lucienne finally said. "You and Catherine and Kurt can come over here to see me if you come right now." Catherine steeled herself. She had to make her decision. This might be her only opportunity.

"We'll watch out for you," said Kurt. Catherine raised her eyebrows as if to punctuate her doubt that anyone could protect her from Lucienne. Nervously, she said, "Yes." She would go with her brothers.

Kurt and Eddie each came over and kissed Bob and me. Catherine watched them from where she was seated on the edge of a bed. She stood up and walked the few steps to the chair where Femme was seated. She put her arms around her mother and kissed her. Then she walked the few steps to Jon, who was half leaning on the bureau, and did the same. When the door banged behind them, I saw tears running down Femme's cheeks. Jon had taken her hand and was patting her arm.

"What's the matter?" I asked, confused.

"I can't remember the last time she kissed me. It was probably the day she got married over ten years ago. Just that kiss was worth this trip."

The three siblings left. Jon and Femme, Barbara and Cath returned to their respective rooms. We waited.

ဆ 23 ℃ℛ

The Reunion

ABOUT TWO HOURS LATER, EDDIE CALLED US from the cab as they were returning to the hotel. The visit had gone well. During little snatches of time during the next twenty-four hours, he filled Bob and me in on the details of that visit, the shock of the circumstances in which they found their mother.

The only other time he and Kurt had seen Lucienne was in the pristine environment of the hospital a few months earlier. This was different. They found themselves in a barracks-like complex of unkempt two-story dwellings. The place reminded Eddie of a government dormitory at best, and a tenement at worst. He and Kurt and Catherine bypassed the front door and went down a few steps, as Deborah had instructed them to do, to a basement doorway. Lucienne was there waiting for them, peeking from behind a dirty glass pane. She wore a faded flowered dress, a cross between a nightshirt and a mu-mu. Kurt and Eddie's first impressions were that she appeared healthier than the deathbed image they carried in their heads. This was a relief. A quick calculation led each of them to believe she was physically capable of coming to the hotel, if only they could break through whatever resistance was causing her to refuse. Her face was neutral as she pushed open the door and looked hard at each of them. Her gaze lingered on Catherine, whom she had not seen since

1971. Lucienne did not react immediately, but seemed to pause to collect her thoughts. And then, "So I finally see you all together. What a sight," she said, shaking her head in disbelief or awe, they couldn't be sure. They all smiled, and gingerly followed her down a narrow cinder-block corridor that had been carelessly painted beige. Kurt and Eddie kept Catherine between them, knowing her anxiety and how hard this meeting was for her.

Lucienne shuffled along, and then stopped at one of the many steel-gray metal doors along the hallway. She pushed on the door.

Deborah stood just inside a small windowless room that served as the living room and kitchen. Lucienne, a bit breathless now, made her way to a large overstuffed chair and sat down. Stains had bled into the upholstery, and what looked like syrup from medicine was crusted on the vinyl footstool on which she propped her shoeless feet. A soiled kitchen towel thrown across the back of the chair served as a headrest. They could see tufts of cotton batting poking through the threadbare upholstery. Next to her, on a pine box, was a framed picture of Eric, taken when he was in his thirties. In it he was holding his guitar on his lap.

Kurt was startled by the picture. This was the one Deborah had described to Eddie during Lucienne's hospitalization two months earlier. He felt he was looking at himself. The same lanky frame, the same soulful eyes and dark clipped beard, even the way Eric was holding the guitar, tenderly balanced over crossed legs. Next to the framed photograph, propped against a dirty white candle, were two other loose snapshots, frayed at the edges and begging to be dusted, of Eric and Lucienne. Nailed to the wall behind the pine box was a painting of Jesus, giving the whole arrangement the feel of a primitive altar. Several plastic containers of pills were lined up on a chipped wooden table that stood against the wall. The TV blasted a game show. Lucienne told Deborah to lower the volume. Next to her chair were the remnants of a tuna fish sandwich and several empty coke cans. Alongside, on the floor, was her Nintendo game. The room was hot, and they could hear the radiator hissing steam over the sound of the TV.

They started to talk, with Lucienne taking the initiative. She was still angry with Catherine and Eddie. She was unwilling to abide by anything but total devotion to her, and she had rightly intuited Catherine's ambivalence and

Eddie's struggle with his anger. Kurt was another story. He looked so much like Eric that he entranced her. She reserved her warmest feelings for him.

In a withholding mode when they first entered her apartment, Lucienne soon displayed her feisty spirit. They pleaded and cajoled and joked with her, and, after an hour or so, Lucienne relinquished her stubbornness and agreed to come to the hotel for the reunion.

The boys agreed to return after showering and changing, to pick her and Deborah up at the apartment and accompany them. Having had to cancel the original meeting room reserved for us during the day, now Eddie quickly called the hotel and arranged for a private room that we could use at 7:00 p.m. We would all meet there and then go to the restaurant. Eddie requested a piano.

Everyone loves a reunion, and the hotel manager was no exception. He gave us the entire mezzanine, generally reserved for cocktail parties or weddings. Business was slow, the room was available, so he had his staff turn on the lights, remove the cover from the baby grand piano, and unlock the keyboard. "Return the key to my staff when you're finished with the room," he said, patting Eddie on the back and wishing him well.

The three children quickly showered and changed their clothes and returned to Lucienne's apartment to bring her to the hotel. At 6:45 the rest of us gathered outside the bank of elevators that serviced the mezzanine, one of which would bring Lucienne to us.

I had no image of Lucienne in my mind. All the years she floated in the periphery of my life, ethereal and ghostlike, the embodiment of the unknown. I had never seen her picture. I had never heard her voice, nor had I constructed in my mind's eye a face or a body. Subconsciously I seemed to need her to remain without flesh and blood that required reckoning with.

There were a few groupings of chairs to the left of the bank of elevators, and we were a flock of nervous wrens perched on the edges of our seats, waiting. The four elevators faced the glass doors of the restaurant where we had reservations for dinner. To the left of the elevators was the lounge area, which doubled as the hotel's ballroom. It opened out like a huge shell scalloped into the architecture. The ceilings were over twenty-feet high, and the windows were covered by red velvet drapes, giving an operatic quality to the drama about to unfold. A black-lacquered baby grand piano placed in the far corner of the room was the lone witness to our waiting. A soft chime sounded each time one of the elevators stopped. We could hear it from our sentinel spot around the curve of the lounge. Rising in a wave, the six of us hastened to where we could see the elevator doors opening. The lead person, usually Bob, would turn around and report—"It's not them."

Then that final chime, the lingering red light above the elevator door as Kurt and Eddie each grasping one of Lucienne's arms, got her ready to emerge from the oak and mirrored cube of the elevator. Catherine and Deborah came out first. Each hesitated, and with a backward glance spontaneously held open one of the automatic doors of the elevator to keep it from closing too quickly. Lucienne, with Kurt on her right and Eddie on her left, stepped proudly from between the doors being held back for her by her two daughters.

Her face was white as chalk, like a Madonna or a witch. Her blouse was black, as were her slacks. She wore gray wool socks and men's black slippers. From the leg of her pants hung an opaque tube supplying oxygen to a small device clipped to her nostrils. Kurt was carrying a small canvas bag that held the oxygen supply that allowed her lungs, most likely dried as raisins, to tolerate the world.

Her coat was fur. I remembered seeing a raccoon that had been skinned by a farmer when I was just a girl, how he hung the pelt on the wash line then went about butchering the meat for his family of malnourished children. It seemed the same small matted and diseased pelt was covering Lucienne's shoulders. I watched her approach. Her sons looked huge in their winter coats as they bent solicitously towards her, each holding one of her arms, steadying her like a delicate china doll as she put one foot in front of the other. They whispered to her as they brushed snow from her gray hair, and helped her remove a faded woolen scarf. I started to walk toward them.

Mostly it was her eyes that I remembered. At first she squeezed them shut, tightly, as though she was going to cry. But no tears rolled down her cheeks. As the squeeze unscrewed itself, her eyes became visible and seemed to roll back in her head, as if she was searching for something written inside the dome of her skull. When she apparently found it, she began to speak. Her jaw worked around her toothless mouth and she uttered something we could not understand and which might or might not have been meant for us to hear. While she spoke, her head was bent back, and she seemed to be talking to the heavens. We waited for her to finish and then took turns greeting her. I heard Kurt say to Lucienne, "This is our mother, Marion."

I bent down, and said, "Hello, Lucienne."

She reached up and put her arms around me. She felt as small and fragile as a broken bird as she embraced me. She whispered, "Thank you, thank you" into my ear, not once but many times. Joy and relief flooded me as I heard those two words. Of the millions of words in the English language, I could not have chosen better. *She knows. She knows*, I thought dizzily. When I stepped back, or she released me, I could not say which, our boys were standing nearby, and they were smiling.

She was not strong enough to tolerate standing for too long, and we made our way with her into the restaurant. The maître d' had set up a long table to accommodate everyone. Kurt carefully held the vertical tube of oxygen and balanced the canister with his foot while Eddie helped her slip her arms out of her coat. Working together, they maneuvered the canister of oxygen under her chair, and she slid into the seat at the head of the table.

Kurt sat on her left and Eddie on her right. Deborah and Catherine sat alongside their brothers. Deborah's friend Trina sat on her right, across from Barbara and Cath. At the far end of the table, Jon and Femme were on one side facing Bob and me on the other. The boys read the hotel menu with its assortment of offerings to Lucienne and Deborah. After ordering for her, they leaned close as she spoke, so as to catch every word she uttered. I felt removed, like a distant figure painted into the background of some surreal canvas as I watched Lucienne and her children.

Once the food arrived and before picking up her fork to eat, Lucienne reached out for the four hands of her children as if to sanctify the moment. A ripple of silence cascaded down the row of chairs to the opposite end of the table where I sat. Once again, her eyes rolled back in her head. She intoned a long rambling personal prayer, all the while tilting her head toward the ceiling. I could see quizzical glances pass between Kurt and Eddie and Catherine, as each gave up their hands and waited for whatever was going to happen to happen. Only the whites of Lucienne's eyes were visible, the pupils hidden under her upper lids. Fascinated by her willingness to take control of the table, we all followed her lead and tentatively joined hands. Offering grace before a meal at home was not foreign to the boys or to Bob and me. However, we had never prayed in a restaurant! Maybe this woman could teach me something, I thought ironically, as I placed one hand into Jon's and the other into Bob's and bowed my head. If ever there was a time for prayer, it was at this first supper, a quarter-century in the making.

This group acquiescence to her will seemed to strengthen Lucienne as she gazed down the long hushed table. Although she had appeared reticent upon emerging from the elevator, by now her inhibitions were gone. Before long she was telling bawdy jokes and laughing heartily while draping her arms around her boys. She no longer looked fragile. She was having the time of her life.

The table seemed divided by an invisible line, with Lucienne and her children on one end, the rest of us on the other. Bob and I and Jon and Femme engaged each other in conversation. An unspoken agreement had evolved between us to be careful and not infringe on Lucienne's time with her four children. Each of us, as biological parents as well as adoptive parents, could put ourselves in her place, alone with her four children, breaking bread—like a family. There was a sense of finality to the scene taking place at the other end of the table, an intimation that this opportunity was a once-in-a-life-time event. Lucienne deserved to have her time. After all, she had given birth to them, and that was everything.

Gradually the young people got up, and once again Kurt and Eddie were twin attendants, helping their mother back into the open ballroom of the mezzanine. Eddie sat down at the piano for what I knew was the long-fantasized moment when he would play for his mother. Suddenly the cavernous room resounded with a repertoire of popular music. From the doorway I could see Lucienne with a heartfelt smile on her face as she sat herself next to Eddie on the piano bench. Kurt stood behind them, whispering into Lucienne's ear. Not quite knowing where I belonged, I haltingly tucked myself into the deep curve on the opposite side of the piano and stood facing them. Catherine took a place next to me, and the rest of the group spread out along the perimeter of the piano. Lucienne's eyes were closed, and she had a dreamy look on her face as her

The meeting in Canada. Bob, Kurt, Lucienne, Deborah, Eddie, Marion, Catherine, Jon, and Femme.

The meeting in Canada. Deborah, Lucienne, Eddie, Catherine, and Kurt.

243

shoulders swayed in rhythm with the music. When the beat got hot, she half rose from the bench and began to dance in place, hips rotating, arms raised above her head, hands flapping like tiny wings, the oxygen tube, forgotten, bobbling on her thigh. Catherine, momentarily snared by the music, let go the reservations that had kept her a few steps behind her brothers all evening and danced in place. Amazingly, through the music, she became a mirror image of the mother she was having so much trouble accepting.

Eddie changed the pace. Suddenly "Rhapsody in Blue" filled the room. Lucienne, moved by the music or by a flash of insight, looked directly at me across the piano.

"I couldn't have given him this," she said.

"You did." I responded. "It's in his genes."

She liked that, and took the compliment graciously. "Yes, I know the genes are there, but the training is what I could not have given him."

In that incredible exchange lasting less than a minute, made possible by some combination of the right medication, the will of her children, and the prayers of two mothers, we shared our sons. This was the ultimate moment for me, the one memorized like a poem that trembles the heart.

After "Rhapsody in Blue," the strains of something beautiful and new, something I had never heard before, burst forth from the piano. Suddenly, tears welled up in Eddie's eyes.

"What?" I said as I made eye contact with him across the piano.

"This is for you," he mouthed.

I was taken aback as Eddie continued. "I wrote it for you and waited for the right moment, and tonight is the right moment."

But was it? Sudden panic coursed through me as I thought of the difficulty this child of mine had had in figuring out boundaries as a child. Although I felt near to bursting with gratitude and love, I was afraid Lucienne might have heard those words. This was her night, and I did not want to blemish it for her. But she showed no sign. Her eyes were closed again, her face relaxed with that faraway dreamy look.

It was a complicated moment. I could not help but wonder if this music, this song, was the sublimation of Eddie's anger that had been simmering for years. Was this his way of saying to Lucienne, "See, look what you missed out on. This could have been meant for you?"

My heart was beating wildly. Secretly, I had wanted a token, something to reassure me that I would not lose my sons, physically or emotionally, to this woman. Was this Eddie's way of saying, "Have faith, Mom. It's going to be okay"?

* * *

SOON EDDIE WAS TAKING REQUESTS. Can you play "Piano Man?" Do you know any Beatles songs? He played and played one song after another.

I saw the hotel manager with a few waitresses standing in a little semicircle nearby, smiling as they observed this reunion to music. It was getting late; the staff were all taking a peek before their shift ended. Everyone got their favorite song played. Finally, Jon made a request, and, as befitting a minister, it was a hymn—"Amazing Grace." Although, through the years I had heard it hundreds of times, I never heard it in quite the same way as I heard it that night.

"Just hum a few bars to get me started," Eddie said to Jon.

As the opening chords filled the room, Jon began to sing the words. He reached for Femme's hand, and she also began to sing. All at once, as though choreographed and rehearsed, Catherine put her arm around my neck and moved closer, and we both began to sing. Kurt, still standing behind Lucienne, who had remained seated next to Eddie on the piano bench, began to sing. So did Lucienne. Bob, who was standing next to Kurt, one hand lightly resting on Eddie's shoulders and the other on Kurt's back, was singing. Deborah left her friend's side and stood behind her mother, next to Kurt. She joined in. Barbara and Cath were standing alongside Catherine, singing. Everyone seemed to know the words.

> Amazing Grace, how sweet the sound
> That saved a wretch like me
> I once was lost but now am found
> Was blind but now I see
> Through many dangers, toils and snares

I have already come
'Tis grace has brought me safe thus far
And grace will lead me home.

As these last words cascaded from our throats, I felt Catherine begin to tremble. Her brothers, the brothers she had longed for, the brothers she had never given up on, were there. They were singing with her.

I once was lost and now am found . . .

Catherine laid her head on my shoulder and quietly began to sob, as words written a hundred years before she was born filled the room, and filled each one of us with the amazing grace of the night.

"Play it again, Eddie," someone said.

He did, and we sang and sang in that cavernous ballroom on an ordinary spring night. Out of the losses of the past, this disparate band of travelers was braided together in timeless moments that, having happened, could never be undone.

❧ 24 ❧

Afterwards

IT HAD BEEN A MAGICAL EVENING—an evening lived completely in the present, where ties to the past, both distant and recent, were relinquished. It
was as if that ballroom was at the center of some parallel universe, outside the
dimension of time. That night was the last time I laid eyes on Lucienne.

At around 11:00 p.m., Bob and I said good-night and left for our room
on another floor of the hotel. The decision to leave was a complicated one. In
part, I wanted to exit on a high note, with "Amazing Grace" echoing in my
mind, as if by leaving I could preclude any last-minute disaster that might
descend upon the evening. In addition, knowing the conflict Kurt and Eddie had
experienced over their two mothers, I could not help but wonder if my presence
was constraining them in some way. And lastly, a kind of giddiness flooded me.
I felt magnanimous. I wanted to give Lucienne her time in that room, alone with
her four children. That was the wonder of the night for me—that somehow the
core of my misgivings and anger dissipated, and I was overflowing with gratitude to Lucienne for my sons and for their happiness. It was one of those
moments, sacred in a sense, and so infrequent in life, when everything was right
with the world. As unexpected as they are sustaining, they flash, permeating that
part of memory that serves as the bedrock of hope—that they will come again,
full of their own wonder and awe.

And so the night ended for me. But the story continued. Kurt, Eddie, and Catherine took a euphoric Lucienne home around midnight and settled her into her chair amid the clutter of the tiny apartment. They promised to return Sunday morning to spend the day with her. Bob and I flew home.

Weeks later they told me about the changes that took place in Lucienne between Saturday night and Sunday morning. Still in her cotton night shirt, her unwashed face wrinkled with sleep, her teeth sitting in a dish next to her chair, she lumbered towards them. As Kurt bent to kiss her, she raised her arms and placed them around his neck, pulling him down from his six-foot height to her level. With a strength that surprised him, she pulled his mouth to her, and then thrust her tongue into his mouth. Terror seized him. *What the hell was going on?* He disengaged without reacting.

"Here, have a doughnut," he offered, as he pushed the white bakery bag he was holding towards her.

She didn't do it to Eddie, didn't freak him out in the same way. But what was obvious to both of them as the afternoon wore on was that Lucienne was unable to separate Kurt from his biological father, Eric. She flirted, told inappropriate stories, repeated over and over how Kurt looked like and sounded like Eric, her immortalized, idealized dead husband. Although Kurt had made it clear that he no longer drank, she tried to cajole him into having a beer, chiding him for his refusal to drink with her and Deborah. She had Deborah open a cold can of beer and put it in front of him. Deborah, in spite of her avowed disdain for alcohol, was drinking herself, drinking hard. She, according to Kurt, went off on an alcohol-induced rant, "mocking me for not drinking."

The line between reality and fantasy must have blurred for Lucienne, and she was acting out her own long-suppressed impulses. Kurt and Eddie were baffled. They asked themselves and each other what had happened in the few hours since they had delivered her to her apartment the previous night. Perhaps the excitement from Saturday had set off some sort of manic response, or she had forgotten to take her medicine. Maybe she had just been on good behavior when she "met the parents," and, like a teenager set loose, had decided to abandon caution and have an unfettered good time in the safety of her own home. Regardless, Kurt and Eddie, like soldiers sweeping a mine field, carefully stepped around what was confusing or upsetting to them. They were determined to accept her as she was, for better or worse.

Lucienne loved talking about Eric. That afternoon she told the boys stories about how he could have made it big as a musician, but he had been scammed. It seemed there was a Country Western singer who frequented the same bars as Eric. When Eric was down on his luck, he sold the songs he wrote, one by one, for a beer or a few dollars. The singer supposedly went on to have several hits in the United States and Canada. Lucienne knew some of those hits were songs that Eric had composed and bartered away for a beer.

Curious, when he got home to New Jersey, Eddie checked out the famous name Lucienne gave him on the Internet. Sure enough, he found the singer, and details of geography and timing did fit Lucienne's story. This was interesting to Eddie and Kurt but no longer compelling. Both of them knew their own talents, and were at peace with where they were musically. Especially for Kurt, relinquishing the desire for fame and for a famous father was part of his past.

They listened, in quiet horror, as Lucienne told them about herself. She detailed her abused childhood, a tale so extraordinary that it was tempting for them to ascribe it to the realm of fantasy or delusion. The history of her father selling her to a Chinese landowner in the backwoods of Canada when she was barely in her teens and her life as this man's sex slave were lurid and disturbing. Lucienne told them of the four children she bore this man, or one of his many friends, she couldn't be sure. She had so dissociated herself from that part of her past that she laughed as she spoke, in long rambling sentences, about what must have been a series of rapes that had happened fifty years ago. She told them of her cunning, how she eventually ran away from this abuser and the children she had borne while still a child herself. She believed that by escaping, she had the last laugh. Kurt and Eddie and Catherine listened in horror. Yet they remained skeptical.

Hearing this history from Kurt and Eddie when they returned from Canada, I was also horrified. For many years I had worked in a Woman's Trauma Program where I bore witness to women's histories, one after another, histories so traumatic as to be unspeakable. And so I tended to believe Lucienne's history, and in doing so I could not help but admire the fact that she had survived. But like most trauma victims, she had survived at an incredible cost to herself, both in terms of her mental health, and to those with whom she came in contact, especially her children.

When Kurt and Eddie left Lucienne that night, it was with promises to write, to call, to visit their mother at least once a year, and to send her copies of the photographs taken over the course of the weekend. Yet, within a few months, Kurt and Eddie broke those promises and severed all contact with Lucienne and Deborah.

On Mother's Day of 1998, a few short weeks after the reunion, Catherine, the reluctant daughter, picked up the telephone and called Lucienne. The possibility for a relationship between Catherine and her mother had evolved during the reunion. It was as though a great flood had receded, and Catherine was trying to salvage, from the debris left on the shore, the material with which to build a bridge to her mother. She was trying. She wanted to feel that she belonged to this broken family her brothers were trying to resurrect.

Everyone had taken pictures at the reunion, and we all promised to send our random snapshots to the others as if any moment captured on film might turn out to be the one moment of truth, the ultimate portrait that the others could not live without.

But it was Catherine's misfortune to send her pictures out first. Eddie and Kurt received their photos; Lucienne's were delayed even though Catherine sent them from the Yarmouth Post Office at the same time. When learning from the boys that they had received photos, Lucienne took her non-delivery of mail as a personal affront, a deliberate and evil act on Catherine's part. Unaware of her mother's perceived slight, Catherine innocently called Lucienne on Mother's Day.

"Hap-hap-happy Mother's Day," Catherine said with the slight stutter that sometimes broke through when she was nervous.

A blast of expletives and insults erupted from Lucienne. "You sent the damn pictures to your brothers and not to me," she said.

For a minute, Catherine told me, she was speechless. At the same time, tears of rage rolled down her cheeks. She made one attempt to defend herself. "But I did send the pictures to you the same day I posted them to Kurt and Eddie."

"Like hell you did. Then why aren't they here? You're not my child. I want nothing to do with you."

Catherine was finally and irrevocably defeated. Stunned, she hung up the phone. With that action not only Mother's Day ended, but also any future that might have followed for her and Lucienne.

Upon hearing about the debacle of this phone call from their sister, Kurt and Eddie's reactions were simple. Based on their experiences as one of five siblings, each of them had learned long ago that you defend your brother, you defend your sister. You fight for them when the world treats them unfairly. And so they fought for Catherine. At first they tried to reason with Lucienne, explain the unreliability of mail service and the good intentions of her daughter. They let her know that insulting Catherine was insulting them.

Now it was Lucienne's turn to hang up on her sons, who were not willing to join her in maligning their sister. She "wasn't going to listen to this crap." Once again, a conversation with their mother left them drained and bereft. Still, they kept trying.

Deborah wanted to come to New Jersey for a visit. Kurt and Eddie invited her for a week in August, just three months after the reunion. The plan was for Deborah to stay with Kurt and his wife. However, as the summer went on, the boys had second thoughts. It had become obvious during phone calls that Deborah was drinking or using drugs. Kurt was still working on maintaining his own sobriety and was concerned about how he would handle Deborah if she were actively drinking while staying with him and Cath.

The boys decided to postpone the visit. Deborah and Lucienne were furious, and a series of harassing calls, with Deborah screaming, "You're not my brother. I hate you," shattered Kurt and Eddie's desire to try anymore.

And so it ended, like a short fizzle at the end of fireworks. They let Lucienne go. They let Deborah go. Within days, Eddie wrote a final letter to Lucienne. In it he defended Catherine and her misunderstood attempt to share her photographs. He explained his and Kurt's need to cancel Deborah's visit, and he expressed his anger about Deborah's phone tirade. Speaking for Kurt and himself, the final paragraph read—

"We now understand why we were placed for adoption and are grateful that we had the opportunity to meet the both of you. This is an experience that neither of us will have again. It has made our relationship stronger and better than ever. We appreciate each other and our limitations much better. We are both happy to put the matter of who we are and where we come from to a rest."

The letter was signed, "Eddie & Kurt Goldstein."

The act of writing the letter was empowering for the boys. During their early years, they had internalized Lucienne's failures as evidence of their own deficiencies. Now it was different. They could choose to put an end to the pain she continued to inflict. By cutting her out of their lives, they were no longer her victim. In a very real sense, they were freer than they had ever been before. The unknown that periodically haunted them was now known, and the truth was easier to live with than the fantasies that spawned endless questions. Catherine, their sister, had found them, and she needed and loved them. Reciprocating was easy. In giving themselves to her, their lives were enriched. She and her family became their focus for the future of their biological heritage.

✻ ✻ ✻

MEANWHILE, BEING REUNITED WITH KURT and Eddie infused Catherine with a new-found courage. At the time of the reunion, while they were at Lucienne's apartment, Lucienne had rummaged through an old trunk and ferreted out three baptismal certificates. She handed over a yellowed document to each of the three children. Catherine read hers closely. She was baptized in St. Ambrose Cathedral in Yarmouth. In wonder, she took notice of the names of her godparents. She read:

Godfather - Tom Deveau. Godmother - Ceal Deveau

A shock of recognition stirred in Catherine. She knew a Tom Deveau! He was the father of one her first schoolmates in Yarmouth. Catherine, like Kurt and Eddie, had always been aware of the surname of her biological family. Although Deveau was a common name in Canada, Catherine had long and secretly sensed a connection between her and this family, but was too shy and reticent to pursue it. Now, bolstered by the two brothers who loved her, she found new courage.

"I decided to dig deeper," Catherine said to me in one of our period-ic telephone conversations. She called up Tom Deveau and told him she had found her two brothers, Kurt and Eddie. She asked him if he knew of them.

He did, oh, how he did! Tom revealed that he was Eric's younger brother; the one who was closest to Eric. There were two more brothers, Wilfred and John, as well as two sisters, Rita and Cecilia. All were married and had families. So, in addition to ten aunts and uncles, Catherine discovered she and Kurt and Eddie had twenty-four cousins. Most of the cousins were mar-ried with children. The number of relatives grew exponentially. For Catherine, it was as though long rains had suddenly ended a draught and painted the desert into a flowering field of color.

Now Catherine learned that she, Eddie, and Kurt had been the skeletons in the family closet. Tom Deveau had known about Catherine's whereabouts, but had never revealed himself to her. Perhaps it had something to do with an alle-giance to Eric's first wife and her four children, who continued to be very much a part of the family long after Eric had deserted them for Lucienne. Perhaps there was a shame that the family carried because they failed to intervene and assist Catherine and Kurt and Eddie when they were babies in Yarmouth. Perhaps they remained silent in those early years to protect Catherine from Lucienne's reach.

Regardless, the news that Catherine had found her brothers was spreading through the Deveau family like fire in a field of wheat. This vast extended family tumbled out of every province in Canada to lay claim to the three lost children. Now they opened their hearts to Catherine. They opened their arms to Kurt and Eddie.

Letters started to arrive in New Jersey from different parts of Canada, warm, loving, down-home epistles that spoke to the intimate details of life in this Canadian family. Trying to catch the boys up on their thirty-year absence, they wrote of all things, great and small: of Aunt Carolyn's arthritis and Uncle John's retirement from the Canadian Mounted Police, of the quilting that had to be done, the flowers planted, the cakes baked, of star gazing on winter nights, of the hikes in the woods to cut down their own Christmas tree, of the epidemic of frostbite cases in the burn unit where one of the cousins worked as a nurse. They sent pictures, one a snapshot of the one-room schoolhouse where Eric's mother, Katie, their biological grandmother, taught school in the early nineteen hundreds. And finally they sent a complete genealogy with more names than the boys or I could fathom, tracing the family back to 1623.

Now the boys had roots extending back to the Renaissance. It made them dizzy, it made them laugh, the irony of it all. Through the fall of 1998 and into the spring and summer of 1999, these letters came, supplemented by calls from people who wanted them back in their lives. It was a heady experience for all of us.

* * *

KURT AND EDDIE HAD PROMISED CATHERINE that they would travel to Yarmouth to meet her husband and her children. In the summer of 1999, the boys and their wives drove to Bar Harbor, Maine, and took the ferry across the Bay of Fundy into Yarmouth. A few hours later, they fell into the outstretched arms of Catherine, who was literally dancing on the dock as she waited for them. Oh, how they loved to be loved by Catherine.

They had a full week planned, and it included a visit to their father's family, who so wanted to meet these sons of the prodigal Eric. There were invitations—lunch at Aunt Carolyn's with several family members, dinner with Aunt Ceal and Uncle Billy with more family members. They went curiously and gratefully. At one luncheon, they found themselves across the table from Susan, Eric's eldest daughter by his first marriage, i.e., their half-sister. It was overwhelming.

Along with the invitations, there were demands. Foremost was a pressing desire of their new found aunts and uncles to have the boys visit Uncle Wilfred, Eric's oldest brother, who was near death in a nursing home. Every conversation included the pressure to make time to visit Uncle Wilfred. There seemed to be a need for the family to complete some circle, a closure on Wilfred's life more symbolic than real, since he was barely conscious and unable to communicate.

Kurt and Eddie refused to visit the nursing home. Neither of them were comfortable around death. They did not want to spend an afternoon of their vacation at the deathbed of an uncle they never knew. Regardless of how many times they were told about how deeply Uncle Wilfred cared for them thirty years ago, the fact was, he let them go. They held no animosity towards him or members of the family, but it was difficult for the boys to buy whole-heartedly into these sudden affections, to reconcile this surging desire of the family to know them with the draught of involvement in the early years of their life. Additionally, the fact that, over the years, no one had reached out to Catherine, even though she was living right in their own backyard, in Yarmouth, was difficult to understand. Although Catherine was included in all the invitations that week, it was clear to all three of them that Kurt and Eddie were the main attraction.

They were struck by the fact that not one baby picture of them exist-ed in any of the family albums pulled out that week by aunts and uncles bent on providing them with their proud family history. Like all of us, who look for evidence of our former selves preserved in old photographs, they would have loved to come upon a moment from their past, or the past of their par-ents, preserved in one of those albums, but they found nothing. Eventually, they grew weary of hearing about and gazing at photographs of people they never knew. Try as they might, they were unable to relate, and the effort made them acutely aware of having been eradicated from these people's lives.

A final rupture took place the day before they were scheduled to return home. They received a call at their hotel to come to a particular restaurant for lunch. It was another claim on their time, but this was their last day in Yarmouth, and they had already made plans for a packed day. Kurt answered the phone and declined the invitation, saying they were just about to leave for a drive through the countryside. Ten minutes later, another call came, this time from Uncle Billy, demanding they show up, hollering over the phone, berating their thanklessness, and berating them for not going to visit Uncle Wilfred in the nursing home.

The tirade was hurtful. Enough was enough. They did not go to the restaurant. Months later they would learn that over fifty family members had gathered from far and wide as a surprise. In their well-meaning enthusiasm for making the most of Kurt and Eddie's visit to Yarmouth, these relatives did not consider the plans already made by the boys. Kurt and Eddie's failure to show was a grave disappointment. It would result in another long silence from the family, as letters and phone calls ceased. Unfortunately, Catherine would be blamed for monopolizing their time and once again would find herself ostracized by her relatives.

* * *

That same afternoon, with Eddie at the wheel, the four of them drove around Yarmouth and the surrounding countryside for a long last look before leaving the next day. Nothing was familiar. Of course, things had changed dramatically in thirty years. Roads had been paved, more houses had been built, and urbanization had pushed into the suburban areas. As they rounded a bend in the road, Eddie suddenly stopped short and pulled the car to the side of the road.

"What's up?" the others asked, thinking they might have blown a tire.

"I have a funny feeling, like I know this place," Eddie said, breathing heavily. He opened the door and jumped out of the car.

"Do you feel anything, Kurt?" Eddie said to his brother.

Kurt rolled his eyes, calmly looked around, and shook his head. "Not a thing."

"Something's happening to me," Eddie said. Beads of perspiration started to form on his forehead. He began to walk along the side of the road, tentatively at first and then more swiftly, as if he knew where he was going. The others followed. Kurt was amicably rolling his eyes at the absurdity of his brother's sudden detour. They came to a house. Eddie hesitated, as if lost, then walked up the front path, past fir trees and bushes, up the wooden steps and onto the porch.

"Where do you think you're going?" an embarrassed Kurt whispered from behind Eddie.

"I have a feeling we used to live here," Eddie said. "I'm going to see if anyone's home." Kurt and Barbara and Cath stood quietly to the side as Eddie knocked on the door. A woman answered.

"Yes?" she asked quizzically as she took in the four of them standing sheepishly on her porch.

Eddie took a deep breath and after a few false starts mumbled, "Did you ever hear of Ardis or Allen Morton?"

"Who are you?" the woman asked.

256

"We're two foster children that they took care of almost thirty years ago."

She gasped. "Allen, Allen, come quickly."

In the next moment, Allen Morton appeared before them.

"We're Kurt and Eddie."

Allen paled. He caught his breath. Tears streamed down his face. He put up his arms and hugged them, the two boys he had known as babies, now towering over him. He started to cry. "I never though I'd see you again," he said, as he shepherded them inside. As they entered the front room, it was as if they had suddenly jumped back into an ocean of memories; all those days with Ardis and Allen came rushing back in waves.

After they all calmed down, Allen told the boys that they were the first of thirty foster children Ardis and he had taken in. Ardis was dead now. He introduced them to his second wife. He quickly phoned his daughter, the child Ardis was pregnant with at the time of their adoption. She and her husband quickly drove over to meet them. Yes, she knew all about Kurt and Eddie. Her parents talked of them often. She had seen their pictures. This reminded Allen of something. He walked across the room and reached into a small cabinet. He pulled out an album containing perfectly preserved photographs of Kurt and Eddie. "Here you are—you can keep them," he said, handing them back their small selves in portraits taken at the local Sears Roebuck store just days before they left Canada.

"Ardis and I were going to send these pictures with you to your new parents, but we couldn't give them up."

The boys had found someone they weren't even looking for, a person who knew them and loved them and cherished their memory. The following day it would be Allen who showed up at the dock and stood next to Catherine, waving madly, as the ferry pulled out of Yarmouth for the return trip home to New Jersey.

They told Bob and me that a sense of completeness coursed through them as they waved from the deck of the ferry. Finding Allen was like discovering the last piece of a puzzle left lying through all sorts of weather, under the porch table where it had faded into the rug. Now whole, the puzzle could be safely packed away.

Of course, they knew they would see Catherine again. In fact, the next reunion was already in the planning stage. It took place the following summer, when Catherine, her husband George, and their eldest son, George Junior, came to New Jersey and spent a week with Kurt and Eddie during which they proudly introduced our whole family to their sister

Meanwhile, the letters from their father's family ceased. Catherine was benignly ignored by all except the youngest daughter of Eric's first wife, a woman named Charmagne. She had returned to Yarmouth around 1999, a self-proclaimed black sheep, and had sought out Catherine. They became best friends, and Catherine felt like she had found a sister. Occasionally, Kurt heard from Ricky, Charmagne's brother, and they spoke about what they had in common, their striking resemblance to Eric and their skill with the guitar.

In late April of 2000, Catherine, after a long period of silence, received a letter from Aunt Carolyn. There had been no contact since the day of the ill-fated surprise luncheon that had been aborted. As Catherine opened the letter, a newspaper article fell out of the envelope. It was Lucienne's obituary. She had died in St. John on April 6, 2000. By the time the obituary reached Catherine, Lucienne was buried. Deborah had never reached out to any of the three siblings to notify them of their mother's death. Kurt and Eddie received the news from Catherine with regret but not sorrow. When I asked them about it, Eddie said, "It was over, Mom. We had already buried her." He then repeated the words he had said those months ago. "I know they say blood is thicker than water, but it really isn't true."

I am reminded of this each year on Mother's Day. After Catherine calls Femme, she calls me and we have a little heart to heart, both of us knowing that it might have been otherwise.

✷ ✷ ✷

As the years went by, I continued to mine books for the gold in the ore of others' spiritual journeys. I searched for the unique combination of words that would speak to me, that would evoke a numinous moment when yearning for the divine was fulfilled, before dissipating into desire once again.

One such moment occurred when I read the words of Pope John XXIII: "All language in relation to God—including the title Father—is by way of analogy, since God transcends all human experience." These words gave me the latitude to relinquish my need to wedge an infinite God into my finite ability to understand. They allowed me to remain open to rare moments of personal revelation, when ordinary experience seemed sacred and wrapped in mystery.

Science has already taken us beyond the limits of comprehension of the natural world. The origin and destiny of galaxies, the evidence that time does not pass but is merely a dimension through which we pass, and sub-atomic particles that exist in two places at once, are but a few of the concepts that defy understanding. To accept the possibility of a supernatural world beyond comprehension in this one seems a logical leap of faith. I have learned to live with the questions and have lived my way—if not into the answers—into a sort of peace supported by prayer.

Over the years my faith in prayer has looped and circled and doubled back. Sometimes falling, sometimes soaring, prayer has come to exist as a reality—as though it has substance. Like galaxies existing light years away that are known only by their effect on our solar system, I have felt the effects of prayer, even if the effect is only to calm my fear or move me in the direction of acceptance or letting go.

And so words gleaned from others have become the underpinnings of my intellectual search for God, while intuition, those feelings caught in the updrafts of awareness, reinforce a sense of transcendence. They happen, these moments of unexpected light, the sudden knowing, like the most elusive word in a cross-word puzzle shining out of the swirl and roil of language surrounding it—transforming the fractured world on the page to a whole.

The poet T.S. Eliot wrote:
> "What we call the beginning is often the end
> And to make an end is to make a beginning.
> The end is where we start from."

I end this book where I started, with a child I do not know.

After having three biological children of their own, my son Dennis and his wife, Beth, applied to adopt a baby from China. They waited for nearly two years as their file worked its way through the bureaucracies of the U.S.

and China. Disappointment followed disappointment. Then the wonder of it—finally, the long-awaited news arrived. When Dennis called me, bubbling with joy, he told me, "I know three things. Her name is Tian Hua. She's from Hunan Province, and she was born on September 4th, 2006."

I gasped. A chill ran up my spine as memory returned me to September 4th, 2006.

It was my mother's ninety-fifth and final birthday. Four months later she was dead. The whole family traveled through a hurricane to mark the occasion with her. Frail and barely aware, my mother had smiled as she extended her arms to encircle the great-grandchildren gathered around her wheelchair as we all sang "Happy Birthday." I realized now that while my mother and the

The next generation with Marion and Bob. Top row: Ryan, James, Tristan, Devin, Casey, Sara; Middle row: Brendan, Colin, Cara; Bottom row: Annie, Irene, and Zachery.

children blew out the candles for the last time, halfway around the world, a woman was giving birth to a girl who would become the newest member of our family.

Call it fate, call it coincidence, call it luck, call it divine intervention, but we must call it something, this wonder of lives crossing. Anna Louise Tian Hua, our Annie, joined her siblings Ryan, Devin, and Sara, and eight cousins. There are Robert's children, Brendan, Cara and Colin; Kathleen's children, Tristan and Casey; Eddie's children, James and Irene; and Kurt's son, Zachery. Can you picture them running around my house, just as their parents did all those years ago? Blood pales when compared to the tie that binds them, invisible as ions in a magnet, but undeniable, the astonishing force of love pulling them together.

ഊ • ര

Epilogue

IN JANUARY OF 2008, DEBORAH, who was still living in St. John, contacted Catherine through Facebook. A relationship began to grow between them. In the previous ten years, Deborah had gotten her life together. She developed relationships with friends who urged and supported her to reconnect with her family. She gradually began to understand how her life had been shaped as an infant in the moment Lucienne carried her out of the hospital. She was no longer hostile to her siblings. Catherine brought Kurt and Eddie into her newfound relationship with their sister and tentative calls and emails have begun between them. In the spring, Catherine traveled to St. John, and she and Deborah spent a weekend together. On one occasion, after a sisterly heart-to-heart, Deborah told Catherine, "You and Kurt and Eddie were the lucky ones. I never had a chance until now."